"*Race, Gender, and Culture in International Relations* opens
national relations to the world – where people carry s
their lives and where national hierarchies are built on these social divisions and
then magnify them. It is impossible to imagine 'international relations' without
race and gender, without imperialism and the urge for freedom. But, of course,
that's how IR is often understood. This book shows why IR has, largely, been
too myopic and why IR needs to expand its vision."

Vijay Prashad, Trinity College, USA

"This is the first and much-needed textbook to emerge in IR that introduces
the undergraduate student to postcolonialism. It has the added advantage of
focusing in a sustained way on how Eurocentrism intersects with race and gender thereby bringing a wider critical perspective to the student. This is a deeply
impressive book that should be a go-to resource for all lecturers and students
who are interested in this rapidly-rising area within IR."

John M. Hobson, University of Sheffield, UK

"By bringing together race, gender and postcolonial critique, this textbook radically expands the vantage points and critical considerations currently offered in
introductions to International Relations. Teachers and students alike will find
the material challenging, thought provoking, and above all, timely and relevant."

Robbie Shilliam, Queen Mary University of London, UK

"This important textbook brings together contributions from outstanding
scholars to advance our understandings of the cultural constitution of global
politics through the intersections of race and gender. Drawing from postcolonial theory, indigenous theory, and feminist theory, the volume contributes in
significant ways to enhancing our understandings of some of the key concepts
and processes of International Relations – the nation-state, sovereignty, security,
global capitalism, colonialism, and violence."

Shampa Biswas, Whitman College, USA

Race, Gender, and Culture in International Relations

International Relations theory has broadened out considerably since the end of the Cold War. Topics and issues once deemed irrelevant to the discipline have been systematically drawn into the debate and great strides have been made in the areas of culture/identity, race, and gender in the discipline. However, despite these major developments over the last two decades, currently there are no comprehensive textbooks that deal with race, gender, and culture in IR from a postcolonial perspective. This textbook fills this important gap.

Persaud and Sajed have drawn together an outstanding lineup of scholars, with each chapter illustrating the ways these specific lenses (race, gender, culture) condition or alter our assumptions about world politics.

This book:

- covers a wide range of topics including war, global inequality, postcolonialism, nation/nationalism, indigeneity, sexuality, celebrity humanitarianism, and religion;
- follows a clear structure, with each chapter situating the topic within IR, reviewing the main approaches and debates surrounding the topic and illustrating the subject matter through case studies;
- features pedagogical tools and resources in every chapter – boxes to highlight major points; illustrative narratives; and a list of suggested readings.

Drawing together prominent scholars in critical International Relations, this work shows why and how race, gender and culture matter and will be essential reading for all students of global politics and International Relations theory.

Randolph B. Persaud is Associate Professor, School of International Service, American University, Washington, DC, USA.

Alina Sajed is Associate Professor of International Relations, McMaster University, Canada.

Race, Gender, and Culture in International Relations

Postcolonial Perspectives

Edited by Randolph B. Persaud
and Alina Sajed

Routledge
Taylor & Francis Group

LONDON AND NEW YORK

First published 2018
by Routledge
2 Park Square, Milton Park, Abingdon, Oxon OX14 4RN

and by Routledge
711 Third Avenue, New York, NY 10017

Routledge is an imprint of the Taylor & Francis Group, an informa business

British Library Cataloguing in Publication Data
A catalogue record for this book is available from the British Library

Library of Congress Cataloging in Publication Data
Names: Persaud, Randolph B., 1959– editor. | Sajed, Alina., editor.
Title: Race, gender, and culture in international relations : postcolonial perspectives / edited by Randolph B. Persaud and Alina Sajed.
Description: Abingdon, Oxon ; New York, NY : Routledge, 2018. |
Includes bibliographical references and index.
Identifiers: LCCN 2017049219 | ISBN 9780415786423 (hbk) |
ISBN 9780415786430 (pbk) | ISBN 9781315227542 (ebk)
Subjects: LCSH: International relations–Social aspects. |
International relations and culture. | Postcolonialism.
Classification: LCC JZ1251 .R33 2018 | DDC 327.101–dc23
LC record available at https://lccn.loc.gov/2017049219

ISBN: 978-0-415-78642-3 (hbk)
ISBN: 978-0-415-78643-0 (pbk)
ISBN: 978-1-315-22754-2 (ebk)

Typeset in Bembo
by Out of House Publishing
Printed and bound by CPI Group (UK) Ltd, Croydon, CR0 4YY

From Randy – to Maya, Thea, and Dolly
From Alina – to Sophia

Contents

List of figures and tables   xi
List of boxes   xii
List of contributors   xiii
Acknowledgements   xvi

1   Introduction: Race, gender, and culture in
    International Relations   1
    RANDOLPH B. PERSAUD AND ALINA SAJED

2   Postcolonialism and its relevance for International
    Relations in a globalized world   19
    SANKARAN KRISHNA

3   Race in International Relations   35
    SRDJAN VUCETIC AND RANDOLPH B. PERSAUD

4   Gender, race, and International Relations   58
    AYTAK AKBARI-DIBAVAR

5   Gender, nation, and nationalism   80
    NIVI MANCHANDA AND LEAH DE HAAN

6   Postcolonialism and International Relations: Intersections
    of sexuality, religion, and race   99
    MOMIN RAHMAN

7   Race and global inequality   116
    NAEEM INAYATULLAH AND DAVID L. BLANEY

8   Discourses of conquest and resistance: International
    Relations and Anishinaabe diplomacy   135
    HAYDEN KING

9   Security studies, postcolonialism and the Third World   155
    RANDOLPH B. PERSAUD

10 'It is not about me…but it kind of is:' Celebrity
    humanitarianism in late modernity   180
    AIDA A. HOZIC, SAMANTHA MAJIC, AND
    IBRAHIM YAHAYA IBRAHIM

    Index   200

List of figures and tables

Figures

6.1 The modernization progress model of LGBT identities
and rights   101
6.2 The social structure of heteronormativity   103
6.3 The triangulation of homocolonialism   106
6.4 Muslim LGBT as intersectionality   108

Table

3.1 Western views of itself and Others   37

List of boxes

2.1	What is the Third World?	29
2.2	Chapter 2 Key points	31
3.1	From Rodney's *How Europe Underdeveloped Africa*	45
3.2	Race and immigration	46
3.3	Chapter 3 Key points	51
4.1	Definition: Hegemonic masculinity	60
4.2	Definition: Andro-Eurocentrism	61
4.3	Definition: Liberal feminisms	62
4.4	Definition: Gender mainstreaming	65
4.5	Sojourner Truth (1797–1883): Ain't I A Woman?	66
4.6	Definition: Patriarchy	68
4.7	Definition: Heteronormativity	69
4.8	Definition: Social reproduction	70
4.9	Definition: Subaltern	73
4.10	Definition: The traditional African-American quilt pattern	75
4.11	Chapter 4 Key points	76
5.1	The exclusivity of nationalism	93
5.2	Chapter 5 Key points	94
7.1	Story box	130
7.2	Chapter 7 Key points	131
8.1	Chapter 8 Key points	151
9.1	Massacre at Amritsar, India, 1919	162
9.2	Snapshot: Violence against the Third World	171
9.3	Chapter 9 Key points	173
10.1	Chapter 10 Key points	183
10.2	Story box	195

List of contributors

Editors

Randolph B. Persaud is Associate Professor of International Relations at American University, Washington, DC. He specializes in the areas of race and international relations, hegemony and counterhegemony, postcolonialism, human security, and immigration and identity. He is the author of *Counter-Hegemony and Foreign Policy* published by the State University of New York Press. His research has also been published in *Cambridge Review of International Affairs, Globalizations, Latin American Politics and Society, Alternatives, Race and Class, Conn. Jour Int'L Law*, and *Korea Review of International Studies*. He co-edited, with R.B.J. Walker, 'Race in International Relations' – *Alternatives,* Vol. 26, No. 4, 2001. Persaud and R.B.J. Walker also recently co-edited a follow-up special issue on the subject of 'Race, De-Coloniality and International Relations. *Alternatives*', Vol. 40, No. 2, 2015.

Alina Sajed is Associate Professor with the Department of Political Science at McMaster University. She researches on and teaches decolonization, politics of the Third World, and political violence. Her research has been published in *Review of International Studies, International Studies Review, Globalizations, Third World Quarterly, Citizenship Studies, Cambridge Review of International Affairs*, and *Postcolonial Studies*. She is the author of *Postcolonial Encounters in International Relations. The Politics of Transgression in the Maghreb* (Routledge, 2013); and the co-author (with William D. Coleman) of *Fifty Key Thinkers on Globalization* (Routledge, 2012).

Chapter authors

Aytak Akbari–Dibavar is a PhD Candidate and 2016 Pierre Elliot Trudeau Scholar with the department of Political Science at York University. She specializes in International Relations and Gender Studies. Her research investigates the trans-generational transmission of political trauma and politics of silencing and memory in authoritarian states. Her research has been published in *Journal of Time and Society* and *Critical Security Studies*. She is currently a Research Fellow with the York Centre for Refugee Studies.

David L. Blaney is G. Theodore Mitau Professor of Political Science at Macalester College. He works on the social and political theory of international relations/global political economy. More specifically, he explores the constructions of identity, time and space central to the discipline of International Relations. He is the author of numerous scholarly articles and books. His most recent publications are *Thinking International Relations Differently* (co-edited with Arlene Tickner) (Routledge, 2012) and *Claiming the International* (Routledge, 2013).

Leah de Haan completed her Masters in International Relations Theory at the London School of Economics and Political Sciences in August 2017 after a BA in Politics and International Relations at Macquarie University, Australia. She is currently working as an editorial assistant at the Royal Institute of International Affairs, Chatham House, in London. Her academic interests include queer, narrative and post-structural IR theory.

Aida A. Hozic is an Associate Professor of International Relations with the Department of Political Science at the University of Florida. Her research is situated at the intersection of political economy, cultural studies, and international security. Her current project, however, explores the resurrection of the old Ottoman trade routes in contemporary Balkans, the accompanying political violence and instability, and the role of the Balkans in the world economy. She is the author of *Hollyworld: Space, Power and Fantasy in the American Economy* (Cornell University Press, 2002) and a number of articles in journals and edited volumes.

Naeem Inayatullah is Professor of Political Science at Ithaca College. His research focuses on poverty and inequality in the global political economy, with a focus on Hegelian and Marxian dialectics, and on the cultural political economy. Additionally, he writes on pedagogy, popular culture, and autobiography. He has published numerous scholarly articles and books. His recent book is *Savage Economics* (with David L. Blaney) (Routledge, 2010).

Hayden King is Anishinaabe from Beausoleil First Nation on Gchi'mnissing in Huronia, Ontario. He has been teaching Indigenous politics and policy since 2007, and is currently in the Faculty of Arts at Ryerson University, with an appointment as adjunct research professor at Carleton University. He is also a Senior Fellow at Massey College. His research, analysis and commentary on Indigenous nationhood and settler colonialism in Canada is published widely.

Sankaran Krishna is Professor of Political Science at the University of Hawai'i at Manoa. His work so far has centered on nationalism, ethnic identity and conflict, identity politics, and postcolonial studies, located primarily around India and Sri Lanka. He is currently working on some essays dealing with the partition of the Indian subcontinent in 1947, the culture of Indian foreign policy making, the silent presence of race in discourses of international relations, diasporic forms of Indian nationalism, and other eclectic topics. He has published numerous scholarly articles. He is the author of *Globalization and Postcolonialism* (Rowman and Littlefield, 2009) and *Postcolonial Insecurities: India, Sri Lanka and the Question of Nationhood* (University of Minnesota Press, 1999).

Samantha Majic is Associate Professor of Political Science with the John Jay College of Criminal Justice at the City University of New York. Her research lies in gender and American politics, with specific interests in sex work, civic engagement, institutionalism, and the nonprofit sector. She is the author of *Sex Work Politics: From Protest to Service Provision* (University of Pennsylvania Press, 2014) and the co-editor (with Carisa Showden) of *Negotiating Sex Work: Unintended Consequences of Policy and Activism* (University of Minnesota Press, 2014). Her research has also appeared in numerous political science and gender studies journals.

Nivi Manchanda is a Lecturer in International Politics at Queen Mary, University of London and co-convener of the BISA Colonial, Postcolonial, Decolonial Working Group. Her research interests include race, gender and the legacies of colonialism in International Relations. She is currently working on a book manuscript entitled *Imagining Afghanistan: The History and Politics of Imperial Knowledge Production* which is based on her award-winning PhD thesis. She is the author of 'Queering the Pashtun: Afghan Sexuality in the Homonationalist Imaginary' *Third World Quarterly* (2015), 'Rendering Afghanistan Legible: Borders, Frontiers and the "State" of Afghanistan' *Politics* (forthcoming), and co-editor of *Race and Racism in International Relations: Confronting the Global Colour Line* (Routledge, 2014).

Momin Rahman is Professor of Sociology at Trent University in Canada. He has published *Gender and Sexuality: Sociological Approaches* (2010, with Stevi Jackson), *Sexuality and Democracy* (2000) and numerous articles on LGBT issues, including work on queer representations of David Beckham (2004) and in sports celebrity more generally (2011). He is currently working on the tensions between Muslim cultures and sexual diversity.

Srdjan Vucetic is Associate Professor at the Graduate School of Public and International Affairs, University of Ottawa, Canada. His research interests revolve around the politics of international hierarchy. He is the author of *The Anglosphere: A Genealogy of a Racialized Identity in International Relations* (2011).

Ibrahim Yahaya Ibrahim is a PhD candidate in Political Science and a research associate with the Sahel Research Group at the University of Florida. His academic interest relates to Comparative Politics, Islam and Politics, Political Stability, and International Development in the Francophone Sahelian countries. His current research focuses on political contestations and Islamic discourses in the Sahel, with particular focus on Mali, Niger and Mauritania.

Acknowledgements

Dr. Persaud would like to thank Research Assistant Shayna Vayser (American University, Washington, DC) and students from his classes – 'Identity, Race, Gender and Culture', and 'From Empire to Globalization'. He would also like to acknowledge the support of his colleagues at American University – Amitav Acharya, Akbar Ahmed, Amanda Taylor, Christine B.N. Chin, Patrick Thaddeus Jackson, James Mittelman, Vidya Samarasinghe, and Ann Tickner. Dr. Sajed would like to thank the students in her fourth year seminar on Non-Western IR for engaging so passionately in discussions around issues of race, gender, and culture. While in Romania, Alina also benefitted from the love and support of her mother, who created a space for her to work on this project without having to worry about the burden of daily chores. We also gratefully acknowledge important comments received from Catherine Baker, Alexander Davies, John Hobson, Audie Klotz, Craig Murphy, Ajay Parasram, Mustapha Kamal Pasha, and three anonymous reviewers. Many thanks also to Nicola Parkin and Lucy Frederick of Routledge for their constructive input and support. The 'Village' at the International Studies Association is a major source of support and inspiration to both of us, and we register our sincere thanks.

1 Introduction

Race, gender, and culture in International Relations

Randolph B. Persaud and Alina Sajed

Introduction	1
Classic works of postcolonialism	2
Critical theory	5
Gender dimensions of the postcolonial	7
Conclusion	13

Introduction

The most impactful things in our lives often exist in plain sight and yet cannot be readily recognized (Henderson 2015). Yet, the lack of obvious visibility does not in any way take away from the power exercised by these social forces. In fact, it is the hidden form, plus the lack of objectivity, and the impossibility of scientific verification that allows these social forces to have the influence that they wield in society. Race, gender, and culture are three of the most powerful such conditions in our lives (Chowdhry & Rai 2009). They exist and operate at multiple levels, the local (village or town, or city); the national (the nation state), the regional (usually contiguous countries bounded together by assumptions of a similar history or language), and the global, meaning that which has universal appeal or is presented as having trans-historical and transnational authenticity. Despite their extraordinary significance, none of the three is organic, meaning none is natural. We can say, therefore, that race, gender, and culture have one common denominator, that is, they are all products of human thinking and human actions. In many ways, race, gender, and culture are simultaneously personal and shared, sedimented and dynamic, unconscious/conscious, in your mind and mentality, as part of who you are, that is your *being*. Through speech and action, you are also a carrier, a transporter and transponder, and thus you pass the codes of meaning on to others, all the while perhaps not knowing. The dynamics of race, gender, and culture can and have been the basis of extraordinary solidarity or *Otherness* (Inayatullah and Blaney 2004; Chowdhry and Nair 2004; Vucetic 2011), resulting in both cooperation and conflict, peace and violence, boundaries of insides and outsides.

International relations as a discipline is very much influenced by race, gender, and culture. This much, in fact, has been widely accepted, even by those scholars who are more concerned with "objective" phenomena that can only be observed and measured. Many textbooks on International Relations have some discussion, if not an entire chapter on gender and culture, and occasionally race. This book advances the discussion on these problems in ways that both build upon and go beyond much of the existing scholarship. Specifically, the authors present postcolonial perspectives on International Relations, with a focus on these three topics. It should be noted at the outset that a postcolonial perspective is not, and cannot be separated from, other critical bodies of literature in International Relations, nor for that matter is it possible to construct postcolonial arguments while ignoring the standard literature, much of the latter characterized by Eurocentric assumptions.

The main claims of postcolonial International Relations are:

1. The Third World has been a maker of the international system as much as it has been made by it.
2. Postcolonialism is part of a larger critical tradition in International Relations (and beyond it), and cannot be separated from that literature.
3. The modern world system including the global economy and the modern state system are not the product of evolution from a single source (i.e. the West), but from multiple sources.
4. Colonialism and neo-colonialism, and imperialism and neo-imperialism, were and continue to be central forces in the making of the world order.
5. Racism as a practice and ideology has been central to the making of the modern world order. Racism is invariably gendered.
6. Domination and exploitation based on gender have been central to European colonization and imperial intervention.
7. Racialized and gendered ideas and actions have been central to various nation-building projects around the world, to the global economy, to foreign policy making and strategy, and to security practices (such as wars and humanitarian interventions).
8. Powerful actors in the current Euro-centered world order are reacting to defend the status quo both at the level of the international, and in societies where Eurocentric politics, culture, and ideologies dominate. This conservative and regressive reaction is taking multiple forms, including white nationalism and populism.

Classic works of postcolonialism

Aside from its close attention to the intersections of race, gender, and culture, postcolonialism also investigates both the historical processes associated with European colonialism, and its impact on contemporary politics, such as immigration, globalization, development discourses and practices, nation-building, and foreign policy, among others. Since colonialism is central to understanding postcolonialism, what then is colonialism? Ania Loomba (2005, 2), in *Colonialism/Postcolonialism*, defines colonialism as 'the conquest and control of other people's lands and goods.' While a useful starting point, if we limit ourselves to this definition, we might conclude that colonialism is a timeless process as old as human history since there have always been conquests and empires. The claim of postcolonialism is rather that colonialism is a historically specific set of processes and practices associated with the expansion and conquest by European powers of most areas of the world, which arguably started in 1492 with the conquest of the Americas, and then continued with the conquests and domination of Africa, major parts of Asia and the Middle East, and the settling of the Americas, Australia, and New Zealand. What, then, makes the European colonial empire so different from previous empires and conquests (e.g. the Mongol Empire, the Aztec Empire, the Roman Empire, the Ottoman Empire)? Is it its sheer size, namely that it encompassed most of the globe? Is it that it was more violent? Is it that it possessed military or technological superiority?[1]

There are a couple of elements that indicate the specificity of the European colonial project. One element is indicated by Loomba who writes that '[m]odern colonialism did more than extract tribute, goods and wealth from the countries that it conquered – it restructured the economies of the latter, drawing them into a complex relationship with their own, so that there was a flow of human and natural resources between colonized and colonial countries' (Loomba 2005, 3). In other words, European colonialism introduced the capitalist system as the dominant mode of production, which altered – with indelible and long-term consequences – the economic, social, cultural, and political dynamics of many societies around the world. The European colonial empire, then, has taken the capitalist system from a local system of economic exchange, and transformed it into a global economic system where virtually no territory or society has remained unaffected by its operations (see Chapters 1 and 7).

Aimé Césaire (1955), in his now classic critique of colonialism, *Discourse on Colonialism*, discussed the devastating impact of capitalist expansion on the colonies where raw materials and human labor were extracted under regimes of slavery, systematic violence, and ruthless exploitation from colonial societies. *Discourse on Colonialism* is considered one of the foundational texts of postcolonialism, being one of the first texts to openly and publicly contest the so-called 'humanist' claims made in defense of the colonial project. The latter asserted that European colonialism served to civilize colonial societies and their supposedly backward peoples, and some of these claims are still being made today. In a devastating critique of the so-called 'civilizing mission', Césaire provides an inventory of the atrocities committed by European colonialism while also providing incontrovertible evidence that the latter not only did not civilize non-European societies, but in fact, it de-civilized them. Césaire thus illustrates that the specificity of European colonialism lies not simply in its expansion throughout all continents of the world, but also in its intrinsic impulse to dehumanize those considered inferior to Europe. Put differently, what drove the

European colonial empire was not simply the desire for profit (capitalism), but also an unquestioned belief in its own superiority and in the inferiority of all those others it encountered (racism).

Frantz Fanon, a psychiatrist and philosopher born in the small Caribbean island of Martinique, examined the racist underpinnings associated with colonialism, in its political, economic, social, and even psychological manifestations. In *Black Skins, White Masks*, published in English in 1967,[2] Fanon explores the psychoanalytical mechanisms of the black person's lived experience *as* black. Here, he delves into the profound dehumanization experienced by the black subject as an individual, which results in feelings of dependency and into an internalized complex of inferiority since blackness is always negatively juxtaposed to whiteness. In *Wretched of the Earth* (1963), Fanon's best-known work, he takes up the topic of colonial racism and dehumanization, and investigates it on a larger scale – that of French colonialism in Algeria. The book is arguably one of the most famous and widely used texts in postcolonial studies but also beyond, inspiring political leaders and activists ranging from Steve Biko in South Africa to Malcolm X and the Black Panthers in the United States, and to Ernesto Che Guevara in Cuba. Here Fanon examines the structural mechanisms through which the colonized are dehumanized by colonial domination and denied both human worth and any sense of historical agency in their own societies. He also discusses at length the means through which the colonial project denies any value to local cultures and traditions thus introducing and maintaining an internalized sense of inadequacy and backwardness when compared to Western cultures and civilizations. Fanon thus investigates the psychological effects of such dehumanization and internalized inferiority complex on the colonized through a discussion of the psychiatric conditions induced by the sheer violence of colonialism. Thus, in his first chapter 'On Violence' (the most widely read – and also the most controversial – chapter of this work), he suggests that since the violence of the colonial system is so overwhelming in its political, economic, social, and psychological effects, the only path through which the colonized can regain their humanity and dignity is through violent resistance.

Another key feature of European colonialism, which distinguishes it from previous forms of domination and conquest, is also, aside from its dependence on capitalism and racism for its survival and sustenance, its systematic production of a body of academic knowledge that underpins and justifies – ethically and 'scientifically' – the enterprise of colonialism as a meritorious and worthy enterprise. Edward Said's *Orientalism*, another foundational text of postcolonial studies, discusses, with a special focus on literary texts, the ways through which various academic disciplines propagate racist and patronizing representations of the Orient/East as despotic, lascivious, irrational, fanatical, backward and deceitful. Orientalism is then the systematic representation by Western scholarship of the East through a series of patronizing clichés and stereotypes that reduce a variety of societies and cultures to an unchanging essence. This representation becomes entrenched not only in scholarship, but also in public imagination, in the formulation of foreign policy and strategy, and, equally importantly, internalized by the colonized themselves (Inayatullah and Blaney 2004).

Well before Fanon, and going back to the turn of the century and then right through the onset of decolonization – commencing around World War II – a number of other scholars and activists contributed to what we know as post-colonialism today. It was W.E.B. Du Bois (1994, 24), the African American soci-ologist, who delineated the twentieth century as marked by the color line. While Du Bois was predominantly concerned with racial domination in the United States, he was also very much involved with the Pan-Africanist move-ment, which saw African Americans teaming up with like-minded individuals from the colonies to challenge colonial and imperial rule. The late nineteenth century was marked by resurgent imperial expansion, not least because of the aggressive entrance of the United States into the world politics of empire building. This was also the period of a new scientific racism, which sought to divide the world between '…Anglo-Saxons or Teutons and the inferior races…' (Vitalis 2015, 26) – a construction tremendously legitimized because this type of knowledge came from reputable scholars working at the Ivy League univer-sities. Du Bois resisted the racial thesis and 'began in the late 1890s to explain hierarchy instead as the outcome of history, specifically colonial and mercantile capitalist expansion and of the transatlantic slave trade that secured the domi-nance of the West' (Vitalis 2015, 27).

Critical theory

Although Fanon is widely known for his analysis of the impact of racial domi-nation on the colonized, he also focused a great deal on economic exploitation, and the ways in which social classes mirrored the racial profile of colonial soci-eties. The big difference between Fanon and many of the Marxists, who were also concerned with economic questions, was that he did not see a direct cor-respondence between classes and politics, because other things, and especially race, 'rubbed up' in between. Race was thus both a constitutive and mediat-ing factor, meaning that race contributed to the making of the class structure, but also acted as a filter which would allow race to develop an independent dynamic, or relative autonomy. Specifically, Fanon argued that the colonized working classes who formed the administrative core of the colonial state could not be relied on to wage a struggle for freedom. The main reason is that these workers were mostly urban. Urban life meant proximity to the culture and even to the imagination of the colonial rulers and the local elites associated with them. For this reason, Fanon broke away from the typical Marxist argu-ment which sees the working class as the main engine of change. Instead he felt that the rural populations (peasants) combined with the 'lumpen proletariat' would form the leading edge of decolonization. The cultural aspect included dimensions of gender and sexual relations between the colonizer and colonized. The colonial architecture was massively gendered with women on the inside of the colonizer's desire, but on the outside in all other matters of social existence (Persaud and Chin 2016). Colonial societies were dependent on borders, and gender complicated the separation between inside and outside. As Anne McClintock has noted, it is important to remember that the colonizer erected multiple borders between the colonized man and woman where the latter 'belonged…in anachronistic space, lagging…at least 500 years behind their men' (McClintock 2001, 26). Of importance to us here is the fact that one of the early postcolonial writers felt compelled to theorize the intersections of race, class, and gender.

While Fanon was both inside and outside of the Marxian paradigm, other scholars in this tradition were principally concerned with the ways in which global capitalism drew in non-capitalist societies through Euro-American expansion. Simply put, the relevance of Marxist thought to international relations was limited to the ways in which the capitalist world economy kept on expanding. The principal international relations of concern here were restricted to imperialism and anti-imperialism. Even so, Euro-Marxists tended to accept European modernity as the global standard of what constituted 'civilized life', and as Hobson has argued, this led to a rather paternalistic form of anti-imperialism (Hobson 2012). As Chapter 3 in this book shows, later writings within the Marxian tradition did incorporate race, with the most significant contributions coming from Andre Gunder Frank and Barry K. Gills, and then from some Neo-Gramscian scholars whom we shall soon examine.

Frank and Gills' work is noteworthy on race and IR because it grew out of dependency and world systems theory which had hitherto not factored in race in a systematic way. Their first iteration came in a 1992 paper, published in the *Humboldt Journal of Social Relations*, in which they squarely rejected Eurocentric IR. The key points made by Frank and Gills were as follows:

1. The modern world system is itself part of an older and more (geographically) expansive *world history*. They suggest that it is better to think of world history in terms of five thousand, rather than five hundred years.
2. Against the claims of writers such as Immanuel Wallerstein and Samir Amin, modern capitalism is not unique in the 'ceaseless' accumulation of capital.
3. There have been multiple hegemonic centers through world history, but some may be characterized as super-hegemonic.
4. Race, ethnicity, and gender are important elements in the constitution and reproduction of the world system and must be incorporated into the new world historiography.
5. The totality of the above means that '…we should discard the usual Western Eurocentric rendition of history, which jumps discontinuously from ancient Mesopotamia to Egypt, to "classical" Greece and then Rome, to medieval Western Europe, and then on to the Atlantic West, with scattered backflashes to China, India etc.' (Frank and Gills 1992, 20).

Another dimension of critical theory with links to postcolonial IR came through neo-Gramscian theory, and especially neo-Gramscian international political economy. The impetus came through the work of Robert W. Cox from York University in Toronto. Cox's principal challenge to mainstream IR theory was against its pretention to be scientific. Cox labeled the new structural realism of Kenneth Waltz 'neorealism', a label that became widely adopted. In contradistinction to neorealism's supposed scientific credentials, Cox argued that this theory was influenced by Cold War politics—a conclusion reflected in his now famous aphorism 'theory is always for someone and for some purpose' (1981, 126). Although postcolonial theorists have major differences with Coxian critical theory (Hobson 2012), they still agree with his idea that theory is not politically neutral. The second dimension of neo-Gramscian IR of relevance to us here is the theory of hegemony, which, in contradistinction to 'problem-solving theory', places strong emphasis on the cultural aspects of domination in capitalist societies. While the neo-Gramscians stress the cultural aspect of hegemony in general, some directly incorporated the weight of race and/or gender (Augelli and Murphy 1988; Mittelman and Pasha 1997; Chin 1998; Persaud 2001; Slater 2004; Peterson 2003; True 2003; Whitworth 2004). The third aspect of neo-Gramscian theory that warrants attention in terms of its connection to postcolonial IR perspectives concerns its emphasis on consensus by most neo-Gramscians (Gill 1992). The idea behind the consensus argument is that elites have managed to get the working classes and the poor to 'buy into' the key assumptions, practices, and promises of capitalism as a social system. The OECD countries have almost perfected this framework of state–society relations. The IR aspect refers to the globalization of the consensus model whereby less developed states, though subjected to coercion, nonetheless joined in the key 'global hegemonic institutions' often through multilateral organizations.

While our main focus here is to connect postcolonialism to critical international relations as in the case of the neo-Gramscians above, it is nonetheless important to acknowledge the groundbreaking work of the Subaltern Studies School in India. The scholars involved in the Subaltern Studies School embarked on a long-term project of producing a new historiography and new histories of India from the perspective of everyday Indian life, with a good deal of emphasis on the lives of peasants. For Ranajit Guha (1994), the existing elitist historiography of Indian nationalism 'fails to acknowledge, far less interpret, the contribution made by people *on their own*, that is, *independently of the elite* to the making and development of [Indian] nationalism' (1994, 3). Importantly, while the early Subaltern scholarship did not directly involve International Relations, it formed the basis for postcolonial IR.

Gender dimensions of the postcolonial

One cannot engage the issue of the subaltern without discussing the issue of women and women's contributions to postcolonial studies. Since a number of chapters in this textbook (see Chapters 4, 5, and 6) examine both the relevance of gender to international relations, and its enmeshment with race, class, and culture, we would like to highlight a few of the seminal interventions made by women in postcolonial studies. We focus here on two scholarly contributions to the voices of women in colonial/postcolonial societies that had a major impact in postcolonial studies and gave rise to important debates: Chandra Talpade Mohanty's article 'Under Western Eyes', and Gayatri Chakravorty Spivak's article 'Can the Subaltern Speak?'. Mohanty (1984) takes to task the existing literature on Third World women by Western feminist scholars, and highlights the glaring mis-representations of Third World women as passive, backward and needing to be rescued by their liberated white sisters. Moreover, she also draws attention to how Third World women are consistently lumped together into a homogeneous category without any consideration of their varied experiences of oppression, their different socio-economic standing (class and race do matter a great deal), and of the different understanding they might have of liberation. Mohanty's core argument can be neatly captured by Aihwa Ong's (2001, 108) felicitous statement: '…for [Western] feminists looking overseas, the non-feminist Other is not so much patriarchy as the non-Western woman'.

Spivak (1985) engages the issue of recovering the voice of the subaltern woman. More to the point, she makes the case that the subaltern, by definition, cannot speak since their position in a system of power relations is so marginal that their voice is simply inaudible. To make her argument, she looks at the case of the *sati* in colonial India,[3] and remarks that the *sati* – spoken for both by the British colonial administration, and by the local patriarchy – constituted in some ways the ultimate example of subalternity, someone utterly deprived of voice or agency. She thus concludes that it is impossible to recover the voice of the subaltern or of the oppressed colonized. Spivak's article caused many reactions, with some postcolonial feminists severely criticizing her argument. Benita Parry (1987), for example, accuses Spivak of 'deliberate deafness to the native voice where it *can* be heard' (quoted in Loomba 2005, 196). Spivak's essay and the vivid reactions it elicited speak directly to a number of questions central to postcolonial studies, which are in fact engaged in various ways in this textbook:

> To what extent did colonial power succeed in silencing the colonised? When we emphasise the destructive power of colonialism, do we necessarily position colonised people as victims, incapable of answering back? On the other hand, if we suggest that the colonial subjects can 'speak' and question colonial authority, are we romanticising such resistant subjects and underplaying colonial violence?
>
> (Loomba 2005, 192–193)[4]

Thus, at the core of reflecting on intersections among race, gender, and culture are the following questions: 'To what extent are we the products of dominant ideologies, and to what extent can we act against them? From where does rebellion arise?' (Loomba 2005, 193). The latter is taken up by Black feminism.

According to Patricia Hill Collins (1990), Black feminism is a school of thought that starts its theorization of gender from the lived experience of *racialized* women. It thus acknowledges that understanding gender is inseparable from understanding race and from understanding class. This inseparability of gender, race, and class is called intersectionality, a term coined by Kimberlé Crenshaw (1989; see Chapter 4). More specifically, Black feminism can be historically traced to two historical moments in the United States: the civil rights movements of the 1960s and 1970s, and the rise of feminism as an ideology in the same period. Black feminists took issue both with the sexism of the former (the exclusion of women's voices from the civil rights discourses and events), and with the racism of the latter (the exclusion of black women/women of color's voices and experiences from feminist discourses). Black feminist scholars/activists such as Angela Davis (1983) and bell hooks (1984) focus in their works on the inseparability of race, gender, and capitalism, showing how racial hierarchies and gender oppression are made possible and perpetuated by capitalism and its system of class inequality.

Since its first use by Hamza Alavi to theorize forms of state in the Third World, postcolonialism has allowed for critical analyses of forms of domination in both pre- and post-independence periods. Postcolonial theory is now at the center of what might be broadly seen as forms of resistance and counterhegemonic practices in the world system, and especially so within the gathering momentum of globalization. In Chapter 2, Sankaran Krishna provides a *contrapuntal* interpretation of international relations, meaning that the history of the modern global system must be understood as deeply connected. Contrapuntal analysis is a major focus of postcolonialism. Its key claim is that there was no 'West' – over here – and an 'East' – over there, that is, separate spaces governed by their own internal dynamics of development. Rather the East and the West, the South and the North, the Orient and the Occident, though historically connected, are marked off by differential relations of power. In practical terms the 'West' – though itself, internally divided, has held a common view of itself as superior, and has acted in history (that is, in reality) as if it were superior. Mainstream International Relations scholarship has generally brushed off this 'singular fact'. A postcolonial, contrapuntal reading exposes the Euro-centeredness of these IR knowledges, and introduces the violent and exploitative dimension of the long historical relationships between Orient and Occident – between Euro-America and its various Others. Krishna offers a poignant and very useable idea that postcolonialism is that which has occurred since 1492, which for him, is a better starting point for analyzing the making of modern International Relations. Following most postcolonial scholars, Krishna rejects 1648 as the original moment of the modern world system.

Srdjan Vucetic and Randolph B. Persaud in Chapter 3 trace the presence of race in global relations, both as lived history, and also as a construct in the literature broadly related to colonialism, imperialism, and empire. They place considerable emphasis on the shifting and variable meaning of race as both a conceptual and classificatory category, including a discussion on whether to continue or discontinue the use of race as an analytical tool. Of interest, is their analysis of Eurocentric assumptions about supposedly essential attributes of the West and Third World peoples. Vucetic and Persaud introduce the idea of *actually existing racism* as a practical way of dealing with the usual disagreements about what race means, and how it should be defined. Chapter 3 also discusses in some detail the relationship between race, global development, and security.

Chapter 4, by Aytak Akbari-Dibavar, provides a definition of gender as a category that helps us make sense of certain dimensions of social relations, and looks at the ways in which identities are shaped by gendered expectations and assumptions. Moreover, it explores both the definitive and ambiguous roles played by gender in world politics, and not least in the ways in which gender-based activism has become generative of long-term changes in social, political, and cultural relations in multiple parts of the world. If we accept the premise that the discipline of International Relations is masculinist in structural, behavioral, and ideological terms, we must still probe the types of masculinities that are privileged in disciplinary understandings of world politics and their consequences. Akbari-Dibavar plumbs the depths of Black feminism with special emphasis on its agential and emancipatory dimensions to provide guidance on the complex entanglements and intersectionalities in which gender is always deeply imbricated. Black feminism has a distinctive history, much of it based on the stubborn refusal of white supremacist masculinity to acknowledge the diabolical character of slavery with its attendant pertinent gendered and racialized post-slavery effects. Akbari-Dibavar also explores the territorial confinement of this body of knowledge, and couples it with the broader postcolonial/feminist literature. The undoubtable basis for the epistemological fusion is that both literatures have common elements in the coloniality of oppression, and most importantly, they both have authentic emancipatory genealogies.

In Chapter 5, Nivi Manchanda and Leah de Haan follow up on the analysis in the previous chapter on the meaning of gender, with a focus on the ways in which gender shapes visions of 'the nation' and informs practices of nationalism. Whether in the construction of Western nations, in national wars of liberation, or in various independence movements around the world, the nation is almost always feminized, that is, imagined as a woman in need of protection. One of the central questions pursued here is the ways in which feminization actually is the harbinger for masculinist militarism, xenophobic nationalism, racialized nativism, anti-immigrant hysteria, and the reproduction of institutionalized patriarchal authority. Following critical overviews of theories of nationalism, with specific attention to primordialism, modernism, and ethno-symbolism, Manchanda and de Haan cull theoretical wisdom from noted critical, postcolonial, and 'Black' feminists, including Crenshaw, Hill-Collins, Butler, Mohanty, and True, in their interrogation of the multiple technologies employed in the gendering of the nation. The work of Homi Bhaba and Frantz Fanon are also used to establish the connection between nation-building and decolonization, and 'nationness' as a heterogenous enterprise, rather than one that is built on hegemonic homogeneity.

In Chapter 6, Momin Rahman disturbs taken-for-granted notions of gender/sexuality/identity and complicates the picture of world politics by applying the *problematique* of 'hetero-normativity'. The discussion reflects on how hetero-normativity shapes expectations of masculinity and femininity, and how such expectations profoundly influence political processes ranging from nation-state building to activism and to conflict. The questions explored here are the following: what is hetero-normativity? How does it impact political processes? What was the role of hetero-normativity in the process of colonialism and with what long-term consequences? In answering these questions, Momin Rahman fleshes out multiple sites of domination. For instance, he shows the ways in which Western dominance expresses itself through homocolonialism, whereby the secular, modern West assumes a global responsibility to proliferate LGBT rights, notwithstanding the homonationalist impetus of both formal state action and those of INGOs and even NGOs. 'Pinktesting' is a new litmus test for not only measuring commitments to democracy, but also a tool of assessment for modernity, where the latter is taken to mean broad acceptance of Western values. LGBT rights has, therefore, surfaced as a new platform of neocolonial incursion and corresponding resistances, this being especially so in majority Muslim nations. Rahman is careful to point out that the critique of homocolonialism is not necessarily a defense of internal resistances to LGBT rights in Muslim countries. The chapter also pays attention to the Muslim diasporas.

In Chapter 7, Naeem Inayatullah and David Blaney draw on a variety of classical, neoclassical, and then critical/postcolonial writers in the contemporary period, to examine the emergence of global capitalism and Western modernity. The 'global', in 'global capitalism' is linked first to European, and then American expansionism. The works of Kant, Hegel, Adam Smith, Marx, and Hayek (among others) are situated within the historical unfolding of capitalism and modernity. Marx, though critical of capitalism as an exploitative system, did accept much of modernization, not least because he felt that industrial capitalism would hasten the development of a revolutionary working class, that is to say, closely following the spread of capitalism into the Third World. Inayatullah and Blaney insert race into the picture, a move that disrupts the construction of Western modernity as a product of pure reason and practical wisdom. Put simply, the European Enlightenment actually fostered reason and race as two sides of the same coin. Key differences among classical thinkers are highlighted, a point that is overlooked in critical/postcolonial literatures. Chapter 7 also discusses the writings of L.S. Stavrianos, Eric Wolf, and Anievas and Nişancioğlu – all of whom are decidedly critical of both racializing and exploitative aspects of global capitalist modernity.

The problematic of indigeneity is systematically interrogated by Hayden King in Chapter 8. A key question answered is what it means to be indigenous, and how the term is related to Western colonialism. Indigeneity reveals the limits of International Relations theory, including strands of critical theory that acknowledge the indigenous moment in the constitutions of the modern world system, but do not systematically follow through with any sustained engagement. More specifically, King explores the linkages among indigeneity, the blatant omission of indigenous histories and perspectives from IR analyses, and the discipline of IR as an enduringly colonial enterprise. On the other hand, a reconstructive and emancipatory engagement with indigenous histories as part of world politics, allows us to re-think not only notions of political community, of voice and agency, but also of alternative worldviews. The latter requires us to adopt a different perspective of history, of what constitutes territory, space, and relations of solidarity and domination. For example, when Epeli Hau'ofa, the Fijian scholar, prefers the term 'Oceania' rather than the 'Pacific', he insists on an understanding of the Oceanic world as a space of numerous islands inhabited by multiple cultures, languages, polities, and histories, interconnected both among themselves and to the wider world. The historical experiences and philosophical worldview of the Anishinaabe amplifies the difference not only from Euro-American IR, but also from critical, Marxist, and postcolonial theoretical perspectives.

In Chapter 9, Randolph B. Persaud insists that violence has been at the center of all global relations/politics between Euro-America and its Others. Hundreds of millions have perished and entire peoples have been destroyed. Most explanations of violence focus on state-against-state wars, a move that in one fell-swoop leaves out entire categories of violence in the historic encounters between peoples and civilizations. Persaud re-situates violence in a wider context, such that both state-based and non-state forms of violence are considered. Importantly, he emphasizes that some of the foundational concepts in Euro-American security studies are only partially capable of accounting for the violence visited on what we know as the Third World and this, during several periods in the historical development of the modern world system. Persaud shows how, on numerous occasions, the 'West' embarked on systematic violence against non-Western societies when there was absolutely no threat to the survival of any Western country. Conquest and intervention have as much, if not more, explanatory power than 'survival' and 'anarchy' in accounting for most of the violent confrontations that Euro-America has had with the Third World. Moreover, he argues that racism rather than reason has been the fulcrum of the *coloniality of oppression*. Chapter 9 also shows how various forms of racializations have played important roles in the causes, legitimation, and conduct of war and of other forms of organized violence at the global level. To substantiate claims of 'Eastern' agency, the chapter looks at the impact of the Mongols in the making of a 'world order' that preceded 'Columbian' and post-Columbian world orders by some 300 years. The democratic peace, sanctions, humanitarian intervention, terrorism, and war, receive specific attention, with the focus being on contrasting a critical and postcolonial perspective on these matters. All of them carry elements of neo-coloniality.

The final chapter adds a unique take on International Relations by addressing issues related to construction of the Third World in popular culture. Aida Hozic, Samantha Majic, and Ibrahim Yahaya Ibrahim examine the discursive and material practices of humanitarianism with an emphasis on celebrity humanitarianism, a topic that is far more controversial than either the 'stars' or fans might have ever imagined. In some ways, the intervention of celebrities is occasioned by the urgent need for basic goods and services in time of emergencies, such as hurricanes, floods, and other natural disasters, as well as in famine and war, these usually the outcome of complex relations of economic, political, and cultural power. The entry of celebrities is intended usually to bring urgent attention to the disaster at hand, but also to use their fan base to exert passive political pressure on elected officials and even corporations, the latter cutting in with donations underwritten by a discourse of 'corporate social responsibility'. On other occasions, such as the time of this writing, forms of cultural politics may become evident in celebrity humanitarianism. At the time of writing, late September 2017, Puerto Rico is reeling from an extraordinary disaster having just been hit with Irma, a category five hurricane. Irma devastated the island populated by American citizens. Only 5 per cent of the island has electrical power, and there are credible reports of dire shortages of food, water, medicine, and also of security. The island has not received significant help until today – September 28. In fact, even the usual carpet-to-carpet television coverage now normal with 'breaking news' is absent. Critics argue that the delay has something to do with President Donald J. Trump's ardent and vociferous promotion of white nationalism. The demographic politics of white nationalism disqualifies Latinos from the inside, and renders them less than full citizens. In stepped mega star Jennifer Lopez, a Puerto Rican by birth, and a pop icon on the American mainland and Latin America, if not beyond.

Hozic, Majic, and Yahaya Ibrahim capture the kind of situation in which celebrities like J-Lo step in to mobilize attention across a spectrum of actors. In the Puerto Rican case, J-Lo and Marc Anthony immediately formed *Somos Una Voz* (*We Are One Voice*). These interventions, however, are not unproblematic, and this chapter weighs the arguments for and against celebrity humanitarianism. Of particular concern is the extent to which the presence of celebrities sensationalizes disasters, converting them into survival dramas, complete with big-name actors and actresses. Moreover, Hozic, Majic, and Yahaya Ibrahim cast the celebrities in a wider spectrum of entertainment, moving from the culturally elliptical career of Barbie, to the movie-making industry both as a platform of neoliberal rationality and its opposite, namely, a postmodern critique of decadence. Particular attention is placed on human trafficking and famine in the chapter.

Conclusion

As a matter of everyday life, race, gender, and culture have always been central to International Relations. The recognition of this basic fact, however, took much longer to be accepted in the discipline of IR, and headway has only been made through exceptional efforts at multiple levels by determined actors. As we noted above, the imbrication of race, gender, and culture as experience and in scholarship does not mean that there is universal acceptance for it; and in fact, many major writers in traditional IR reject their import. Constructivists have perhaps made the most headway in registering the impact of culture in IR, albeit most often through the concept of ideas. In fact, constructivism has made such forays into the discipline that it became the third platform of IR theory, replacing Marxism after the end of the Cold War. Thus, while most IR syllabi, especially at the graduate studies level, carry realism, liberalism (and their neos) and constructivism, problems of gender and race are still on the margins. These observations are particularly true in the United States.

The silence on race and gender in the IR academy, though less so now, was always justified on the basis that either the scholarship on those problems is not scientific, or that it does not impact the key issue areas of International Relations – taken to be war, and other state-to-state interactions. Against this, Shiera S. el-Malik (2013, 118) builds on Tickner's (1997) critique of IR's epistemological reifications, by suggesting that the 'present-hind-sight' of anti-colonial struggles by women can reveal a good deal of knowledge into the coloniality of oppression. Put differently, these struggles have unique insights into the making of the recent/current world order that constitutes what el-Malik (2013, 104) calls 'crevice moment' – that is 'a moment of disruption in hegemonic forms of discursive consolidation'.

Many students of International Relations legitimately ask why they should study colonialism and imperialism, and other forms of domination that existed in the distant past. The question is legitimate not only because it is difficult to make connections to a past that is complex, but also because there always appear to be pressing problems in the present – hunger, inequality, nuclear weapons, invasions, humanitarian crises due to hurricanes, floods, earthquakes, and the like. Moreover, many students also correctly ask, what does one do with these postcolonial critiques, articulate and insightful though they may be. These questions are asked even by those who are wont to challenge hegemonic knowledge be it in its masculinist, patriarchal, or colonial/imperial forms. The concerns exist, therefore, on both problem-solving and critical grounds.

First, on the question of why focus on the distant past. Postcolonialism is keen on the past because it thinks that the current world system is built on multiple layers of institutions, experiences, practices, and most importantly, memories of those experiences and practices from the past. Hundreds of millions of people in the world today have direct experience of colonialism, and this is so both in the North and South, or East and West if you prefer. Except for Latin America, most of what we know as the Third World only became independent after World War II. Colonialism is not something from the distant past. Further, imperialism, meaning foreign intervention to achieve national interest objectives, is ongoing. Postcolonial scholars and also constructivists and many liberals generally agree that invasion and occupation are acts of modern day imperialism. Keep in mind that Iraq's modern borders were largely established by British imperialism after World War I.

Secondly, and still on the question of why focus on the past, postcolonial scholars insist that the current body of mainstream IR knowledge is also based on a past, actually one that is far more distant. Little Eurocentric IR writing goes beyond Western scholars, almost always starting with the likes of Thucydides, Machiavelli, Hobbes, Kant or Locke – all writers from the 'distant past'. Moreover, Eurocentric IR almost always builds history or IR on the experiences of the 'West' at the center. There is no reason in epistemology, ontology, or methodology that forces this beginning. It is a choice made by mostly Western, and almost always scholars who are Eurocentric in their worldview.

Thirdly, and now on the question of why focus on the past when, in fact, there are things in the present that deserve urgent attention. Let us note that a focus on the past is joined to an understanding of the present. Is it possible, for example, to understand the current Israeli/Palestinian conflict, or current problems in the Middle East without going back to the Sykes-Picot Agreement of 1916? The answer is actually yes, but only if one wants to pretend that the United Kingdom and France did not participate in World War I, and that after the War, they did not undertake a major reconfiguration of the Middle East – everything from creating new states, to taking over the oil, and instituting authoritarian rule – sometimes in the form of monarchies, as was the case with Saudi Arabia. Instead of history, a good deal of explanation of the Middle East by Eurocentric IR theory is focused on religion, with a special enchantment with Islam (Pasha 2010).

Fourthly, current gendered renditions of the East–West have their roots in colonialism and modern-day imperialism. Western war-*fighting* is often articulated in converting the enemy into a dark, effeminate figure whose only value is to be saved from the diabolical Third World man. Other enemy constructions run in the reverse, such as the notion of the deranged Muslim terrorist who we are told, commits to fighting, including suicide attacks so he can pick up seventy-two virgins in heaven. In the current period, and more on questions of economic development, Skalli (2015) shows the ways in which the 'girl factor' is premised on ideas of rescuing the Muslim woman from her own supposedly civilizational worldviews of self-marginalization. Das Gupta (2006) goes further and implicates not only 'development' with imperialism, but also argues that Women's Studies in the United States is an enabler of 'empire building'.

Finally, perhaps there would be much less need for postcolonial scholars to continue with vigorous intellectual interventions in International Relations and beyond if the defense of colonialism, imperialism, racism, patriarchal domination, and civilizational claims of superiority had been abandoned. They have not. One way or another, they keep coming back in different forms. Empire, like global capitalism, is extremely adaptable and innovative. Countering domination has to be even more so, as it has been in the long history of liberation.

Notes

1 Some of these questions are explored by a number of scholars. See, for example, Abu-Lughod (1991) and Frank (1998).
2 The original French version was published in 1952.

3 *Sati* designates a past practice (now illegal) whereby widows were expected to commit suicide or immolate themselves on their husband's funeral pyre.
4 For further engagement of these questions in IR, see Sajed and Inayatullah 2017, and Hobson and Sajed 2017.

Suggested readings

Barkawi, T. (2006). *Globalization and war*. Lanham, MD: Roman & Littlefield. This book is significant not only because it is written by one of the most insightful and prolific postcolonial thinkers in IR, but also because it is about war, an area of inquiry that postcolonial theory needs to urgently deepen.

Chowdhry, G. and Nair, S. (2004). *Power, postcolonialism, and international relations*. London: Routledge.

Fanon, F. (1963/1961). *The wretched of the earth*. Trans. by C. Farrington. New York: Grove Press. One of the founding texts of postcolonialism. Fanon, a psychiatrist by training, was directly involved in wars of decolonization and independence movements. Although he shows that violence was the signature of colonial domination, he also insists that culture was a technology of submission. Most importantly, Fanon points to the mechanisms, structural and personal, through which the colonized must fight oppression in all its forms.

Inayatullah, N. and Blaney, B. (2004). *International relations and the problem of difference*. London: Routledge. This is a landmark book in postcolonialism and IR. The great strength of the book is that is connects several strands of the international/global in ways that allow the reader to intellectually experience the making of relations of difference.

Mills, C. (1999). *The racial contract*. Ithaca: Cornell University Press. Provides a penetrating analysis of the ways in which European thought is deeply implicated in the production of a comprehensive philosophical and political system of race and racism. Moreover, the book shows how the naturalization of racism was a condition of possibility for the emergence of the idea of Europe and its Others.

Said, E. (1978). *Orientalism*. New York: Vintage. The urtext of postcolonialism. Shows how knowledge about the Middle East is inextricable from Western economic and political interests there. And yet hews to the possibility of more ethical, more principled and more accurate scholarship even in the face of such challenges.

Bibliography

Abu Lughod, J. (1991). *Before European hegemony: The world system. A.D. 1250–1350*. Oxford: Oxford University Press.

Augelli, E. and Murphy, C. (1988). *America's quest for supremacy and the Third World*. London: Pinter.

Césaire, A. (2001) [1955]. *Discourse on colonialism*. Trans. by J. Pinkham. New York: Monthly Review Press.

Chin, C. (1998). *In service and servitude*. New York: Columbia University Press.

Chowdhry, G. and Nair, S. (2004). Power, postcolonialism, and international relations. London: Routledge.

Chowdhry, G. and Rai, S. (2009). The geographies of exclusion and the politics of inclusion: Race-based exclusions in the teaching of international relations. *International Studies Perspectives*, 10, 84–91.

Collins, P.H. (1990). Defining black feminist thought. In P.H. Collins (Ed.) *Black feminist thought: Knowledge, consciousness, and the politics of empowerment* (pp. 19–40). New York: Routledge.

Cox, R.W. (1981). Social forces, states, and world orders: Beyond international relations theory. *Millennium*, 10, 126–155.

Crenshaw, K. (1989). Demarginalizing the intersection of race and sex: A black feminist critique of antidiscrimination doctrine, feminist theory and antiracist politics. *The University of Chicago Legal Forum*, 140, 139–167.

Das Gupta, M. (2006). Bewildered? Women's studies and the war on terror. In R. Riley and N. Inayatullah (Eds.). *Interrogating imperialism: Conversations on gender, race, and war* (pp. 129–153). London: Palgrave Macmillan.

Davis, A.Y. (1983). *Women, race & class*. New York: Vintage.

Du Bois, W.E.B. (1994). *The soul of black folk*. Mineola, NY: Dover Publications.

el-Malik, S.S. (2013). Intellectual work 'in-the-world': Women's writings and anti-colonial thought in Africa. *Irish Studies in International Affairs*, 24, 101–120.

Fanon, F. (1967) [1952]. *Black skins, white masks*. Trans. by C.L. Markmann. New York: Grove Press.

Fanon, F. (1963). [1961]. *The wretched of the earth*. Trans. by C. Farrington. New York: Grove Press.

Frank, A.G. (1998). *Reorient: Global economy in the Asian age*. Berkeley and Los Angeles: University of California Press.

Frank, A.G. and Gills, B.K. (1992). The five thousand year old world system: An interdisciplinary introduction, *Humboldt Journal of Social Relations*, 18, 1–79.

Gill, S.R. (1992). *American hegemony and the Trilateral Commission*. New York: Cambridge University Press.

Go, J. (2016). *Postcolonial thought and social theory*. New York: Oxford University Press.

Guha, R. (1994). *Subaltern studies: Writings on South Asian history and society, Vol. 1*. New Delhi: Oxford University Press.

Henderson, E.A. (2015). Hidden in plain sight: Racism in international relations theory. In A. Anievas, N. Manchanda and R. Shilliam (Eds.). *Race and racism in international relations: Confronting the global colour line* (pp. 19–43). New York: Routledge.

Hobson, J.M. (2012). *The Eurocentric conception of world politics: Western international theory, 1760–2010*. Cambridge: Cambridge University Press.

Hobson, J.M. and Sajed, A. (2017). Navigating beyond the Eurofetishist frontier of critical IR theory: Exploring the complex landscapes of non-western agency. *International Studies Review*, 19, 547–572.

hooks, b. (1984). *Feminist theory: From margin to center*. Cambridge, MA: South End Press.

Inayatullah, N. and Blaney, D. (2004). *International relations and the problem of difference*. London: Routledge.

Loomba, A. (2005). *Colonialism/postcolonialism* (2nd edition). London and New York: Routledge.

McClintock, A. (2001). *Double crossings*. Vancouver: Ronsdale Press.

Mittelman, J.H. and Pasha, M.K. (1997). *Out from underdevelopment revisited: Changing structures and the remaking of the third world*. London: Palgrave Macmillan.

Mohanty, C.T. (1984). Under western eyes: Feminist scholarship and colonial discourses. *boundary*, 2, 333–358.

Ong, A. (2001). Colonialism and modernity: Feminist re-presentations of women in non-western societies. In K.-K. Bhavnani (Ed.) *Feminism and 'race'* (pp. 108–120). New York: Oxford University Press.

Parry, B. (1987). Problems in current theories of colonial discourse. *Oxford Literary Review* 9(1–2): 27–58.

Pasha, M.K. (2010). In the shadows of globalization. Civilizational crisis, the 'global modern' and 'Islamic Nihilism'. *Globalization, 7*, 173–185.

Persaud, R.B. (1997). Frantz Fanon, race and world order. In S.R. Gill and J.H. Mittelman (Eds.). *Innovation and transformation in international studies* (pp. 170–184). New York: Cambridge University Press.

Persaud, R.B. (2001). *Counterhegemony and foreign policy: The dialectic of marginalized and global forces in Jamaica.* Albany: SUNY Press.

Persaud, R.B. and Chin, C.B.N. (2016). *From sexation to sexualization: Dispersed submission in the racialized global sex industry. Cambridge Review of International Affairs, 29,* 270–289.

Peterson, S.V. (2003). *A critical rewriting of global political economy: Integrating reproductive, productive, and virtual economies.* London: Routledge.

Said, E. (1978). *Orientalism.* New York: Vintage Books.

Sajed, A. and Inayatullah, N. (2017). On the perils of lifting the weight of structures: An engagement with Hobson's critique of the discipline of IR. *Postcolonial Studies, 19,* 201–209.

Skalli, L.H. (2015). The *Girl Factor* and the (in) security of coloniality: A view from the Middle East. *Alternatives, 40,* 174–187.

Slater, D. (2004). *Geopolitics and the post-colonial.* Malden, MA: Blackwell.

Spivak, G.C. (1985). Can the subaltern speak? Speculations on widow-sacrifice. *Wedge* (Winter/Spring), 120–130.

Tickner, A. (1997). You just don't understand: Troubled engagements between feminists and IR theorists. *International Studies Quarterly, 41,* 611–632.

True, J. (2003). *Gender, globalization, and postsocialism.* New York: Columbia Press.

Vitalis, R. (2015). *White world order: Black power politics: The birth of American international relations.* Ithaca: Cornell University Press.

Vucetic, S. (2011). *The Anglosphere: A genealogy of racialized identity in international relations.* Stanford: Stanford University Press.

Whitworth, S. (2004). *Men, militarism, and US peacekeeping: A gendered analysi*s. Boulder: Lynne Rienner.

2 Postcolonialism and its relevance for International Relations in a globalized world

Sankaran Krishna

Introduction	19
The given wisdom	19
What difference does postcolonialism make?	21
The way forward	28
Conclusion	31

Introduction

This chapter considers the relevance of postcolonialism as a perspective to understand the world in which we live. After first delineating the hegemonic or dominant narrative (as constituted by the discipline of mainstream International Relations, or IR) about how different peoples and regions of the world interact with each other we move to describing what is distinctive about postcolonialism as an alternative perspective seeking to describe that same reality. We consider some of its main preoccupations, questions and concerns, and assess its key contributions. We end by foregrounding some of the challenges facing this perspective that (like any other) has to constantly adapt and evolve to remain relevant in a dynamic and changing world.

The given wisdom

The discipline of International Relations (IR) constructs a certain view of the world, one that is anchored by methodological nationalism: it sees our world as comprising of nation-states locked in competition amidst an overall milieu of anarchy. Following this premise, maintenance of national security becomes the non-negotiable *sine qua non* of every state, and furtherance of national interest at every opportunity becomes its *raison d'être*.

According to the story IR tells of itself, an important moment in the emergence of this (initially European) world of competing states was the Treaties of Westphalia (1648) that concluded three decades of warfare in Europe. As a result of the treaties, vertical ties connecting European sovereigns and their territories to the Papacy in Rome were loosened and created the impetus for the secular idea that religious affiliation or preference of each kingdom was a 'domestic' matter. From thereon they interacted horizontally with each other as putatively equal and sovereign states, with no higher entity to govern them, giving rise to the system of interacting nation-states we know today.

This depiction of a world of self-interested nation states in the discipline of IR is paralleled by an analogous description of the world by neoclassical economics as one populated by selfish individuals or self-interested firms locked in competition. Together, these depictions of the political and economic domains were integral to what one might call a modernist epistemology, or the way in which we understand ourselves in the contemporary world. Indeed, such self-interested utility-maximizing actions by individuals or firms or nations came to be defined as the essence of reason or rationality itself (Ashley 1983 & 1984).

This picture of a world of self-interested, individuals/firms/nation-states competitively interacting in an anarchic milieu arose from and was powerfully augmented by a wider episteme that might be accurately described as 'Social Darwinism' – that is, not just humans and nations, but nature itself can be seen as comprising entities and species locked in an endless and competitive quest for survival and self-advancement. In this world, the 'fittest' – those most adaptable to their environment and with the ability to out-compete others for finite resources – are not merely the winners: their victory is seen as both normatively (or morally) just and necessary for the perpetuation and advancement, or evolution, of all life forms on the planet.

Self-interested competition is the engine or source of our desire to excel, to master nature, and to overcome natural and social adversity. Such competitive instincts must not be reined in, but rather allowed to flourish (barring some sensible precautionary guard-rails provided by a minimalist state, of course) as they work to the collective benefit of all of us. In other words, a form of asocial sociality constitutes the locomotive of history and undergirds the evolutionary trajectory of the liberal imagination and construction of our world.

Among the many consequences of such a world-view, two need emphasis at this point. First, there is a conservative or consequentialist bias inherent in this perspective. That is, the 'winners' of such a supposedly rational and competitive world are, by definition, the ablest or those most capable, and the 'losers' are those who are less worthy. There is little inclination to pause and consider whether we as individuals or as nations or a planet are headed along the right track; whether 'winning' in the short run may be tantamount to losing over the longue durée; whether we are moving in a direction that is suicidal or fundamentally wrong. Similarly, there is no capacity to entertain the idea that the 'losers' may embody values and resources that are worth preserving and learning from.

Secondly, since many of these qualities – self-interest, competitiveness, and anarchy, to mention three – are seen as timelessly human and true, IR has a 'presentist' bias: that is, it regards history, or the past, as nothing other than prior instances of this story of anarchy, competition and self-interest. To give just one instance, realism or the emphasis on a power-politics understanding of the world, has an unbroken continuity in mainstream IR literatures from the Peloponnesian wars of ancient Greece, as outlined by Thucydides, through the internecine politics of early modern Italian city-states, as depicted by Machiavelli, to understanding the Cold War in the twentieth century, as theorized by someone such as Hans Morgenthau, to analyzing the rise of China and the possible end of US hegemony by someone such as John Mearsheimer. In other words, there is no need to belabor the specifics of different times and places, or to consider the possibility that societies may have been ordered on principles that have little or nothing to do with competitive self-interest (Polanyi 1944). History is essentially the same story of might being right; of self-interested actions coalescing to collective good; of competition as the engine of progress and evolution; and it is basically a cautionary tale littered with the failures of individuals and states who forgot these timeless lessons.

This conviction regarding the deeply static and essentialist character of peoples and spaces produces in IR a desire to discover the invariant laws that govern their relations (i.e. a 'theory' of International Relations modeled on the natural sciences), rather than regard our knowledge practices as illocutionary statements (or self-fulfilling prophecies) that produce and reify the very worlds we seek to describe. Perhaps most importantly the point of view from which this story of the international system is narrated, its unmarked locus of enunciation if you will, is that of the large and powerful nation-states of the international system (Waltz 1979).

What difference does postcolonialism make?

First, in contrast to a mainstream narrative of IR that sees the present world as having been timelessly that way and qualities such as self-interest and competitiveness as essential to human nature, postcolonialism sees our modern world and such values as having emerged out of a cataclysmic set of events or conjoined historical processes over the last five centuries that may be initially glossed as colonialism and capitalism. The 'discovery' of the new world by Christopher Columbus' voyages in 1492 inaugurated a violent process of the extraction of valuable minerals and raw materials from there as their native populations were exterminated by genocide and disease. It set in motion the trans-Atlantic slave trade as black Africans were exported to the new colonies to work mines and plantations. It impelled further voyages that discovered a sea-borne trading route from Europe to Asia going around the southern tip of Africa. Through these processes, it provided wealth and markets for certain classes of people in Western Europe who would, in time, propel the industrial revolution and the spread of capitalism across that continent. As Robbie Shilliam (2015, 185) succinctly puts it, the genealogy of '…global capital starts with colonialism … a plantation on expropriated land next to a provision ground – and not in a factory next to an enclosure'.

The emergence of capitalism and industrial society in the northwest corner of the European continent profoundly changed the world – for both better and worse. More than mere money, capital is a social relationship whereby some people who own the means of production (machinery, raw materials, factory sites, land) are able to employ the labor of others to make profit and use that for further rein-vestment and expansion. In comparison to any previous form of production (such as hunting-gathering, slavery, or feudalism), capitalism has proven to be the most innovative, dynamic and exploitative. In large part this has hinged on the fact that competition lies at the very core of the system and because its coercive aspects are ideologically camouflaged by the illusion that labor is free and has the option to not work. This freedom is illusory because under capitalism laboring classes have no other way of ensuring their own survival except by working for wages.

Secondly, given this understanding of a world irrevocably shattered by the events of 1492, postcolonial is synonymous with post-Columbian. It is a per-spective that sees colonialism not as something that happened in the past and has ended but rather as very much part of our ongoing present. Postcolonialism does not mean '*after the end* of colonialism' but rather '*after the onset* of colonial-ism' seen to have begun in 1492 and still relevant in our present-day world.

Thirdly, the fact that the 'west'[1] was the first region to experience the related processes of industrialization and capitalism meant that it surged ahead of the rest of the world in terms of productivity, material affluence, and the ability to militarily, economically, politically and culturally dominate the rest of the world. Such evidence as there is from historical accounts, travel memoirs and other sources indicate that prior to 1492 the world was nowhere near as unequal as it would become thereafter. In fact, it was the fabled riches of the East that ener-gized western travelers like Marco Polo and Christopher Columbus to embark on intrepid voyages to find them. Yet this surge of the west was not a self-contained or indigenous process but integrally related to and based upon the simultaneous underdevelopment of the rest. In other words, west and non–west were produced coevally and through a dialectical relationship to each other.

Fourthly, consequent upon this understanding, postcolonialism radically dis-rupts the methodological nationalism of mainstream IR, that is, the tendency to view the world as populated exclusively by self-contained nation-states. It instead suggests that economic development, political movements, cultural productions, ideas and ideologies, everything about our material and social lives, have to be understood contrapuntally, that is, as results of global and inter-related processes that suffuse the entire world. Historical events and processes cannot be understood in their national isolation but rather as interactions that span across time and space and transform the entire planet (Krishna 2009).

To give one example of the related process of western development and under-development in the rest of the world, the first industrial revolution (often dated to the period 1770 to 1830) was initially propelled by the accumulation of capital in the hands of entrepreneurial classes (or an emerging bourgeoisie) in England who, as we saw above, drew their wealth from a global set of processes: long-distance trade with Asia, the trans-Atlantic slave trade, plantations, mines, and investments in the Caribbean and elsewhere in the new world. As England industrialized, artisanal and small-scale manufacturing outfits across her captive Indian colony were de-industrialized and put out of business since the colonial regime imposed free-trade or laissez-faire preventing the Indians from protecting their industries from this onslaught of cheap imports. As England's booming factory towns like Liverpool and Manchester sucked in displaced serfs from her own countryside she underwent a process of urbanization – whereas in India the destruction of handicrafts and artisanal industries due to cheap English imports led to the decline of towns and cities and the population moved in the opposite direction (i.e. ruralization was the result). As England urbanized, her agriculture was revolutionized by the application of industrial technology due to the growing scarcity of labor in the countryside and the increasing size of agricultural holdings. But in India, as a flood of people abandoned declining towns and cities to return to their villages, the consequent 'over-population' meant smaller and smaller landholdings which exercised a brake on the application of technology to agriculture. The presence of cheap 'surplus' labor flooding the rural sector in India removed the need for mechanized agriculture making it less dynamic and productive over time.

By the late eighteenth century as England was on her way to becoming the factory of the world, she imported raw cotton from all over the world – while India, once renowned for her textiles, prints, and calicoes, was now converted into an exporter of raw cotton to England and an importer of finished goods from there. Hence, one can argue England's industrial revolution was not mainly the product of her national genius or the peculiar skills, attributes and intelligence of her people, or because of the providential wealth of coal and iron ore in her land. Rather the world's first industrial revolution occurred there as a result of a set of economic, social, and political processes that spanned the entire globe; and its impact too, for better and for worse, radiated out into a world far beyond that island. Similarly, India's descent into poverty and 'over-population' is not a sign of its inferiority or its peoples' lack of capacity for development: her failure to develop was produced by the very processes that underlay the success of Britain (Krishna 2014).

One way of understanding the depth of India's underdevelopment during its colonial period is by focusing on the frequency of famines in that country throughout the nineteenth and early twentieth centuries, culminating in the Great Bengal famine of 1943–45 during which as many as three million perished. While these famines are routinely described as the results of 'natural' phenomena such as monsoon failures or drought, there is impressive historical evidence that this was not the case. A British colonial regime wedded to the ideology of laissez-faire refused to intervene by lowering prices during times of drought, and it was common for regions in India to be exporting food grains out of the country even as neighboring regions were seeing starvation and deaths in the hundreds of thousands. The onerous levy of land tax was often not reduced during these times of famine nor would the colonial regime undertake to move food grains to areas of shortage due to this commitment to laissez-faire (Davis 2002). This contrapuntal reading of something like the first industrial revolution, seeing it in its global interconnections, could not be more different from the ahistorical methodological nationalism of mainstream IR narratives (Said 1993).

Fifthly, the material bifurcation of the world into a developed, affluent, capitalist and industrialized west versus an underdeveloped, poor, overpopulated and agrarian east was inevitably accompanied by the preponderant ability of the former to narrate the history and the likely future of the world in its own image, and to locate the latter as weak, pre-capitalist or pre-modern, and in need of tutelage to achieve, through mimicry, what the west had already accomplished. In other words, colonialism (and later on modernization theory) became the vehicle through which the west translated its growing material domination of the world into a civilizational process with itself as the center and the non-western world as the backward periphery. One of the signal contributions of postcolonialism is to place the discipline of IR squarely within this intellectual tradition of modernization theory: like that body of work, when mainstream IR considers the third world at all, it primarily configures it as a zone of lack, and in need of aid and tutelage to become more like the west (Krasner 1985; Jackson 1991).

This ability of the industrialized and capitalist west to represent itself as the epitome of modern civilization and cast the rest of the world as provincial, second-order mimics can be termed Eurocentrism. Eurocentrism is vastly more than mere xenophobia or prejudice or suspicion of strangers and foreigners that all societies have entertained presumably for a very long time. After the industrial revolution and the advent of capitalism, European views about their own innate superiority or civilizational advance were buttressed by an enormously powerful material foundation. Eurocentrism is, if you will, xenophobia on steroids. Perhaps most significantly the past and present of Europe were now held out to be the desired future for the rest of the world whose task would be the emulation of the supposedly self-contained genius of Europe.

Mainstream IR is quintessentially Eurocentric in that it is written from the viewpoint of the advanced nations. Its ideological purpose is to sanctify, depoliticize, and normalize the domination of the rest of the world by the west. By speaking endlessly and ahistorically about a system comprising self-interested and competing nation-states that are supposed equals within an anarchic milieu, mainstream IR draws our attention away from the deeply hierarchical, racist and colonial character of the interactions between different peoples and parts of an interconnected planet. Through its contrasting narratives that emphasize colonialism, racism, genocide, conquest and economic inequality as results of a conjoined and contrapuntal history, one that is avowedly global and not locked within methodological nationalism, postcolonial theory represents a fundamental adversary or critique of Eurocentrism. Hence, in contrast to the image of *equal* states interacting in a competitive and *anarchic* world system portrayed by the mainstream, postcolonialism foregrounds the highly *unequal* and deeply *hierarchical* nature of the world system.

To put it differently, from a postcolonial perspective, the glories of the west – modern industry, science, democracy, rationality, the nation-state, liberty, individual rights, the welfare state, to mention some – which are conventionally seen as arising out of a hermetically sealed and self-referential genius of

Europeans – are regarded as emergent from an interactive and thoroughly contrapuntal planetary history. All too often the costs of these glories were visited upon the non-west while their benefits were confined to the west. To give a concrete example, it was easier for Britain to gradually accede to the demands of her own rising working class movement for wages, rights to unionize, and access to power within its own country because of its ability to exploit laboring classes across its colonies where its power was unrestrained and there were no pretensions to being democratic or inclusive.

Western democracy then was not so much a characteristic intrinsic to such societies but rather underwritten by the super-exploitation of peoples elsewhere. The inability to view democracy from such a global perspective continues to this day. Thus, it is routine in the US media to refer to the Middle East as a place rife with authoritarian governments and equally routine to attribute this to Islam's alleged incompatibility with democracy, inability to tolerate dissent, or a lack of respect for individual rights, etc. In contrast, the US is positioned as a bastion of democracy and defender of human rights on a global scale. Yet, the fact that nearly every Middle Eastern dictatorship is underwritten by US military and political support barely gets mentioned. While the Saudi regime is rightly excoriated for its export of an extremist Wahabi form of religious fundamentalism, the fact that it would swiftly collapse without the support of its staunch ally over the last seven decades, the United States, is assiduously ignored (Khalidi 2005).[2] Methodological nationalism is not just the liability of a discipline like mainstream IR; it suffuses our media and is part of our common sense and the way in which we have been taught to view the world.

The postcolonial critique of Eurocentrism recognizes the incredible difficulty, one might even say impossibility, of the task at an epistemological level. For it is a fact that nearly everything we know about the world today, and even of the history of the non-west, has come to us through discourses that are, at their core, Eurocentric. To recover the religious traditions of India, or the histories of kinship and social relations in Africa, or the rituals and customs of the indigenous peoples of the Americas, when so much of what we think we know about these matters have been gained through centuries of scholarship that were marked by both colonialism and Eurocentrism is a difficult task (Viswanathan 1989; Sinha 1995; Mamdani 1996; Mani 1998; Chakrabarty 2000; Mignolo 2005). Added to this is the fact that the intellectual classes of non-western societies, often at the forefront of movements for political independence and autonomous scholarship, are themselves educated in Eurocentric institutions and traditions. Postcolonialism thus views Eurocentrism as a reality that cannot be wished away, an intimate structure that informs one's own intellectual formation, and therefore as an archive that has to be read against the grain – one that has to be critically interrogated rather than accepted as truth. Further, this deconstruction of Eurocentric knowledges needs to be done without lapsing into belief in a pre-contact pure nativism or truth, that is, the idea that only Africans can write authentic histories of Africa, or other such claims to a superior knowledge because of one's identity. One way then of dealing with the inescapable reality of Eurocentrism is to view every knowledge claim from a postcolonial perspective that is sensitive to the global or contrapuntal character of our material and ideological worlds.

What all these various attributes of postcolonialism add up to is this: it regards the discourse of mainstream IR not as a truthful discourse about the world but rather as an ideological formation that needs to be deconstructed from a certain perspective, one that foregrounds the conjoined histories of capitalism and colonial conquest. Does this mean postcolonialism itself gives up any claim to be an objective, impartial, and scientific description of the world? To a certain extent, yes, it does. It regards knowledge as always inextricably intertwined with power, and in that sense, it regards every act of representation that claims the status of truth for itself as a deeply political (if also predictable) move that ought to be contested. How then does postcolonialism sustain the claim that its own depiction of the international realm is either normatively or empirically better than that of mainstream IR? The answer to that excellent question takes us into the work of one of the most influential theorists from within the postcolonial oeuvre, Edward Said.

On the one hand, Said's (1978) landmark work *Orientalism* shows how the west constructs the Orient as a space that is a different, inferior, feminized, untrustworthy, emotional, dangerous and lascivious counterpoint to an Occident that is rarely named but serves as the invisible eye/I that constitutes the locus of enunciation. This occidental self is correspondingly depicted, more by contrast and implication than explicitly, as superior, civilized, rational, trustworthy, calm, and in control of its emotions. Said is beholden to the idea of discourse, that our representative practices are always interlaced with considerations of power, and hence he abjures epistemic realism, that is, the idea that there is a 'truth' out there about the Orient or the Middle East, that can be excavated if only one relied upon the native informants, or acquired greater mastery over its languages, or consulted better and more authentic sources, etc.

Yet, on the other hand, in a tension or even contradiction with his position on the impossibility of epistemic realism, Said remains committed to the position that 'better' scholarship on the Middle East, one that is less complicit with western interests, less contaminated by empire, relatively more objective or impartial, or even 'more truthful' in some empirical sense, is still possible. Said is aware of this contradiction in his epistemology, owns up to it, and then carries on with his efforts at 'better' scholarship. Said's position here is well captured by a paraphrased observation from the Nobel laureate economist Robert Solow about the difficulty of achieving objectivity in social science: the fact that a perfectly aseptic or sterile operating theater is impossible does not mean one conducts surgery in a sewer. In related vein, even as one acknowledges that all scholarship is tainted with the interests and worldviews of the powerful, one should continue to strive for scholarship that is relatively more detached, more objective and less in bed with power than the dominant forms of representation or the mainstream.

This pragmatic resolution of an intractable epistemological knot makes sense if one remembers that for Said scholarship was not merely a matter of arriving at better and more accurate descriptions or representations of the Middle East just for their own sake. As a Palestinian-Christian born in Jerusalem thirteen years before the creation of Israel as a nation-state at the expense of the Palestinian people, and whose life thereafter was that of an exile unable to return to his ancestral home, Said's scholarship and political activism have always been intertwined. He sees the creation of Israel as a form of western penitence for its long history of anti-Semitism, one that culminated horrendously in the Holocaust – but a penitence that came at the expense of Palestinians and their homeland. The gradual takeover of Palestinian lands by Jewish settlers, which gained momentum in the first decades of the twentieth century, was itself possible because as a British colonial protectorate, Palestinians had lost their sovereignty. In other words, the 'Palestinian problem' (which should more properly be called the 'Israel problem') is a legacy of colonialism (Said 1979). Said's political and intellectual life were animated by the desire to help recover the Palestinian nation for its rightful inhabitants, and to redirect the state of Israel from its growing Zionism towards a just two-state solution.

The luxury of an omniscient, detached, and objective Archimedean standpoint (that invisible locus of enunciation from which so much of mainstream IR is written) is not one available to Said, and like him, to most who adhere to a postcolonial standpoint. Scholarship is always wedded to a normative or principled political agenda; that does not however mean it is either dishonest or somehow always corrupt. Laying out your political predilections openly, and yet striving to read the empirical world with as much impartiality and honesty as possible, remains a worthwhile and feasible endeavor.

Said's simultaneous commitment to a political cause (the recovery of the Palestinian nation for its people) *and* to a meta-critique of power wherever and whenever it manifests itself, including the cause to which one is committed, is best reflected in an episode at a conference honoring his work. After many speeches that lavishly praised him for his scholarship and commitment to the Palestinian cause, in his response Said captured the essence of the postcolonial standpoint: he said he would fight relentlessly for the establishment of a Palestinian nation-state so that, upon its very formation, he could become its foremost critic.

In sum, postcolonialism offers a historical and normative alternative to abstract and economistic theories of mainstream IR invariably written from the perspective of the dominant societies of the world and from a framework that we have characterized as methodological nationalism. It contrapuntally describes a world in which east and west, poor and rich, underdeveloped and developed, are coevally produced and reproduced. By centering the five centuries-long intertwined processes of capitalism and colonialism, a postcolonial perspective is animated by a normative or principled desire to move the relations between peoples of varied nations, regions, classes, genders, religions, and other identities in a less racist and more egalitarian direction (Persaud & Walker

2001; Chowdhry & Nair 2003; Jones 2006; Anievas, Manchanda & Shilliam 2014; Sajed 2017; Pham & Shilliam 2016).

The way forward

A theoretical perspective has to constantly evolve in sync with a changing world if it is to remain relevant and postcolonialism is no exception. In this final section, we look at two contemporary encounters that show postcolonialism to be an invaluable resource for progressive change: global warming and first nations.

One of the most compelling aspects of Naomi Klein's (2015) book *This Changes Everything* is her demonstration that our planetary survival and our economic system (capitalism) are at loggerheads. If we continue along the road that every nation should look out primarily for its own self-interest in a context of ever freer trade we are doomed because the rate of global warming will soon cause coastlines (where the majority of the world's population lives) to be inundated and temperatures to rise to the point where human life will be impossible.

In a powerful example, Klein details how over two decades ago the province of Ontario in Canada embarked on an ambitious state-funded program to secure most of its energy from the sun and greatly reduce fossil fuel emissions. The government induced one of the world's best manufacturers (in terms of efficiency and quality) of solar energy panels to relocate to Ontario. The new plant was housed in abandoned automotive factories that had left Ontario for countries with lower labor costs and fewer environmental regulations; it generated employment for many who had been laid off when the auto plants closed; and it sourced much of its raw materials from within the region. Solar energy seemed an ingenious solution to recession: environmentally responsible, creating good jobs, and growing the local economy.

Yet the Ontario venture was shut down because it was in violation of WTO's principles proscribing government subsidization of domestic industries and the most favored nation clause that requires a country to treat all trading partners equally. There could not have been a clearer demonstration of how the commitment to smaller government and to liberal free trade principles enshrined in the WTO, and at the heart of a liberal free-market economic model, went directly counter to what was best for Ontario and for the environment. Klein's book is full of other examples of how our economic logic puts us on the road to planetary suicide.

The postcolonial critique of economistic, selfish, utility-maximizing logic; of the methodological nationalism of conventional IR; and especially of the diabolical role that a commitment to free trade has played in the history of genocide in the Third World, outlined in previous sections, powerfully converges with the work of activists such as Klein. Her argument that we need a mass, internationalist social movement that aims for nothing less than the total overhaul of capitalist logic is one that postcolonial scholars have been making for decades now.

Box 2.1: What is the Third World?

In the period of the Cold War (1945–1991), it was common to refer to the countries in Africa (with the exception of white South Africa), Asia (with the exception of Japan), Oceania (with the exceptions of Australia and New Zealand) and Latin America as the 'Third World'. This was in contrast to the western, affluent, capitalist democracies of the first world, and the centrally-planned, authoritarian, communist countries of the second world. Most Third World countries had low GDP per capita incomes; were largely agrarian rather than industrialized; had lower levels of life expectancy, literacy, nutrition, and housing; and populations that were overwhelmingly poor. In addition, most of the regimes that governed them were either military dictatorships or autocracies of various hues.

With the collapse of the Soviet Union and communism in the East bloc generally, and the full entry of China into the liberal capitalist world order, the term 'Third World' no longer has the same salience. In addition, the success of countries like South Korea, Taiwan, and Singapore further complicated the picture of poor developmental records across these continents.

Today, it is common to hear 'Third World' evoked as a negative or pejorative metaphor in much political rhetoric in places like the United States or in the west more generally. It is routine to hear politicians say that the infrastructure of the United States is approaching that of a Third World country or that its health care crisis is going to make it a Third World nation in the near future or that parts of the rust-belt Midwest are now a Third World region. In such rhetoric, Third World is synonymous with third rate, that is, something that is palpably inferior, substandard, and to be avoided at all costs.

In 1991, the chief economist of the World Bank, Lawrence Summers (who would go on thereafter to become Treasury secretary under Bill Clinton and later on the President of Harvard University) in an internal memo to his colleagues suggested that the west use the Third World as a toxic waste dump. After all, he argued, life expectancy in such countries was already very low to begin with, and one could argue that in comparison to the west they were 'under polluted'. He averred that the logic of using the Third World as a western garbage dump was economically 'impeccable'.

In all such comments, the Third World is not merely out there – distant, away from the west – but also a space that is somehow responsible for its own ailments and whose people are at fault for choosing to live the way they do. Third World people are seen as filthy, undemocratic, authoritarian, superstitious, lazy, over-populated, uncivilized, corrupt – the list of pejorative adjectives is endless.

> Postcolonialism reminds us that the Third World is not an inert fact of nature, it was not always there, and not always that way. The Third World was produced by the very same historical processes that produced wealth, hygiene, democracy, human rights, science, and civilization in the developed or western world. The Third World is the necessary obverse of the first, its tethered shadow, its possibility condition, as it were.
>
> Postcolonialism also reminds us that the bulk of the world's population lives in the Third World: to be contemptuous of the people who live there is to be contemptuous of most of humanity. There is no way for the west to claim that it is civilized, democratic, non-racist, and a champion of human rights as long as it sees the Third World as external to itself, and not its responsibility.

The issue of climate change is intertwined with that of first nations or indigenous peoples all across the planet today. In many instances, the pursuit of cheaper fossil fuels or of rare earths needed for continued industrialization pits nation-states and corporations against indigenous peoples living on lands rich in these minerals and over which many of them have regained a semblance of sovereignty after decades of protests and struggle. From a postcolonial perspective, many of the self-anointed champions of human rights and democracy – such as the United States or Canada – are themselves settler colonies built on genocide and expropriation of indigenous peoples. That violence has not ended but is ongoing. Supporting the rights of indigenous peoples – be it in the Arctic Circle or Alaskan wildlife preserves or on the issue of the Dakota Access Pipe Line – to decolonization and to sovereignty over their lands is one way to address the conjoined question of climate change and first nations.[3]

As many have detailed, the postcolonial perspective initially focused more on the experience of racial minorities in western, developed societies, especially that of migrants who arrived in the west in the latter half of the twentieth century, and was relatively inattentive to the first nations or indigenous peoples of many of these societies. In its more recent forms, postcolonialism as a perspective has evolved to realize that (a) the consolidation and reproduction of racial dominance in societies such as the United States or Canada or Australia depends on the myth of assimilation of racial minorities, and (b) that this myth of assimilation and that of the model minority is enacted largely at the expense of indigenous inhabitants of these countries. In other words, the indigenous is pitted against what Jodi Byrd (2011) calls the arrivant (immigrant) even as the white order remains in place. The struggle against global warming and climate change has forced us to realize that indigenous sovereignty over their lands may be a critical component in the struggle against a new wave of corporatist accumulation based on the more intensified exploitation of fossil fuels.

> **Box 2.2: Key points**
>
> 1: Postcolonialism does not mean 'after the *end* of colonialism' but rather refers to the condition of the world as a whole 'after the *onset* of colonialism' that began in 1492 and is still ongoing.
> 2: Phenomena such as the emergence of capitalism, industrialization, economic growth, poverty, and climate change are poorly understood if viewed through a cartography that emphasizes the nation-state. These are phenomena that are always already interactively global in their origins and their further development needs to be understood at that level.
> 3: We live in a world where our economic systems (largely premised on the idea that doing what is best for oneself in a competitive milieu drives everyone to excellence and the world to a better place) and our ecological systems are at loggerheads with each other. Selfish, utility-maximizing behavior may be 'rational' on some narrow economistic definition – but it spells extinction for us as a species.
> 4: Scholarship is always motivated in the sense that it is for some purpose and to achieve some end. Postcolonialism aims for a more just, egalitarian and less racist international system.

In analogous fashion, 'emerging' economies like Brazil, India, and China are displacing indigenous peoples in their own industrialization drives thus replicating the western experience. A struggle such as that of the Dongria Kondh in Niyamgiri in India to protect their land from a multinational corporation like Vedanta intent on mining it for bauxite has counterparts in the Amazon basin in South America, all along the frontiers of China, and in much of Africa. By pointing out the continuities between contemporary forms of violent dispossession of indigenous peoples with their historical antecedents, postcolonialism can support such struggles for legal and political redress (Krishna 2015).

Conclusion

The parallel logics of neoliberal capitalism and mainstream International Relations have brought the planet to an economic and political impasse. We find ourselves in a situation where what is best for each of us – as individuals or nations – along these allegedly rational and realist nostrums is also that which dooms us to extinction. The liberal imagination may be said to have reached an apocalyptic dead end. Overturning this belief in the rational, self-interested, competitive actions of each collectively producing the best outcomes for all is a formidable political and intellectual task – and yet it is perhaps the foremost project for us today. Our very survival depends on whether or not it can be accomplished. At this time when radically different and new ways of conceptualizing our history and imagining our possible futures are direly needed, postcolonialism has much to offer.

Notes

1 The philosopher Kwame Appiah (2016) goes to the extent of questioning whether there is such a thing as 'the west' at all. See his piece in the Manchester *Guardian* titled 'There is no such thing as western civilization', November 9, 2016.
2 In contrast to such facile Orientalist prejudice, the work of a historian like Khalidi (2005) details the multiple political movements towards democracy and liberal politics all across the Middle East in the early decades of the twentieth century. He points out that in many instances it was the actions of the colonial powers that often stymied the rise of such progressive politics and pushed these societies back under authoritarian rulers.
3 This argument is explicitly made by Klein. However, rather than regard indigenous communities as trustees of the land, we need to realize that they are the rightful owners and support the recovery of their sovereignty. In this regard, works such as Coulthard (2014), Byrd (2011), Silva (2004), and Wolfe (1998) offer more radical and promising routes to decolonizing the international.

Suggested readings

Frank, A.G. (1979). *Dependent accumulation and underdevelopment*. New York: Monthly Review Press. One of the earliest and best exponents of the thesis regarding the impact of the discovery of the New World and the slave trade in impelling the rise of the west and the consequent colonization and underdevelopment of the rest.

Rodney, W. (1972). *How Europe underdeveloped Africa*. Nairobi, Kenya: Heinemann. Writing out of a Marxist framework, this book depicts the long-term impact of European colonialism on Africa's economy, culture, and society.

Said, E. (1979). *Culture and imperialism*. New York: Vintage. Offers a dazzling and erudite counterpoint to the emaciated methodological nationalism of mainstream IR. Shows culture and identity to be the products of agonistic encounters between different peoples, spaces, and times rather than abstractly equivalent units.

Sinha, M. (1995). *Colonial masculinity: The 'manly Englishman' and the 'effeminate Bengali' in the late 19th century*. Manchester: Manchester University Press. Muddies our categories of west and east, colonizer and colonized by showing them to be joint imperial cultural formations rather than the one-sided impact of one on the other.

Young, R. (2001). *Postcolonialism: An historical introduction*. Oxford: Blackwell. Remains the most comprehensive reader on classic postcolonial works.

Bibliography

Anievas, A. Manchanda, N. and Shilliam, R. (Eds.). (2014). *Race and racism in international relations: Confronting the global color line*. New York: Routledge.

Appiah, K. (2016). 'There is no such thing as western civilization.' November 9, *Guardian*: www theguardian.com/world/2016/nov/09/western-civilisation-appiah-reith-lecture

Ashley, R.K. (1983). Three modes of economies. *International Studies Quarterly*, 27, 463–496.

Ashley, R.K. (1984). The poverty of neorealism. *International Organization*, 38, 225–286.

Byrd, J. (2011). *The transit of empire: Indigenous critiques of colonialism.* Minneapolis: University of Minnesota Press.

Chakrabarty, D. (2000). *Provincializing Europe: Postcolonial thought and historical difference.* Princeton: Princeton University Press.

Chang, Ha-Joon. (2009). *Bad samaritans: The myth of free trade and the secret history of capitalism.* London: Bloomsbury.

Chowdhry, G. and Nair, S. (Eds.). (2004). *Power, postcolonialism and international relations: Reading race, gender and class.* New York: Routledge.

Coulthard, G.S. (2014). *Red skin, white masks: Rejecting the colonial politics of recognition.* Minneapolis: University of Minnesota Press.

Davis, M. (2002). *Late Victorian holocausts: El nino famines and the making of the third world.* London: Verso.

Frank, A.G. (1979). *Dependent accumulation and underdevelopment.* New York: Monthly Review Press.

Jackson, R. (1991). *Quasi-states: Sovereignty, international relations and the world.* Cambridge: Cambridge University Press.

Jones, B.G. (Ed.). (2006). *Decolonizing international relations.* Lanham, MD: Rowman and Littlefield.

Khalidi, R. (2005). *Resurrecting empire: Western footprints and America's perilous path in the Middle East.* Boston: Beacon Press.

Klein, N. (2015). *This changes everything: Capitalism versus the climate.* New York: Simon and Schuster.

Krasner, S. (1985). *Structural conflict: The third world against global liberalism.* Berkeley, CA: University of California Press.

Krishna, S. (2009). *Globalization and postcolonialism: Hegemony and resistance in the 21st century.* Lanham, MD: Rowman and Littlefield.

Krishna, S. (2014). How does colonialism work? In J. Edkins, and M. Zehfuss (Eds.). *Global politics: A new introduction* (2nd edition). New York: Routledge.

Krishna, S. (2015). Colonial legacies and contemporary destitution: Race, law and the limits of human security. *Alternatives,* 40, 85–101.

Mamdani, M. (1996). *Citizen and subject: Contemporary Africa and the legacy of late colonialism.* Princeton, NJ: Princeton University Press.

Mani, L. (1998). *Contentious traditions: The debate on 'sati' in colonial India.* Berkeley, CA: University of California Press.

Mignolo, W. (2005). *The idea of Latin America.* London, UK: Blackwell.

Persaud, R.B. and Walker, R.B.J. (2001). Race in international relations: Special issue. *Alternatives,* 26, 4.

Pham, N.Q. and Shilliam, R. (Eds.). (2016). *Meanings of bandung: Postcolonial orders and decolonial visions.* Lanham, MD: Rowman and Littlefield.

Polanyi, K. (1944). *The great transformation: The political and economic origins of our time.* Boston, MA: Beacon Press.

Rodney, W. (1972). *How Europe underdeveloped Africa.* Nairobi, Kenya: Heinemann.

Said, E. (1978). *Orientalism.* New York, NY: Vintage.

Said, E. (1979). *The question of Palestine.* New York, NY: Vintage.

Said, E. (1993). *Culture and imperialism.* New York, NY: Knopf.

Sajed, A. (2017). Race and international relations – What's in a word? A debate around John Hobson's *The Eurocentric conception of world politics. Postcolonial Studies* 19, 168–172.

Shilliam, R. (2015). *The black Pacific: Anti-colonial struggles and oceanic connections*. London, UK: Bloomsbury.

Silva, N. (2004). *Aloha betrayed: Native Hawaiian resistance to American colonialism*. Durham, NC: Duke University Press.

Sinha, M. (1995). *Colonial masculinity: The 'manly Englishman' and the 'effeminate Bengali' in the late 19th century*. Manchester, UK: Manchester University Press.

Viswanathan, G. (1989). *Masks of conquest: Literary study and British rule in India*. New York, NY: Columbia University Press.

Waltz, K. (1979). *Theory of international relations*. Reading, MA: Addison Wesley.

Wolfe, P. (1998). *Settler colonialism and the transformation of anthropology: The politics and poetics of an ethnographic event*. London, UK: Bloomsbury.

Young, R. (2001). *Postcolonialism: An historical introduction*. Oxford: Blackwell.

3   Race in International Relations

Srdjan Vucetic and Randolph B. Persaud

Introduction	35
Race as theory	36
Race in global society	40
Race and global economic development	43
Race and security	47
Conclusion	52

Introduction[1]

Race as a concept has always been difficult to define. Racism as a practice, however, has been more easily identified, and this in both historical and contemporary time frames. How could this anomaly exist? Part of the answer may be found in a methodological preference through which scholars seek to define what race 'is', and then proceed to apply it in the real world of experience. A similar observation can be made with respect to the role of race in International Relations. This chapter will allow us to more clearly specify the concept of race and its relationship to International Relations by examining how race has functioned, and with what practical effects.

Our historical-genealogical approach has three advantages. First, it begins with a recognition that it is *in actual history* (not theory or abstract principles) that racism has asserted itself and where race emerged as a general organizing category (Painter 2010). This occurred on a *global scale*, which means that race operates everywhere, not just in some countries. Next, as the anthropologist Michel-Rolph Trouillot (1995) has noted, there is a difference between what happened and what is said to have happened; indeed, the latter always distorts the former, sometimes massively so. The writing of history in the Western Academy has played a major role in shaping how we see the world today, and how that world has come to be, especially as it moved from 'primitivity' to modernity. This directly relates to the third advantage of our historical-genealogical approach – the fact that it is fundamentally in sync with the postcolonial perspectives on International Relations specifically (Chowdhry & Nair 2004; Seth 2013; Pham

& Shilliam 2016), and on world historical development more generally (Young 1995). In our usage, the postcolonial approach is a kind of history from below, or what a group of scholars in India (Guha 1982; Spivak 1988; Chakrabarthy 2000) called *subaltern* history – history whose task is to challenge, modify, and correct the Eurocentric history which is popular in International Relations, and on which basis most of International Relations theory is built. The subaltern turn is obviously built on the critique of Orientalism advanced earlier by Said (1978).

Our argument follows from this perspective: in International Relations, race has two broad avenues of occurrence. One is what we shall call *actually exist-ing racism*, meaning racism that has been practiced as action. The other avenue is International Relations scholarship in which race manifests itself through both commission (what is written and taught), and omission (what is left out, minimized and, indeed, *silenced*) (Chowdhry and Rai 2009; Mittelman 2009). To make this argument, we first discuss the concept of race, and then devote one section each on global society, global development, and security. In the concluding section, we reflect on the future of race and racism in world politics.

Race as theory

The scholarship we read in International Relations has been written only over the past century, and most of this writing has not only taken place in Europe and the United States (with important contributions from Australia and Canada), but also from a Western perspective, by Western scholars, and by and large with the subtle or explicit intention of advocating, defending, and/or legitimizing Western interests, values, and beyond. Why does this matter, and what does any of this have to do with race? Those are perfectly legitimate questions.

Let us start with a premise that race is itself a product of culture, and practices of race and racism recursively feed back into culture. They are, in other words, reciprocally constituted. Culturally, the Western construction of the Third World is more likely to be taken as authoritative knowledge, but not the other way around. Table 3.1 below presents a simplified picture of the ways the West sees the Third World – a.k.a., the 'rest', 'The East', 'the Global South', and itself, across ten sectors of life, ranging from 'civilization' to 'religion'.

The basic take away here is the self-conception of the West as scientific, rational, forward looking and industrious. These attributes are taken to be innate at times, while in other situations they are taken to be a part of European culture, that is to say, a product of European ingenuity. The Third World, collapsed into an undifferentiated mass, is formulated into a backward and superstitious people who are bogged down by the memories of colonialism and slavery. The Third World lacks the basic political equipment, that is, the modern state, needed to bring forth economic and social development (Landes 1990; Harrison 1998).

Such constructions are usually called *Orientalist* – a term originating in the cultural studies of the 1970s and particularly in the work of Edward Said. Orientalist elements can be found everywhere in the Western thought, not just in International Relations (Doty 1996; Walker 2006; Hobson 2012;

Table 3.1 Western views of itself and Others

	The Third World	The West
General description	Developing/backward	Free; developed
Civilization	Ancient to non-existent; anachronistic; reconstructed as Western	Modern
Knowledge	Local; parochial; religious	Universal; philosophical
Technology	Consumers; followers	Producers; innovators
Culture	Folk; superstition; exotic, parochial	Cosmopolitan; rational; scientific, problem-solving
Nation–state	Fragile; corrupt	Strong; functional
Economy and work attitudes	Backward; stagnant; emerging	Advanced, postindustrial
	Mañana, mañana	Industrious
Temporal mindset	Backward looking	Forward looking
Security, war and peace	Rule-breaking; terror-oriented; nuclear states lack rational faculties for successful deterrence	Humanitarian; defenders of the civilized world; global leadership; global heroes
Concept of history	Trapped in colonial era and slavery	Progressive; rational unfolding of Enlightenment values
Religion	Superstition; violent; 'too many of them'	Christianity, especially Protestantism

Source: Vucetic & Persaud.

Pijl 2014). The European philosopher G.W.F. Hegel had some respect for Asian culture but was firm in the belief that others, and especially Africans, have not contributed much to history (Buck-Morss 2009). In more contemporary time, writers such as Samuel Huntington and Lawrence Harrison (Harrison and Huntington 2001) believe that some places such as Latin America are static due to the adherence to Catholic values – a claim that also harks back to a separate style of thought in the Protestant world that Spanish speakers sometimes call the 'black legend' or *la leyenda negra* (DeGuzmán 2005). Thus, Harrison argues that while Catholicism is keeping Latin America back, Asians are developing because they have adopted Protestant values. The key values are apparently thrift, postponement of pleasure, hard work, and a high propensity to save.

Postcolonial scholars critique the Orientalist construction of the Third World, with some more directly arguing that Orientalism is an explicit form of racism. Inayatullah and Blaney in their acclaimed book *International Relations and the Problem of Difference* (2004) link Orientalists' theories of socio-economic development to modernization theory which advocates the globalization of Western development strategies, and especially its neoliberal form. To better understand 'development', we should therefore begin by situating modernization theory in the modern colonial encounter itself, paying due attention to 'both global structures and the meanings and intentions of actors' (Inayatullah and Blaney 2004, 125; also see McCarthy 2007; Sajed 2013; Bhambra 2007).

The postcolonial scholarship, which goes back at least to W.E.B. Du Bois, has offered no shortage of penetrating accounts of the relations between race and racism on the one hand, and labor exploitation, patriarchy, sexuality, militarism, colonialism, and migration on the other. But this scholarship was always resisted. Du Bois, who by any reasonable measure counts as one of the twentieth century's intellectual powerhouses, was effectively silenced throughout his professional life and long afterwards simply because he was African American. Other African American scholars who followed in Du Bois's footsteps – Vitalis (2016) describes some of them in a highly praised book on the origins of American International Relations – had similar professional and personal experiences.

None of this should be surprising. As Vitalis (2016) highlights, what we know today as International Relations was, at its founding, understood to be a discipline dedicated to 'race development'. The journal that we know today as *Foreign Affairs*, was the original journal for American International Relations scholarship, and its title was *Journal of Race Development*. The stated purpose of the journal was to present ideas about what methods 'developed peoples', and specifically colonial administrators, could use to help 'uplift' 'backward' and 'under-developed' races. Indeed, contrary to what almost all standard textbooks say, the object of inquiry that gave rise to the discipline of International Relations was not 'the international' so much as 'the inter-racial'. The goal of that inquiry, in turn, was the protection of *white supremacy* (Mills 2015).

In addition to struggling with their disciplinary history, today's International Relations scholars are also struggling with the concept of race itself (Malik 2009).[2] This, too, should not be surprising. Two scholars can agree that races do not exist in a natural (biological) sense as well as that our world is characterized by actually existing racism, yet they can still disagree about the best way to conceptualize race. Philosophers of race have spent a lot of time thinking about this issue (Vucetic 2015). At one level, conceptualization debates are always about ontology, the branch of philosophy that deals with the issue of the nature of reality. If one is to judge by institutions that help administer justice or wealth, affirmative action policies, national census questionnaires, media caricariturizations of 'identity politics', forensic DNA assessments or personalized genetic genealogies, then race exists – it is 'out there to know.' If one is to talk to natural scientists, however, then race is illusory. We know that phenotypes and genotypes – for example, body hair genes – are not indicative of biological or genetic fixity, they would say. Both perspectives are in fact correct. Race exists as a *social phenomenon*, which means that it exists as a *relation*, not a 'thing'. 'Brown people', 'Caucasians', or 'old stock Canadians' do not exist independently of the acts of categorization, all of which are historically context-dependent.

Thousands of scholars in fields such as anthropology, cultural studies, history, and sociology today devote their entire careers studying *racialization* – social relations and processes that produce race by articulating and legitimizing intragroup unity and intergroup incommensurability.[3] Why were the Irish during the Victorian era racialized as white in India, but as 'less than white' in the British Isles or North America? Are the residents of Moscow who hail from the Caucasus and Central Asia more likely to be racialized as black (*chorni*) today than they were in the Soviet period? Could it be that *hukou*, a system of controlling residency and movement of workers in contemporary China, is in fact racializing the country's urban–rural divide? The goal of such research questions is not understanding what race is (or is taken to be) so much as *what race does* – that is, about the consequences of racialization on the differentiated distributions of power, authority, recognition, wealth, worth, resources, entitlement and opportunity. As Lentin (2015) has argued, understanding this 'performativity of race' is in fact necessary for the success of anti-racist activities today; to challenge the racisms that underpin today's societies, we must first develop an intimate knowledge of how race mutates to fit the contemporary context and time (Kendi 2016).

Social theoretic and social scientific research on contemporary manifestations of racism occasionally appears in books and articles with seemingly paradoxical titles such as 'new racism', 'racism without racists', 'racism without races', and even 'racism without racism'. These effectively emphasize both the longevity and the malleability of racialized realities. Some of this research is also experimental. The scholarship on *habits* – this connects turn-of-the-twentieth century social theory to twenty-first century social neuroscience – shows that humans create and maintain their worlds informally, implicitly and unselfconsciously and that racialized worlds are no exception. Relatedly, many cognitive psychologists have long demonstrated that racial prejudice can be present even among those who consistently reject the existence of races and otherwise hold reliable anti-racist attitudes – the so-called *implicit bias*.

Most reputable news media outlets today do not shy from reporting on how racialized systemic structural advantages and disadvantages impact people's lives on a global scale. Read about the experience of Aboriginal and Torres Strait Islander communities in Australia, Bolivian migrants workers in Argentina, Dalit people in Andhra Pradesh, Hispanics in Arizona or temporarily protected asylum seekers in Austria and you are likely to observe that most majoritarian anxieties over the alleged cultural incompatibilities involving minorities revolve around race and racism. The same goes for the stories about the so-called *culture wars* – what is and is not remembered about the past, and why. For some of you, the most thought-provoking pieces will be those that prompt you to think about your own complicity in racialized relations of power – a piercing editorial on why 'we' should be held accountable for 'their' conflict or poverty, or perhaps an astute op-ed on the meanings of 'white privilege', 'habits of whiteness', 'white ignorance', or 'white innocence'.

When consuming the media reporting on race and racism, it is important to keep a critical mind about the 'latest scientific research on race'. As we show in the next section, the history of the political misuse and abuse of such research is long and sordid. Sample recent newspaper articles about race from the perspective of *genomics revolution* and corollary sequencing of the genomes of human beings (the interpreting of the DNA that make up a person's genome) and you are likely to discover no shortage of misleading and unsubstantiated claims. In some cases, said articles will be authored by professional provocateurs who will try to pick your intellectual pockets with claims that new scientific findings that show that human races are real in the genetic sense or that genetic differences among races may explain changes in social behaviors and institutions during recent evolution. It is also a good idea to read what scientists are actually saying. Recent claims by evolutionary psychologists that race *may* be a by-product of *evolved cognition* of the human brain – meaning the result of evolution by natural selection, whereby tribal identity formation came to depend on some sort of perceptual saliency of skin color – are speculative at best.

This brings us to another major conceptual question that has kept philosophers of race awake: how should we talk about race in the first place? The relevance of this question is self-evident once we accept that language has the power to *reify*, or naturalize, what is socially constructed. Most people tend to be 'conservationists', a term for a position that racial categories should be conserved for the purposes of policy and politics. In contrast, 'eliminativists' contend that such categories should be eliminated from public discourse. This camp includes political liberals who think they live in color-blind and/or post-racial societies, conservative polemicists who think minorities should 'get over it' as well as a relatively small group of social scientists and social theorists who think that the meanings of race could be more effectively subsumed under a 'nearby' category such as class or ethnicity.

The problem with the eliminativist position from the perspective of this volume is that it erases the philosophical and theoretical basis for anti-racist politics that motivates the very idea of postcolonial scholarship in the first place. This was a point Du Bois made a century ago: critical confrontation with race is the necessary step in the possibilities of overcoming the problem of race.[4]

Race in global society

Most histories of race begin with European overseas expansion in the early modern period. What made this expansion possible was mass-scale imperial dehumanization – an effort to affix the indigenous peoples in the Americas and Africa as non-human or less-than-human indistinguishable from livestock for the purposes of their enslavement, dispossession, exploitation and extermination. Behind this effort was a simple cost-benefit analysis: treating some humans as indistinguishable from livestock made social domination easier than accepting their rights and recourse to justice.[5]

Historians of race typically differentiate among multiple but inter-related processes of racial dehumanization that occurred in modernity, thus again emphasizing that race is a relation and not a fixed identity. Depending on the time and place, race could therefore mean 'civilization', 'spirit', 'blood', 'nature', or 'culture', – and sometimes all of the above at once. This is why the word racism sometimes comes with adjectives 'theological', 'cultural', 'biological' and 'scientific' (Frederickson 2002).

The mid-sixteenth century Spanish theological debate on whether the 'Indians' – the newly 'discovered' population of the Americas – were 'natural slaves' or not paralleled much earlier distinctions between *savages* and *barbarians* (Todorov 1999). 'Savages' referred to people who supposedly lacked basic forms of law and order, sometimes even reason. 'Barbarians', in contrast, 'merely' lacked culture and civilization. (The ancient Greek word *bárbaros* – a similar word also exists in Sanskrit and Latin – described people whose foreign language sounded as the onomatopoeic 'bar bar bar'). Along the same lines, early Christian theological discourses on the inferiority of Jews and Muslims later came to inform secular forms of *cultural racism*, including some present-day versions of anti-Semitism and Islamophobia.[6]

The transatlantic slave trade – the human trafficking of Africans across the Atlantic – was an especially important site of modern imperial dehumanization. What matters here is the construction of the human body as the primary site and marker of difference – skin color, hair type, and facial features. Enslaved Africans became the inferior 'black' and European slavers the superior 'whites'. Not all scholars of race will agree that color hierarchies are a modern invention, but they will all agree that slave trade was integral to the development of the so-called *biological racism*.[7] Contemporary media preferences for the white European body – Hollywood – and in fact Bollywood-style whitewashing, for example – are some of the many legacies of this history.

By the late eighteenth century, cultural and biological racisms were being enmeshed in what we today call *scientific racism* – a pseudo-scientific body of thought that in essence sought to prove the inherent superiority of the cultures and races of the West, meaning of Europe and its overseas offshoots (Watson 2001; Painter 2010). A good example of scientific racism is the first volume of *Journal of Race Development*, published in 1910. In it, one can observe how ideas about civilization and color combined with the latest advances in the natural and human sciences – evolution and eugenics, for instance – to inform the politics and policy of colonial management. Many striking examples of scientific racism can be found in the Nazi ideology, starting with Adolf Hitler's division of humanity into Aryan 'founders of civilization' (the 'racially clean and unmixed' North Americans belonged to this group), 'bearers of civilizations' such as the Japanese, and 'civilization-destroyers', principally the Jews.

In this period, scientific racism naturally became enveloped in a so-called *standard of civilization*, a conceptual-legal yardstick, that individual and institutional actors in the West had previously used to adjudicate the relative simplicity or complexity of non-Western peoples with whom they interacted. This concept, originating in the early fifteenth century, is central to understanding the development of modern *international society*. From a Eurocentric point of view, it was European expansionism that unified a number of different regional systems into an oceans-spanning international society characterized by the ideas, institutions and practices first invented or perfected in Europe – those related to diplomacy and international law, for example. As a general rule, only polities defined by themselves and others as 'European' and later 'Western' recognized each other as equal sovereigns – an exclusive club of territorially sovereign states and empires of different sizes (Gong 1984; Grovogui 1996; Shogo 2009; Benton 2010). Put down the Eurocentric lens, however, and you will see a much richer picture of international social life, the outstanding case in point being relations involving indigenous polities (Crawford 1994; Lightfoot 2016).

As the nineteenth century was the high point of European imperialism, the standard of civilization gained power on a global scale and created an *international hierarchy* that in many respects has lasted to this day. To begin with, no colonial intervention could take place without a 'civilization debate' – that is, on whether the target area can be, or should be, civilized through colonization. The US debate over what do in the Caribbean and the Philippines after the Spanish-American war is an example of this (Murphy 2009). Similar debates surrounded colonial partition projects, some of which were continental and sub-continental in scale: the post-1881 'scramble for Africa' or the 'carving up the Chinese melon' after 1895. Even the 1947 division of British India into India and Pakistan can be seen in this light given that it was completed in a month and half by a boundary commission headed by Sir Cyril Radcliffe, a London lawyer who until then had never been east of Paris.

As architects of modern international order, white Europeans considered only themselves to be competent to adjudicate the civilization of others. When the Haitian Revolution, 1791–1804, overturned the slave system in Saint-Domingue, the crown jewel of the French empire and in fact the entire colonial world, most European intellectuals at first refused to believe it. The notion that a successful slave revolt – on this island alone the colonizers had previously quashed at least eight such revolts – could give birth to an actually existing and radically revolutionary black polity in the New World island was simply *unthinkable* to them (Trouillot 1995). Years passed before France moved to recognize Haiti, but only on the harshest of terms for the latter. In 1825, Haiti's government agreed to repay an 'independence debt' to compensate French slave-owners for 'lost property', meaning slaves who had won their freedom – a transaction that was in fact illegal in then French and international laws. To finance this exorbitant sum – with standard adjustments, it hovers around US$30 billion in today's money – Haiti's government also committed itself to working with banking institutions in Paris, with a predictable effect on the fairness of interest rates and fees.[8]

The fate of Haiti speaks volumes about white supremacy. An international society maintained by and for white Europeans could not tolerate an American nation birthed in a revolt of an enslaved people of African descent. This is why no other colonial power with interests in the Caribbean supported Haiti over France; in fact, the colonial powers scrambled together to prevent similar revolutions from occurring elsewhere. Their fear was palpable because Haiti's leaders – many of them enlightened men of letters – had the nerve to outlaw slavery (Article 12 of the 1805 constitution) as well as territorial aggrandizement and foreign interventions (Article 36). Contrast this with the nineteenth-century experience of the United States. Had the new Haitian state been a secessionist white settler colony practicing slavery and expansionism, perhaps it too would have swiftly joined the society of states.

Another example of white supremacy at work is the attempt of the Japanese delegation at the 1919 Paris Peace Conference to insert a '*racial equality clause*' into the Covenant of the League of Nations (Shimazu 1998). At this time, Japan had indeed demonstrated its 'civilized' statehood by behaving like a Western power in every way – its state and society modernized, while its empire expanded. Yet, none of this impressed the white men who dominated the conference proceedings. US President Woodrow Wilson who is widely cited as the great *idealist* of International Relations in fact presided over the meeting that nixed Japan's demand for equal status (Lauren 1988, 80–95; Klotz 2017, 371).

A related, and equally dramatic, example of the operation of the racialized standard of civilization at the same conference was the introduction of a so-called *mandate system* – an arrangement for transferring the former German and Ottoman colonies to new sovereign authorities, namely those of the victorious European powers and Japan, according to the aforementioned standard-of-civilization schema (Shilliam 2017, 290). The mandate system later influenced the UN trusteeship systems (Toussaint 1956, 2–3) and thus today's international state-building debates (Sabaratnam 2017, Ch. 2).

It was after World War II, the Shoah (Holocaust), decolonization, and the rise of human rights that international society began to transform itself into a somewhat more inclusive club.[9] The word 'somewhat' is apt, however. A familiar example of the staying power of racism in the world is the forty-fifth president of the United States, Donald Trump. Following a deeply racist and xenophobic campaign, Trump proceeded to enact white supremacy through White House policy – the 'Muslim ban', a new 'voter fraud' commission, refusals to condemn Nazism and neo-Nazis, etc. In doing so, he fueled racial hatreds to the point of inspiring white supremacists to murder people on American streets. 'UN sounds the alarm over US racial tensions' was a page one headline in *The Guardian* on August 24, 2017. Another striking example of *actually existing racism* today is to be found in the practice of *mandatory and indefinite detention for asylum seekers*, the outstanding case in point being the latest iteration of Australia's 'Pacific Solution' (Vucetic 2012, 211; Lentin 2017). In many ways, racialization is as central for understanding state sovereignty, migration and borders today as it was a century ago (Klotz 2017; also see Box 3.2).

Race and global economic development

There is actually much more critical material on the impact of race and racism on global economic development than there is in international security. A good deal of this is due to the fact that before IR was penetrated by postcolonialism, critical gender studies, critical human security, and the political economy of climate change, Marxist and neo-Marxist were an integral part of the political economy debates of International Relations (Dirlik 2003). That said, most of these scholars saw race (and gender) in terms of class relations, and more broadly within the exploitative relations of global capitalism. Marxists who stressed production rather than trade as the crux of capitalism tended to see race as a form of 'false consciousness', meaning that race was *not* a form of domination that emanated from the contradictions supposedly embedded in capitalism as an economic and social system. For Marxists, the proper corresponding ideology against capitalist exploitation should have been proletarian resistance aimed at a macro-structural transition from capitalism to socialism.

Marxist political economy, despite solid contributions to the critique of imperialism, generally disregarded race as a conceptual and analytical category. Karl Marx himself assumed that global capitalism would benefit places like India because it would transform the local culture, much of it assumed to be tied down by what Marx thought were superstition. In this sense, many Marxists, going back to Marx, and then through the period of Third World decolonization, held on to notions of Western modernity even when offering critiques of militarism and imperialism. John Hobson argues that Marx and Engels explicitly supported imperialism, and further that their view of the non-Western world amounted to 'paternalist Eurocentrism'. Later classical Marxists including Lenin, Luxemburg, Hilferding, and Bukharin though anti-imperialist, had worldviews Hobson calls 'subliminal anti-paternalist Eurocentrism' (Hobson 2012).

Despite these shortcomings, as Blaney and Inayatullah note in Chapter 7 of this book Marxist political economy did not ignore the 'rest' in its accounting of the emergence of the modern world system. Nowhere was this more systematically done than in dependency theory and world-systems analysis. These historically oriented branches of Marxism which were both influential from the 1960s through the mid-1980s, therefore, did make some connections between racist ideology and the relations of exploitation and domination. Andre Gunder Frank and Immanuel Wallerstein drew race into their work more systematically, but only on a systematic basis after 1989. Before that, it was 'Third World' scholars such as Walter Rodney and Eric Williams who were insistent that global capitalism cannot be understood without the extraordinary role that race and racism played. In fact, much of what we would come to know as postcolonial critical political economy was already spelled out in Rodney's *How Europe Underdeveloped Africa*. The quotations from Rodney's book in Box 3.1 paint a good picture of a sort of Marxian postcolonial understanding of the world economic system and more broadly, the general structure of global political and cultural power embedded in the state system. Rodney's thinking illustrates a fusion between Marxian political economy from the 1970s and postcolonial economic critiques.

Immediately following World War II, three major historical developments started almost simultaneously, namely, decolonization, the Cold War, and the dramatic rise of the United States as the unofficial leader of the Western world. All three of these global phenomena had major impacts on economic development, and all three were also implicated in *actually existing racism* that followed World War II. Decolonization ruptured the vertically-organized system of global economic relations between the European and Third World economies,

---

Box 3.1: From Rodney's *How Europe Underdeveloped Africa*

The developed and underdeveloped parts of the present capitalist section of the world have been in continuous contact for four and a half centuries. The contention here is that over that period Africa helped to develop Western Europe in the same proportion as Western Europe helped to underdevelop Africa (p. 75).

Pervasive and vicious racism was present in imperialism as a variant independent of the economic rationality that initially gave birth to racism. It was economics that determined that Europe should invest in Africa and control the continent's raw materials and labor. It was racism which confirmed the decision that the form of control should be direct colonial rule (p. 141).

It can further be argued that by the nineteenth century white racism had become so institutionalized in the capitalist world (and especially in the USA) that it sometimes ranked above the maximization of profit as a motive for oppressing black people (p. 89).

---

though mostly in formal terms. The Cold War imposed a bifurcated, bipolar states system, at least in terms of international security, and especially so in terms of state-to-state security. These three developments formed a historical structure (Cox 1987) which would eventually collapse in 1989. The disappearance of the Soviet Union in turn broadly coincided with the spectacular rise of globalization, which according to Dirlik (2003) is the *form* of a new world order.

Decolonization did not end *actually existing racism* in the global political economy as new forms of racialities emerged, for instance, the legal, political, economic, and cultural imposition of apartheid in South Africa and Rhodesia (now Zimbabwe), as well as in Canada in a milder form, with its reserve system for indigenous peoples. We see the continued racialization of economic development both in theory and practice (Matlon 2016). In theory, the most influential contributors were hyper-modernists, where the latter basically means following Western models, not only of economic development, but also of state society relations, and more broadly culture (Williams, Meth, & Willis 2014). The metamorphoses of the *actually existing racism* led the Peruvian sociologist Anibal Quijano (2000) to propose the concept of the *coloniality of power*, meaning the continuation of relations of domination conjured up in the ideas, institutions, and material practices of global capitalism combined with new form of cultural Eurocentrism.

The racialization of the political economy of development had two principal dimensions, and they still exist today. The sustained anti-immigrant politics in the West, which is dependent on the Third World for both 'cheap' and high-tech labor, is not only a fetter on economic growth, but also a matter of massive insecurity for immigrants and migrant workers (see Box 3.2).

Box 3.2: Race and immigration

It was a typically cold night in Olathe, Kansas on the evening of February 24, 2017. Two engineers, Srinivas Kuchibhotla and Alok Madasani, who worked at Garmin, the company that makes GPS devices, decided to do the usual – take a few drinks after work on a Friday night at Austins Bar and Grill. At 7.30 p.m. a white gunman walked into to the bar and opened fire on the two Indian immigrants. Srinivas, thirty-two, died of his wounds. Alok, also thirty-two, survived, but was seriously wounded. The gunman, fifty-one-year-old Adam Purinton, fled the scene and made his way to an Applebee's some eighty miles away in Clinton, Missouri. He told the staff at the restaurant he wanted to hide because he had shot two Iranians. A third person, Ian Grillot, a white young man of barely twenty-four, was also shot when he attempted to come to the assistance of the two Indians. Like so many immigrants, Srinivas must have come to the United States to enjoy what is called the American Dream. He was on his way to becoming a qualified engineer working at a high-tech company in the American heartland. His family was with him, and he had friends, friends like Alok. Purinton also had a dream, but his was different. His dream, it appears, was to rid America, save America, from those foreigners, those Muslims who are today, and have been for the longest time, portrayed as a fundamental threat to an otherwise ideal society. Before the gunshots the only previous contact between the Indian immigrants and their assailant were the words of Purinton – 'get out of my country'.

www.thehindu.com/news/international/Indian-engineer-shot-dead-in-Kansas/article17359339.ece and/or www.nytimes.com/2017/02/24/world/asia/kansas-attack-possible-hate-crime-srinivas-kuchibhotla.html

The first concerns the right of the Third World states and peoples to govern themselves. Discourses from the late nineteenth century were replete with the widespread belief in the Western world that colored people were not ready for self-government, and certainly not for leadership. The belief was itself ensconced in notions of Western white supremacy, and led to aggressive imperialism with the American military intervention in the Philippines, and the already well-known scramble for Africa. Postcolonial scholars see many strands of post-independence interventions in the Third World as a continuation of the parent/child ideology established in the nineteenth century.

The second dimension of the continuity of *actually existing racism* in the political economy of development is the widespread notion that the Third World is a late comer to modern life, meaning here a combination of capitalist economics, individualism, and everyday ways of life (Landes 1990, 11). The work of Max Weber and W.W. Rostow, though not racialized, did however formulate a temporal model which has allowed other thinkers to treat the Third World as kind of a left-behind deformity, bogged down by backward cultures. At times, the racialization has been expressed in religious terms as in the afore-mentioned claim by Harrison that Latin America has been held back because of Catholicism. Some, such as David Landes go so far as to say that 'success' in Catholic countries were actually achieved by the Protestants, as he claims happened in France and Bavaria (Landes 1990, 12).

The so-called rise of the rest – the ongoing shift in material power away from the West and towards, above all, China – is making race more relevant to world politics, not less. For one thing, like Euro-America before it, China is now practicing its own form of colonialism in Africa, much of it under the guise of economic development. At a minimum, that is what the critics are suggesting.

Race and security

In International Relations, 'security' has traditionally focused on the military and economic security of mostly European great powers. This, too, has to do with a Eurocentric conception of the world. Consider the status of *The Peloponnesian War* by Thucydides in many textbooks. If Greco-Roman culture and civilization are assumed to be the foundations of Europe and the West, then in like manner the face-off between Athens and Sparta described by the ancient Greek general-cum-historian may well be a natural point of departure for 'thinking the international'. Accordingly, many theorists who emphasize the competitive nature of great power politics – the so-called *states under anarchy* model – have long drawn on Thucydides to illustrate their dynamics of system structure, security dilemma, hegemonic transition and other theories and concepts used to explain international conflict. Thucydides's insights are today often deployed in debates about the ongoing tensions between the US and China (Buruma 2017) just like they were used a generation ago to illuminate the dynamics of the Cold War. Even Chinese President Xi Jinping felt compelled to join the fray, declaring, during his 2015 US visit, that the so-called Thucydides trap – a potentially violent escalation caused by a newcomer's rise (Athens, China) and the fear this inspires in an established power (Sparta, United States) – is a myth.

A postcolonial sensibility stops us from falling in the trap of debating the Thucydides trap today (Barkawi 2010). In addition to warning against equating European history and Greco-Roman culture with global developments, postcolonial thinking makes us pause over the concept of anarchy, given its place in the history of anthropological thought and European colonialism (Sampson 2002). But if we must read *The Peloponnesian War* today, then why not subject it to a postcolonial reading? So viewed, the conflict between the Spartans and the Athenians was primarily a clash of opposing *imperial* systems – a democratic maritime empire against an oligarchic land empire. This of course radically changes the content of 'lessons learned' that one draws from Thucydides as the focus of discussion becomes hierarchy, not anarchy – that is, how patron–client relations operate in war, how superordinate polities and their agents mobilize the subordinate, and how such large-scale violence sustains and transforms different political orders (Barkawi 2010).

As Barkawi (2010, 2017) and others have shown, the interconnection of 'security' with empire is overwhelming and multiply connected. For postcolonial scholars, many analytical goals in this area revolve around *structural power*, that is, around the question of how empires produce political, cultural, and social subjectivities. When nineteenth- and twentieth-century colonial agents conducted censuses of the local population and related research, they did so with imperial security in mind but what matters more are the new insecurities they created. Typically, the colonized peoples were enumerated and classified through a mix of interviews with local elites and the methods of scientific racism – skin color assessments and physiognomic measurements, some of which were done via photographs (Metcalfe 1995). In this process, race was in fact grafted onto the intertwined and highly context-dependent local identities – caste, tribal, regional and religious – and the result was a system of knowledge that at once confirmed white supremacy and forced new divisions and discord on the colonized. Suffice it to say, such *divide-and-rule* practices have left a lasting mark on most colonies and on the independent states that replaced them. As Mamdani (2002) argues, we cannot understand the 1994 Rwandan genocide without also understanding the colonial-era racialized identity formation.

A world in which international and inter-imperial relations were simultaneously or even primarily inter-racial relations was replete with *race wars* and *race alliances*, to use two *fin-de-siècle* phrases. Race wars were waged especially in the colonies against the indigenous peoples. One example is the early twentieth century genocide of the Herero and Nama peoples in what was once called German South-West Africa and is today known as Namibia. (This war, note, is now revisited in multiple courts of justice with an eye towards setting a new standard in the idea and practice of international reparations.)

For race alliances, take the Venezuelan crisis of 1895 – a complex colonial territorial dispute that saw Britain and the United States lock horns over their respective spheres of influence in the western hemisphere. From a liberal International Relations perspective, the Anglo–American war was averted in this case thanks to the pacifying effect of democratic norms and democratic political structures – a so-called *democratic peace*. (Realists, in contrast, believe that the crisis was merely a 'near-miss'.) What the historical record shows, however, is saber rattling quickly collapsing under the weight of Anglo-Saxon supremacism. Why would the 'two trustees of civilization', asked one high-ranking US policymaker at the time, 'fight over the mongrel state of Venezuela'? (Vucetic 2011, 34).

Fin-de-siècle beliefs in '*Anglo-Saxon unity*' not only helped resolve other Anglo-American disputes in a peaceful fashion, but they also played a decisive role in the emerging structure of imperial alliances and rivalries, thus influencing the course of world history. In the Spanish-American (1898) and South African Wars (1899–1902), Anglo-Saxonism helped London and Washington act as each other's cheerleaders, which was crucial considering that all other imperial capitals favored, respectively, the Spaniards and the Boers (also see Klotz 2012).

Given that all racial identities are constructed, contingent, and change-able, the line between a race alliance and a race war was often thin. Take the Venezuela crisis of 1902–1903 – a convenient shorthand for an even more com-plex colonial quarrel involving Venezuela, the United States, Britain, Germany and Italy (Vucetic 2011: Ch. 2). Like in 1895, the British and American elites declared themselves the 'two branches of the same race' and ended the tiff. Germany, heretofore touted as a potential member of a broader Anglo-Saxon-Teutonic race alliance, was cast as a *racial Other*, as 'the Goth and the shameless Hun', in the words of Rudyard Kipling who wrote a poem criticizing Britain's choice of allies in this policy situation (*The Times*, December 22, 1902). Exactly a decade later, the same racialized alliance dynamics emerged anew, paving the road to the Great War. On December 8, 1912, Kaiser Wilhelm II convened an Imperial War Council at Potsdam to discuss the future of international order, an event many historians regard as a decisive step to the outbreak of conflict. There, Kaiser spoke of an existential war (*Existenzkampf*) between the Germans ('Austria, Germany') and the Slavs, the latter in alliance with the Latins (a.k.a. 'Gauls') and eventually the Anglo-Saxons as well.

Western scholars sometimes forget that Clausewitz's dictum – war is a con-tinuation of politics by other means – applied to the idea and practice of race wars well into the twentieth century. In World War II, the 'war without mercy' in the Pacific, like the treatment of 'lower races' as soldiers, prisoners of war, workers, and objects of strategy can all be regarded as continuations of the inter-racial politics that began in previous centuries (Horne 2004). US race laws, and not just those associated with the Jim Crow regime in the South, impressed and inspired Nazi jurists in the 1930s. Indeed, the then US racist immigration con-trol policies, anti-miscegenation laws and black disenfranchisement, segregation and lynching practices can be said to belong to the same colonialities of power as the Nazis' own *Existenzkampf* ideology.

Postcolonial perspectives shed new light on many large-scale 'tragedies' that accompanied World War II. Take the case of over three million Bengalis starving to death in 1943. The largest degree of responsibility for this famine – one of the worst of the twentieth century – goes to the British decision-makers. The colonial administrators in India at the time could not be bothered to imple-ment food price controls that would benefit their subjects, and neither could the war cabinet in London, when given a choice to divert food and aid from other theaters to India. British actions look even worse when we consider that no fewer than two and a half million soldiers drawn from British India fought in World War II. As Barkawi (2017) notes, this fact puts a completely different spin on the meaning of the 'British Army'. The same author reminds us that 'World War II' also incorporated many wars of decolonization. Take an extraor-dinary circumstance of soldiers from India, again in 1943, facing each other on the battlefield. On the one side, the British Indian Army fighting to save democracy denied by the same British they were fighting for; on the other side, the (Second) Indian National Army led by Subhas Chandra Bose fighting with Fascist Japan against the British colonizers (Barkawi 2017).

Like critical security studies scholars, postcolonial theorists are focused on non-state and non-military referents of security, hence their occasional use of terms such as world security, cooperative security, comprehensive security and human security (Collins 2016). However, critical security studies scholars sometimes forget that these alternative notions of security have a long lineage in postcolonial theory. It is easy to see why: the history of modern Euro-American empires is defined by systemic violence designed and executed in the name of security – the security of trading routes, of strategic military bases, of settlers – and against various peoples racialized as non-white. Conversely, decolonization meant insecurity and radical changes to the order of things at home. As Barkawi wrote in 2010, 'Vietnam remains the single most important event of the last half of the twentieth century for understanding *US politics*. The Algerian war led to regime change *in France*, as did wars of decolonization in Mozambique and Angola for Portugal.'

Along the same lines, we could again consider the Haitian Revolution and think about its (much-silenced) impact on the events that changed the course of world history (Buck-Morss 2009). These include the votes in France's revolutionary legislatures to give 'full rights for free blacks and mulattos' (1792) and to abolish slavery in the colonies (1794) as well as the debates that later led to the suspension of the international slave trade (Crawford 2002). Even the 1803 Louisiana Purchase, too – a bewildering stroke of a pen that doubled the size of the United States and enabled its 'westward expansion' – has everything to do with the then goings-on in Haiti.

The global expansion of Europe and later its offshoots was at once a configuration of economic, political, cultural, and military power. These aspects of power formed a comprehensive system both during the periods of conquest and colonization, as well as after European colonies (and other forms of foreign rule) were either pushed out or abandoned. In fact, the process of decolonization was quite often a bloody affair with enormous loss of life of Third World peoples. A cursory glance of the death toll of wars of liberation reveals the one-sidedness of the killing. Below, for instance, is one entry from Michael Clodfelter's massive encyclopedia of war casualties between 1494 and 2007. The entry is for 'Wars of Independence in Portuguese Africa: 1961–74':

> Portuguese military and civilian dead – 4,000 in Angola, 3,500 in Mozambique, 1,000 in Guinea; guerrilla dead – 25,000 in Angola, 10,000 in Mozambique, 2,000 in Guinea; – African civilian dead 50,000 in Angola, 30,000 in Mozambique, 5,000 in Guinea.
>
> About 3,265 of the total Portuguese dead in the three wars were *military personnel*.
>
> (Clodfelter, 2008, 599; authors' emphasis)

Although the continuous killing in the Third World since conquest cannot be always directly linked to race and racism (Barkawi 2017), numerous writers, some postcolonial but certainly not all, have shown that Euro-American notions of racial supremacy have indeed influenced the forms and scales of killing. Marnia Lazreg makes the point in compelling fashion when she argues that torture – a practice endorsed with various degrees of enthusiasm by successive US presidents even in this century – 'partakes in the work of the civilization in whose name it is practiced' (Lazreg 2007, 5). Further, unlike critical theories of hegemony which place emphasis on the construction of relations of exploitation through consensus, postcolonial and other critical scholars insist that the horror of violence is a definitive aspect of Western warfighting (Riley, Mohanty, & Pratt 2008; Kumarakulasingam 2017; Mitamura 2017).

On the flip-side, the wars of the others have been thoroughly Orientalized or reduced to cultural or political backwardness. Patrick Porter (2013, 21) for instance, argues that '…Westerners have voiced their fears about themselves, their survival, identity and values, through different visions of non-western warfare'. Postcolonialism sees these same wars as wars of liberation. The wars of liberation were for nothing more than the key ingredient of the modern state system, namely sovereignty. Little wonder that so many theoretical binaries preferred by mainstream security studies – war/peace, internal/external, domestic/international, civil/military – are of limited purchase for postcolonial scholars.

Box 3.3: Key points

- Race is not a biological fact but has been represented as such through pseudo-science such as eugenics. Race is a product of racism and racism is an ideology of power. Race is a signifier and because of that different things can, and for centuries have been, used to designate some populations superior to others.

- Race occurs both in practice and thought. Practice refers to action (anti-immigrant violence; war). The thought aspect can take many different forms, including philosophy, history writing, social and political theories, political rhetoric, and in the everyday thinking of small groups and individuals.

- Ideologies and practices of racial supremacy have been consistently present in International Relations, at least for the past five hundred years. The struggle for racial equality has been a persistent cause among those peoples and nations once colonized or conquered by for powers that claim to be superior.

- Racial ideology and racism have affected almost all aspects of International Relations including – the causes and conduct of wars, conceptions of national interest and foreign policy, global property relations, immigration and refugee policies, and also international cooperation. White supremacy and other forms of racism continue to shape perceptions of those nations and peoples who are other than white. Not talking about race, as in the ideology of colorblindness, tends to perpetuate white supremacy.

Conclusion

This chapter has highlighted the multiple ways in which race and racism have influenced international relations both in terms of structures and actions, meaning both the underlying foundations and behavioral aspects of the international system. Our focus on the relationships among race on the one hand and theory, global governance, economic development, and security on the other, is not by any means exhaustive. This is so because race also affects a whole slew of other sectors of society including gender, class, nationalism, and among other things, the political economy of state finance (issue of welfare, education, healthcare).

Theorizing race is difficult because, as we have shown, there are disputes even about the most basic questions, such whether to continue engaging with the discourses of race or to eliminate it altogether from our discussion. Those who argue for eliminating hold that view because they think that talking about it is another way of guaranteeing its continuity. What is your view?

We have also shown that race and racism have been deeply embedded in governance for several hundred years, and specifically so since 1492 with the advent of European conquest. The period of colonial rule saw direct and often violent structures and methods of governance over societies flung around the globe. Informal empire and imperial interference (such as the US foreign rule of the Philippines) continued where formal colonialism did not take hold. Even after decolonization (especially after World War II), Third World states have been subjected to coercive rule through multilateral mechanisms, such as humanitarian intervention, much of it based on assumptions of the inability of those states to properly govern themselves.

Race has had a devastating impact in terms of security relations broadly defined. Conquest, which marked the beginning of the modern encounter between the European states and others was exceptionally violent, with entire societies and people wiped out through the effects of slavery, European diseases, starvation, psychological trauma, and the direct application of physical violence, including numerous massacres and other forms of large-scale violence. Many scholars are convinced that continuing violent intervention in the Third World, such as in the case of Iraq, is directly related to the racialized assumptions that Euro-American policy makers hold about Muslim societies.

The impact of race on economic development has also been profound. As we have shown, world systems and dependency theorists, and also scholars working within the Marxist tradition, have roundly concluded that the predominant feature of the relation between Euro-America and the Third World has been one of economic exploitation. Marxists have tended to stress the imperialist nature of capitalism as a system. World systems theory and dependency theory, both influenced by varieties of Marxian political economy, provided comprehensive explanations of this economic exploitation through imperialism, but did not always place much emphasis on race. Some Third World historians such as Rodney did, however, factor in racism in the explanation of underdevelopment.

A quick survey of International Relations today would show that the problems of race and racism are still not only active, but also deeply divisive. The most poignant expressions of this are to be found in the general politics of immigration and refugee issues, where Euro-America is again concerned about, and resistant to, more people from the Third World coming in. While some of the concerns are economic, related as it were to competition for jobs, there are deeper feelings of racialized animosities. The latter have found outward expression and structured mobilization in political parties, and other 'civic' groups are imbued with discourses of various forms of white supremacy. The rise of radical conservative politics has been so dramatic that the latest president of the United States will go down in history as someone who openly sided with neo-Nazis and the KKK. Race and racism manifest themselves in the mutable, context-dependent forms, which means that International Relations scholars must continue to develop conceptual and political ways of understanding them, to say nothing of reflecting on their own position as both producers and products of the Eurocentric and ideological base of white supremacy.

Notes

1 We are grateful to Catherine Baker, Alexander Davies, Audie Klotz, and Ajay Parasram for their valuable input during the writing of this chapter. All standard disclaimers apply.

2 Mainstream international relations textbooks, collections and bibliographic compendia have only recently started soliciting chapters on race (see, respectively: Shilliam 2017; Klotz 2017; and Búzás 2017; and compare with Doty (1996), Sampson (2002), Hobson (2012), Henderson (2014), Krishna (2001) and Persaud and Walker (2001).

3 The concept draws on the work of the black Martinican French postcolonial theorist Frantz Fanon, among others (Shilliam 2017, 292).

4 Although conservationists reject attempts to substitute race for class or ethnicity, they tend to readily accept that race, class, and gender – to mention but three relations of power – should be analyzed together. Labelled *intersectionality*, this theory comes from the long tradition of Black feminist thought in the United States. Kimberlé Crenshaw, who coined the word in the 1970s, has argued that this tradition spans nineteenth-century thinkers and activists like Anna Julia Cooper and Maria W. Stewart to the more recent figures like Angela Davis, Audre Lorde and Deborah King. Intersectionality helps advance anti-racist politics without reifying race while also providing a powerful new lens for examining the multiplicity of ideas, discourses, institutions, policies and practices that contribute to the exclusion and oppression of some people and not others in specific contexts.

5 Similar cost-benefit analyses inform Orientalist knowledge we discussed in the previous section. Why critically interrogate colonialism when it benefits the West to pretend that the material circumstances of the Third World are fundamental expressions of an inner culture not consistent with modernity?

6 These forms of racism are ideal types – as abstractions distilled from concrete phenomena that serve to categorize, compare and contrast complex social systems. To better understand how cultural racism relates to other forms of racism as well as other

forms of oppression, see how Martínez's (2008) analysis of the relationship between colonial Mexico's *sistema de castas* and the late fifteenth-century Spanish concept of 'purity of blood' or *limpieza de sangre*.

7   This is why chattel slavery must be seen as qualitatively different from the previous enslavements of people from sub-Saharan Africa and other modern forms of oppressions involving 'black' people (the practice 'blackbirding' in the colonial-era Pacific, for example). For an informative foray into the history of blackness from the perspective of the eighteenth century Atlantic, see Nussbaum (2009).

8   Much like the present-day talk of reparations for slavery, the present-day talk of France repaying some of these extorted moneys to Haiti remains just that – talk.

9   Key developments in the middle years of the twentieth century include the 1950 UNESCO statement on race, the 1955 Bandung conference, Black Power and the US civil rights movement in the 1960s, and the 1963 Security Council decision to sanction apartheid South Africa (Shilliam 2017, 290, 292–3; Klotz 2017, 372–377).

Suggested readings

Du Bois, W.E.B. (1915). The African roots of war www.theatlantic.com/magazine/archive/2014/08/the-african-roots-of-war/373403/. A version of the Hobson-Lenin-Luxemburg theory of the imperialist origins of World War I but with much-needed attention to racism – by one of the giants of social science.

Frantz, F. (1963). *The wretched of the earth.* New York: Grove Press. Finished ten weeks prior to the author's death at the age of 36, this is a pioneering text on race, colonialism, and decolonization.

James, J. (1998). *The Angela Y. Davis reader.* Oxford: Blackwell. A collection of writings by a revolutionary, radical public intellectual and a living witness of the anti-racist struggles of our era.

Jones, B.G. (Ed.). (2006). *Decolonial international relations.* Lanham, MD.: Roman & Littlefield. An excellent volume on decolonizing international relations written by some of the most prominent postcolonial scholars in IR.

Painter, N. (2010). *The history of white people.* New York: W.W. Norton & Co. A highly acclaimed book that traces the historical and intellectual development of race and racism across regions and cultures, with a focus on the emergence of 'white people' as a cultural category.

Bibliography

Barkawi, T. (2010). Empire and order in international relations and security studies. In R.A. Denemark and R. Marlin-Bennett (Eds.). *The International Studies Encyclopedia.* Hoboken, NJ: Wiley Blackwell.

Barkawi, T. (2017). *Soldiers, of empire: Indian and British armies in World War II.* Cambridge: Cambridge University Press.

Benton, Lauren A. (2010). *A search for sovereignty: Law and geography in European empires, 1400–1900.* Cambridge: Cambridge University Press.

Benton, Lauren A. (2010). *A search for sovereignty: Law and geography in European empires, 1400–1900.* Cambridge: Cambridge University Press.

Bhambra, Gurminder (2007). *Rethinking modernity: Postcolonialism and the sociological imagination.* Palgrave MacMillan: Basingstoke.

Buruma, I. (2017). Are China and the United States headed for war? *The New Yorker*. Last modified June 19, 2017. www.newyorker.com/magazine/2017/06/19/are-china-and-the-united-states-headed-for-war.

Chakrabarthy, D. (2000). *Provincializing Europe*. Princeton: Princeton University Press.

Chowdhry, G. and Nair, S. (2004). *Power, postcolonialism and international relations: Reading, race, gender, and class*. New York: Routledge.

Chowdhry, G. and Rai, S.M. (2009). The geographies of exclusion and the politics of inclusion: race-based exclusion in the teaching of international relations. *International Studies Perspectives*, 10, 84–91.

Clodfelter, M. (2008). *Warfare and armed conflicts: A statistical reference to casualty and other figures, 1494–2007* (3rd Edition). Jefferson, NC: McFarland.

Collins, A. (2016). *Contemporary security studies*. New York: Oxford University Press.

Cox, R.W. (1987). *Production, power, and world order: Social forces in the making of history*. New York: Columbia University Press.

Crawford, N. (1994). A security regime among democracies: Cooperation among Iroquois Nations. *International Organization*, 48, 345–385.

Crawford, N.C. (2002). *Argument and change in world politics: Ethics, decolonization, and humanitarian intervention*. Cambridge: Cambridge University Press.

DeGuzmán, M. (2005). *Spain's long shadow: The black legend, off-whiteness, and Anglo-American empire*. Minneapolis: University of Minnesota Press.

Dirlik, A. (2003). Global modernity? Modernity in an age of global capitalism. *European Journal of Social Theory*, 6, 275–292.

Doty, R.L. (1996). *Imperial encounters: The politics of representation in north–south relations*. Minneapolis, MN: University of Minnesota Press.

Fredrickson, G.M. (2002) *Racism: A short history*. Princeton: Princeton University Press.

Gong, G.W. (1984). *The standard of 'civilisation' in international society*. Oxford: Clarendon Press.

Grovogui, S.N. (1996). *Sovereigns, quasi sovereigns, and Africans: Race and self-determination in international law*. Minneapolis: University of Minnesota Press.

Guha, R. (1982). *Subaltern studies I: Writing on South Asian history and society*. New Delhi: Oxford University Press.

Harrison, L. and Huntington, S.P. (2001). *Culture matters*. New York: Basic Books.

Henderson, E.A. (2015). Hidden in plain sight: Racism in international relations theory. In A. Anievas, N. Manchanda and R. Shilliam (Eds.). *Race and racism in international relations: Confronting the global colour line* (pp. 19–43). New York: Routledge.

Hobson, J.M. (2012). *The Eurocentric conception of world politics: Western international theory, 1760–2010*. Cambridge: Cambridge University Press.

Horne, G. (2004). *Race war: White supremacy and the Japanese attack on the British Empire*. New York: New York University Press.

Inayatullah, N. and Blaney, D.L. (2004). *International relations and the problem of difference*. London: Routledge.

Kendi, I.X. (2016). *Stamped from the beginning: The definitive history of racist ideas in America*. New York: Nation Books.

Klotz, A. (2012). The imperial self: A perspective on Anglo-America from South Africa, India, and Ireland. In P. Katzenstein (Ed.). *Anglo-America and its discontents: Civilizational identities beyond East and West* (pp. 81–104). New York: Routledge.

Klotz, A. (2017). Racial inequality. In T. Dunne and C. Reus-Smith (Eds.). *The globalization of international society* (pp. 362–379). Oxford: Oxford University Press.

Krishna, S. (2001). Race, amnesia, and the education of international relations. *Alternatives,* 26, 401–24.

Kumarakulasingam, N. (2017). Metropolitan killings: Laundering a scandal. Paper presented at the 58th ISA Convention, Baltimore, MD.

Landes, D. (1990). Why are we so rich and they so poor? *The American Economic Review,* 80, 1–13.

Lauren, P.G. (1988). *Power and prejudice: The politics and diplomacy of racial discrimination.* Boulder, Colorado: Westview Press.

Lazreg, M. (2007). *Torture and the twilight of empire: From Algiers to Baghdad.* Princeton: Princeton University Press.

Lentin, A. (2015). Racism in public or public racism: doing anti-racism in 'post-racial' times. *Ethnic and Racial Studies* 39, 33–48.

Lentin, A. (2017). "De-racing the border," a blog post, May 11, 2017. www.alanalentin.net/2017/05/11/de-racing-the-border/

Lightfoot, S. (2016). *Global indigenous politics: A subtle revolution.* London: Routledge.

McCarthy, T. (2007). *Race, empire, and the idea of human development.* Cambridge: Cambridge University Press.

Malik, K. (2009). *Strange fruit: Why both sides are wrong in the race debate.* Oxford: One World.

Mamdani, M. (2002). *When victims become killers: Colonialism, nativism, and the genocide in Rwanda.* Princeton, NJ: Princeton University Press.

Matlon, J. (2016) Racial capitalism and the crisis of black masculinity. *American Sociological Review,* 81, 1014–1038.

Metcalfe, T. (1995). *Ideologies of the Raj.* Cambridge: Cambridge University Press.

Mills, C.W. (2015). *Global white ignorance.* In *Routledge international handbook of ignorance studies* (pp. 217–227). New York: Taylor and Francis Inc.

Mitamura, E. (2017). Provoking humanity: Afterlives of mass violence in Cambodia and the United States. Paper presented to the 58th ISA, Baltimore, MD.

Mittelman, J.H. (2009). The salience of race. *International Studies Perspective,* 99–107.

Murphy, E. (2009). Women's anti-imperialism, 'The white man's burden', and the Philippine-American war. *Gender & Society,* 23, 244–270.

Painter, N.I. (2010) *The history of white people.* New York: W.W. Norton & Co.

Persaud, R.B. (2001). *Counter-hegemony and foreign policy: The dialectics of marginalized and global forces in Jamaica.* Albany: SUNY Press.

Persaud, R.B. and Walker, R.B.J. (2001). *Apertura:* Race in international relations. *Alternatives,* 26, 373–376.

Pham,, Q.N. and Shilliam, R. (2016). *Meanings of bandung: Postcolonial orders and decolonial visions.* Lanham, MD: Roman & Littlefield Publishers.

Pijl, K.v.d. (2014). *The discipline of western supremacy: Modes of foreign relations and political economy.* Vol. III. London: Pluto Press.

Porter, P. (2013). *Military orientalism: Eastern war through western eyes.* New York: Oxford University Press.

Quijano, A. (2000). Coloniality of power and Eurocentrism in Latin America. *International Sociology,* 15, 215–232.

Riley, R., Mohanty, C. and Pratt, M.B. (2008). *Feminism and war: Confronting U.S. imperialism.* London: Zed Books.

Rodney, W. (1981). *How Europe underdeveloped Africa.* Washington, D.C.: Howard University Press.

Sabaratnam, M. (2017). *Decolonizing intervention: International statebuilding in Mozambique.* London: Routledge.

Said, E. (1978). *Orientalism*. New York: Vintage.

Sajed, A. (2013). *Postcolonial encounters in international relations: The politics of transgression in the Maghreb*. New York: Routledge.

Sampson, A.B. (2002). Tropical anarchy: Waltz, Wendt, and the way we imagine international politics. *Alternatives*, 27, 429–457.

Seth, S. (2013). *Postcolonial theory and international relations*. London: Routledge.

Shilliam, R. (2017). Race in world politics. In S. Smith, P. Owens, J. Baylis (Eds.). *The globalization of world politics* (pp. 286–300). Oxford: Oxford University Press.

Shimazu, N. (1998). *Japan, race and equality: The racial equality proposal of 1919*. New York: Routledge.

Shogo, S. (2009). *Civilization and empire: China and Japan's encounter with European international society*. London & New York: Routledge.

Spivak, G.C. (1988). Can the subaltern speak? In C. Nelson and L. Grossberg, *Marxism and the interpretations of culture* (pp. 271–313). Basingstoke: Macmillan Education.

Streets, H. (2004). *Martial races: The military, race and masculinity in British imperial culture, 1857–1914*. Manchester, UK: Manchester University Press.

Suzuki, S. (2009). *Civilization and empire: China and Japan's encounter with European international society*. London & New York: Routledge.

Todorov, T. (1999). *The conquest of America: The question of the other*. Tulsa: University of Oklahoma Press.

Toussaint, C.E. (1956). *The trusteeship system of the United Nations*. New York: Praeger.

Trouillot, M. (1995). *Silencing the past: Power and the production of history*. Boston, MA: Beacon Press.

Vitalis, R. (2016). *White world order, black power politics: The birth of international relations*. Ithaca: Cornell University Press.

Vucetic, S. (2011). *The Anglosphere: A genealogy of racialized identity in international relations*. Stanford: Stanford University Press.

Vucetic, S. (2012). The search for liberal Anglo-America: From racial supremacy to multicultural politics. In P. Katzenstein (Ed.). *Anglo-America: Civilizational politics beyond West and East* (pp. 120–141). London: Routledge.

Vucetic, S. (2015). Against race taboos: The global colour line in philosophical discourse. In A. Anievas, N. Manchanda and R. Shilliam (Eds.). *Race and racism in international relations: Confronting the global colour line* (pp. 98–114). Abingdon: Routledge.

Walker, R.B.J. (2006). Lines of insecurity: International, imperial, exceptional. *Security Dialogue*, 37, 65–82.

Watson, H. (2001). Theorizing the racialization of global politics and the Caribbean experience. *Alternatives*, 26, 449–483.

Williams, G., Meth, P. and Willis, K. (2014). *Geographies of developing areas: The global south in a changing world* (2nd edition). New York: Routledge.

Young, R.J.C. (1995). *Colonial desire: Hybridity in theory, culture and race*. London: Routledge.

4 Gender, race, and International Relations

Aytak Akbari-Dibavar

Introduction	58
Gender(less) bodies, gendered bodies in IR	59
Theories of gender in IR	61
Can we talk about race now?	66
Black and postcolonial feminisms	71
Feminist theory versus practice	73

Introduction

On May 9, 1867, in an address to the first annual meeting of the American Equal Rights Association, Sojourner Truth stated 'I have done a great deal of work; as much as a man, but did not get so much pay. I used to work in the field and bind grain, keeping up with the cradler, but men doing no more, got twice as much pay [...] We do as much, eat as much, we want as much'. Born into slavery in 1797, Truth was an abolitionist and women's right activist, who spent her entire 'free' life travelling across the United States, giving speeches on abolition and women's rights. Truth's presence in all her speeches has been described as powerful – strong and truthful tone and earnest gestures – and made her one of the most significant women's rights and anti-slavery activists in American history (Loewenberg and Bogin 1976; Siebler 2010). However, despite Truth's intellectual and political aptitude, her ideas, speeches and activism come to us in scattered fragments, in bits and pieces; this attests to her absence from our political consciousness. Why is that so? Why do people like Sojourner Truth, Anna Julia Cooper, Ida B. Wells-Barnett, Mary McLeod Bethune, Amy Jacques Garvey, Claudia Jones, Barbara Smith, Maria W. Stewart and countless other non-white activists remain absent from our political consciousness? Why do many other women/women of color activists not find their way into our textbooks and in popular culture? What makes them invisible to a searching eye? What turns them into silenced and hidden figures lost in a historical trajectory?

This chapter will introduce the study of gender in International Relations (IR) in an effort to help answer some of these questions and more. There are many ways to think about gender and how gender can inform the study of global politics. However, this chapter will mainly focus on postcolonial and black feminist accounts of IR with a brief summary of prominent mainstream and critical feminist approaches. Part one deals with what gender is and how gender can be employed as an analytical concept in making sense of everyday and world politics. Particular emphasis is placed on showing the limitations of constructing gender as a binary and essentializing category, especially when applied to the 'big questions' of IR, such as war, peace and security. Accordingly, gender goes beyond the biological differences and is rather implicated in relations of power that intersect with race and racisms. Part two focuses on the postcolonial and black feminist critique of white Western feminism, and on the importance of theorizing race and gender together within wider historical contexts. Finally, this chapter provides and accounts for the 'theory versus practice' arguments from a feminist perspective.

Gender(less) bodies, gendered bodies in IR

"Ain't I a woman?"

In examining the field of International Relations, one should ask how gender relations have contributed and informed the conventional construction of the discipline as a whole, which is traditionally occupied by male bodies and by rigid ideas of masculinity. One way to answer this question is to look at the definition of gender and how it differs from sex. The ways in which we understand and conceptualize gender and sex leads to different theories and therefore produces different outcomes. If we understand sex and gender as natural and straightforward categories, then we find ourselves caught up in a very essentialist view of what gender is supposed to mean, what a gender theory should look like, and how it should inform policy. In an essentialized understanding of gender, we miss theorizing about 'gender' itself. In fact, by equating 'gender' with 'woman' we will obscure 'the role of men, masculinity, and patriarchy in the formation of gender in social relations of power' (Agathangelou and Ling 2004b, 26). Whereas, if we understand gender (femininity and masculinity) as a social construct which has been historically informed by social, cultural, political, and religious structures, then we understand why and how gender and gendered practices affect global politics. But, first let us unpack what we mean when we say gender (femininity and masculinity) is a social construct.

Some feminists, such as Laura Shepherd (2010), argue that while sex is natural and biological, gender is something that is created and constructed as a result of socialization. This means that while we may be born with a different anatomy of the reproductive system, and secondary sex characteristics (male/female/intersex), we only learn later on what these different anatomies mean and what social values and roles are assigned to them through socializing with others in society. For example, if one is born with a reproductive system and physical characteristics that are typical of a male body, that person is expected by society to behave in a specific way that is presumed masculine, such as being strong, rational, less emotional, more authoritative. Gender norms and phrases such as 'boys don't cry', 'man up',

Box 4.1

Hegemonic masculinity refers to those institutional and systemic practices and ideas that legitimize heterosexual man's dominant position in society, and the marginalization of women and other ways of being male.

'act like a lady', 'grow a pair', etc. are only few examples of the type of expectation that a society has and values that are assigned based on our sexual anatomy.

Therefore, it can be argued that the perceived binary between man and woman or 'the duality of gender' strictly defines two distinctive categories of human beings and assigns them with their gender roles in both the public and private sphere (Shepherd, 2010). This essentialist understanding of sex and gender manifests itself through a simplistic binary opposition that claims men are stronger, more rational and more authoritative than women, who are depicted as weak, emotional and passive. Although these assigned gender norms and characteristics can shift reflecting different contexts, there is continuity in the unequal power dynamic between genders in many different societies. Hence, the characteristics associated with masculinity are considered to have a greater social value than those associated with femininity. This inequality leads to what is called 'hegemonic masculinity', which simply put, supports male power and female subordination.

Gender in International Relations

By using gender as a category of analysis while examining the field of International Relations, one can see that IR is not immune to these unequal and hierarchical relations between genders. In fact, gendered power dynamics are deeply embedded in the field. The characteristics that are assigned to men such as toughness, power, and aggression have been valued the most in a political conduct (Shepherd, 2010). According to Zalewski (2010, p. 29), when we stop and ask questions such as: 'What concept and categories must be taken seriously in International Relations?' 'Whose life matters the most?', 'What international stories are credible?' – we realize that the answers to those questions come from a highly gendered, racialized and masculine perspective. For example, when it comes to foreign policy (a subfield of IR), advisors are expected to make 'rational', data-based, and 'tough' decisions. They also should be objective about the advice that they are giving and not let their emotions cloud their judgment. According to Sandra Whitworth; 'informed by [the] goal of serving government, scholars of mainstream International Relations have taken as their central concerns the causes of war and the conditions of peace, order, and security. […] The "high politics" of international security policy is […] "a man's world, a world of power and conflict in which warfare is a privileged activity" and from which women traditionally have been excluded' (Whitworth, 2006, p. 90). Given these examples, when it comes to theorizing and talking about world politics, IR privileges certain perspectives – those that belong to *hegemonic masculinity*.

> **Box 4.2**
>
> *Andro-Eurocentrism* is the assumption that masculine and Western ideologies and practices are the central location for knowledge production.

Consequently, IR dismisses or marginalizes other perspectives that do not fit within IR's masculine and Eurocentric framework. Some stories, 'realities', and everyday experiences that do not fit in this 'high politics' talk become invisible, and people turn into numbers and data. These 'realities' remain hidden unless we put a 'gendered' and 'racialized' lens on and are able to identify and think about the lived realities and experiences of the majority of this world's population, those of women, women of color and marginalized groups. Similarly, a gendered/racial lens will enable us to narrate a different IR into existence, 'one in which the experiences and histories of the privileged are read against the histories of the dispossessed and marginalized' (Chowdhry, 2007, p. 106). In 'Race, Amnesia and the Education of IR', Sankaran Krishna (2001) tells us when we start looking at IR beyond the *Andro-Eurocentric* foundation, we can begin to see the histories hidden by abstractions.

Theories of gender in IR

Theories of gender in International Relations aim to understand how gender, as an important category of analysis, informs and shapes not just our day-to-day experiences, but also global politics. In so doing, different feminist/gender theories have different sets of questions when it comes to the origin of women's oppression in global politics. Some gender theories specifically focus on the inequalities between men and women so their aim is to make women visible and equal in IR (Agathangelou and Turcotte, 2010), such as liberal feminism. Other feminists, such as standpoint feminists, emphasize women's marginalized position in society, and aim to shed light on these marginalized locations. Marxist feminists, on the other hand, engage critically with politico-economic structures in capitalist societies to locate the origin of women's oppression, while post-structuralist feminists ask critical questions about the construction of gender and gender roles by socio-political discourses. However, an important question that is missing from these feminisms is the importance of race and of intersectional approaches to understanding gender in theorizing IR.

Liberal feminism

Starting with the suffrage movements, liberal feminism is based principally on legal equality, which translates into equal pay for equal work, equal rights to vote, affording the same rights and protections as men. Liberal feminists argue that there is no reason (natural reason) for women to be excluded from social and political engagements in order to live a fulfilled life. They also reject the idea that women's oppression is due to their passive, caring and/or uncompetitive nature – biologically deterministic – but that it is linked to society's misunderstanding of their nature (Newman and White, 2006). For liberal feminists, the exclusion of women from the public sphere can be remedied through policy and legal interventions that aim to include more women in politics, political institutions, the workplace, and in positions of authority (Newman and White, 2006). Following liberal feminism to its most radical, some argue that if policies, social arrangements, and institutional structures targeted women and granted protections equal to those of men, then there would essentially be no more hierarchical violence against women in society.

Box 4.3

Liberal feminisms draw upon classical liberal ideas of freedom and equality of opportunity. Therefore, they have been characterized as feminism of rights. They believe that equality will be achieved by creating an equal and leveled playing field for both sexes. They also believe that one of the reasons behind women's oppression is that they traditionally belonged to the private sphere rather than the public one, therefore they had no say in the socio-political systems in which they lived. Hence, the solution would be to gender mainstream, meaning have more women in policy-making positions and in offices to include more women's perspectives.

Standpoint feminism

Standpoint feminism maintains that marginalized women are particularly disadvantaged by not only national and international structures, but also that they are systematically overlooked in world politics. Hence, in analyzing the status quo, standpoint feminists ask us to shift our attention from abstract structures, such as states, the European Union, The United Nations, to individuals, with a specific focus on the voices and experiences of marginalized women (Hansen, 2010). Therefore, for standpoint feminists it is not enough to add more women to the above-mentioned political institutions in order to achieve equality, but we also need to shift the foundational notions behind these institutions of power, which are predominantly masculine (Clough, 1994; Hartsock, 1983). The importance of focusing on marginalized women stems from the fact that these individuals are seen as bearers of a different type of knowledge, one that is not included in the larger structures of masculinized knowledge production and without which our understanding and the picture of the world would not be complete (Clough, 1994). For standpoint feminism, the state-centric understanding of International Relations dismisses and silences women and their day-to-day experiences. Therefore, standpoint feminism's basic tenet is to prioritize women's experience, as a counterpoint to the dominance of male hegemony in the traditional fields of knowledge, such as IR. However, one of the important questions being overlooked by some standpoint feminists is the following: are all women's experiences the same? What happens to issues of race, class, ethnicity, and culture when look-ing at gender identity? This question will be answered later in the chapter, when we discuss intersectionality.

Marxist feminism

Marxist/socialist feminism looks into the broader socio-economic structures as the main source of gender-based oppression. Marxist feminists believe that women's oppression is linked to capitalism and private property. Dalla Costa and James (1975), for example, argue that the exploitation of women has played a central function in the process of capitalist accumulation – a process through which one can gather valuable objects such as money, land, surplus value, and use it to gain future profits – insofar as women have been the producers and reproducers of the most essential capitalist commodity: humans as labor-power. Hence, women's bodies and reproductive rights become sites of exploitation. In addition, for Marxist feminists, the shift from feudalism to capitalism and the private ownership of the land has played a pivotal role in making women even more invisible in the public sphere. This shift has fundamentally changed women's relationship with land and forced them into domesticity and the pri-vate sphere, where their labor lost commodity value. Although this does not mean that patriarchal systems have not existed prior to capitalism, the remnants of patriarchal systems from pre-capitalist societies have been utilized to further capitalist agenda. Kollontai (1977) argued that in a capitalist society women's oppression is interlinked with the relations of production – the relationship between those who own the means of production (such as factory owners or the bourgeoisie) and those who do not (the workers or the proletariat). Therefore, the possibilities of emancipation lie within the transformation of these relations.

Poststructuralist feminism

What is the role of discourse – specific use of words, in-built assumptions – in creating and re-creating our ideas of masculinity and femininity as such? For poststructuralist feminists, the question of gendered discourse is an important question as it plays a significant role in the construction of a national identity, security policy and development thinking. Why do we think of a nation as the motherland, for example? What is the significance of attributing femininity or masculinity to a nation-state? Attribution of femininity to a nation-state re-creates a passive, pure and sacred being that needs to be protected from invasion by (male) foreigners. In her study of American nuclear strategists' dis-course, Carol Cohn (1987), observed the gendered discourse around weapons of war used by these strategic analysts, all of whom were men. Cohn refers to this gendered language, used by the American nuclear strategists, as 'techno-strategic' language; a rational, scientific, and gendered discourse around weapons — weapons that are capable of wiping the whole humanity off the surface of the earth. However, use of this sanitized techno-strategic language gives analysts an opportunity to distance themselves from 'the realities of nuclear holocaust that lay behind their world' (Cohn, 1987, p. 690). The attribution of gendered names, sexist phrases and sexual imaginaries such as 'to disarm [means] to get rid of all your stuff', 'vertical erector launcher', 'thrust-to-weight ratios, soft lay downs, deep penetration, and the comparative advantages of protracted versus spasm attack' were only a few manifestations of the gendered language used by the nuclear strategic analysts (Cohn, 1987, p. 693). For Cohn, these sexist discourses and sexual imaginaries in high-security talks are not a standalone phenomenon, but a continuation and re-production of the sexist assumptions that exist in everyday life and in global politics. Therefore, using a gendered lens is very important to acquire a better understanding of issues such as security, peace, peace building, and the global political economy.

Absent questions from most feminist theories

However, one of the main questions not being asked by the above-mentioned gender theories regards the interconnected nature of gender, race, sexuality, geopolitics and economy (Agathangelou and Turcotte, 2010). This speaks directly to the lack of recognition of the historical material processes that facilitated women's oppression. The extent of violence against women at home, in the workplace and in the community, cannot be analyzed separately from significant historical moments such as colonialism, the transnational institutions of slavery, and war. Therefore, gender is not only concerned with the social construction of femininity and masculinity, but is also involved in larger geo-political, racial, and economic processes — underlying notions, structures, and beliefs about whose body, safety, security matters in global politics and why (Chowdhry and Nair, 2004). Gender and the knowledge that is produced around gender should be analyzed intersectionally within geopolitical, racial, colonial and economic (capitalist) structures. By creating theories that focus on individuals rather than states as the main participants in world politics and paying close attention to the gendered and racial aspects of dominant power structures, we can have a deeper understanding of our lives and lived experiences (Agathangelou and Turcotte, 2010). Feminists in IR who tend to *gender mainstream* and 'add women and stir' overlook the profound historical misogyny of international political and economic structures. IR feminisms that are linked to the structural and material struggles of people's daily life are the ones that open spaces for transformation.

Intersectionality

Intersectionality is a term coined by Kimberly Crenshaw, an American scholar and civil rights advocate, to underlie the intersecting of different

Box 4.4

Coined in the UN resolution 1325 as a response to the sex trafficking, rape and other forms of sexual violence that had involved UN peacekeepers, *gender mainstreaming* was promoted as a strategy to include more women within decision-making institutions, so that the interests of women and women's unique perspectives would be represented in decision-making processes. However, as criticized by many feminists, gender mainstreaming is not a solution for the patriarchal structures from which these disasters emerge. Sandra Whitworth (2004) describes gender mainstreaming as simply adding women to the same problematic structures, and stirring rather than profoundly questioning the structures.

social identities and systems of oppression and domination such as race, class, gender, sexual orientation, and culture. Sexism, racism, homophobia and other forms of social inequalities and injustices in a society do not happen on mutually exclusive terrains but historically they intersect with one another and are mutually co-constituted. Hence, when social injustices, such as racism or sexism are reduced to either/or bases, they relegate the multi-dimensional experiences of women of color into a location that is hidden or harder to explain because they use only one category of analyses (i.e. 'gender') instead of looking at how gender, race, and class intersect in specific contexts (Crenshaw, 1991).

This point brings us back to the earlier question raised in the beginning of the chapter about Sojourner Truth and her invisibility in women's suffrage movement. How and why was she absent from our political consciousness and never included in women rights movement? Knowledge production about women suffrage movements in the United States began in 1876, when women agreed to compile a collection of data from their earlier meetings in women's national conventions (Terborg-Penn, 1998). However, these recordings – personal anecdotes, biographical sketches, photographs, state reports from the congressional record – did not reflect, cite or name any African-American women that actively participated and organized these meetings. The first volume was published in 1881 bringing forward the history of women's suffrage movement between 1848 to the late 1860s (Terborg-Penn, 1998). Importantly not one black woman's photograph appeared in this volume. All black suffragists were absent from the report; there was no mention of Sojourner Truth, who, despite resistance from some white suffragists had attended and given speeches in the congress meetings. One of these famous speeches titled as 'Ain't I a woman', very powerfully illustrates what constitutes a respectable woman and a feminized body in American popular culture at the time, and speaks about the absence of black women from this imagination (Collins, 2000). The resistance coming from the suffragettes against the inclusion of their African-American 'sisters' in their movement came from the fear that the abolition movement and the universal suffrage struggles might get confused. Therefore, the National Woman Suffrage Association considered the Northeastern Federation of Colored Women's Clubs as a liability to the association's social and political goals (Terborg-Penn, 1998).

Box 4.5: Sojourner Truth (1797–1883): Ain't I A Woman?

Delivered in 1851 at the Women's Convention, Akron, Ohio.

Well, children, where there is so much racket there must be something out of kilter. I think that 'twixt the negroes of the South and the women at the North, all talking about rights, the white men will be in a fix pretty soon. But what's all this here talking about?

That man over there says that women need to be helped into carriages, and lifted over ditches, and to have the best place everywhere. Nobody ever helps me into carriages, or over mud-puddles, or gives me any best place! *And ain't I a woman?* Look at me! Look at my arm! I have ploughed and planted, and gathered into barns, and no man could head me! *And ain't I a woman?* I could work as much and eat as much as a man – when I could get it – and bear the lash as well! *And ain't I a woman?* I have borne thirteen children, and seen most all sold off to slavery, and when I cried out with my mother's grief, none but Jesus heard me! *And ain't I a woman?*

Then they talk about this thing in the head; what's this they call it? [member of audience whispers, "intellect"] That's it, honey. What's that got to do with women's rights or negroes' rights? If my cup won't hold but a pint, and yours holds a quart, wouldn't you be mean not to let me have my little half measure full?

Then that little man in black there, he says women can't have as much rights as men, 'cause Christ wasn't a woman! Where did your Christ come from? Where did your Christ come from?! From God and a woman!...

Can we talk about race now?

Grada Kilomba (2010), a writer, poet and activist, in her book *Plantation Memories*, describes the psychological reality of everyday racism based on personal accounts and biographical narratives, and deconstructs the normality of racism towards black women's bodies. What does it mean and what is it like to live in a body that has historically been constructed as 'the other'? What is it like to be silenced?

The figure of 'face mask' – an instrument which consists of a bite placed inside of the mouth of the slave, 'clamped between the tongue and jaw, and fixed behind the head with two strings, one surrounding the chin and the other surrounding the nose and forehead' (Kilomba, 2010, p. 16) – is central in Kilomba's depiction of historical speechlessness of black women as it is adequate in capturing the long history of 'imposed silence', interrupted histories, disrupted speeches and 'continual loss urged by colonialism' (Kilomba, 2010, p. 12). This infamous face mask functioned to impose a sense of speechlessness and fear and in that sense it has become an enduring legacy of colonial representation, 'the sadistic politics of conquest and its cruel regimes of silencing the so called "others"' (Kilomba, ibid.)

Who can speak then? What happens when we speak? And what can we speak about? But also, who listens, and who can listen? These become important questions in Kilomba's writings. She argues that the purpose of the face mask, as an instrument, was not solely to prevent the slaves – the others – from speaking, but it also aimed to protect white ears and consciousness from hearing. The master's fear of listening to the black subject, as they might reveal a truth about their own lives that can impose guilt, shame and anxiety on their consciousness, was the purpose of rendering the other silent (Kilomba, 2010, p. 21).

The symbol of the mask and the silences that it represents can be used to illustrate why mainstream theories, including white liberal feminism, resist hearing or including the 'other's voice and knowledge in their theorization. This resistance stems from 'the art of not knowing' or simply deliberately ignoring something you must know, or what you already know. An example of 'the art of not knowing' is the deliberate ignorance of the horrifying conditions of Indigenous reserves in Canada by many Canadians. In these 'unknown' parts of Canada, 'there are 89 Indigenous communities without safe drinking water. On Indigenous reserves, a child is more likely to be sexually assaulted than to graduate high school. The murder rate is worse than Somalia's and the incarceration rate is the highest in the world' (Gilmore, 2017, p. 2). And yet, one rarely talks about these conditions. 'Not knowing' about these horrifying conditions is, in fact, a privilege and a choice. Similar to the purpose of the face mask, the silence that has surrounded these conditions functions also as a means to protect certain ears and consciousness. Because if one hears about them, then one has to acknowledge the devastating impacts of colonialism and slavery and be more serious about the historical responsibility that comes with this acknowledgment. When silenced words and worlds are projected out loud, they leave no room for us to escape. We get entrapped in the Speaker/Listener contract. However, not all who hear listen.

Gender and race

At the end of the 1970s, black lesbian feminist Audre Lorde wrote an open letter to Mary Daly, who was also a radical feminist philosopher:

> Mary I ask that you beware of how this serves the destructive forces of racism and separation between women the assumption that the herstory

and myth of white women is the legitimate and sole herstory and myth of all women to call upon for power and background, and that non-white women and our herstories are noteworthy only as decoration, or examples of female victimization. I ask that you be aware of the effects that this dismissal has upon the community of black women and other women of Color, and how it devalues your own words.

(Lorde, 1984, p. 69)

Lorde's message highlights how white women's focus on their oppression in a patriarchal system is making them blind towards the specificity of other forms of oppression that women of color experience in their daily lives. In addition, it fails to take into account the history of slavery, colonialism and imperial conquest that is entangled with gender-based oppression. The claim that all women share the same experience or that white middle-class women can identify with experiences of women of color ignores the different power hierarchies that cohere to produce different experiences and variations of oppression across space, time, and bodies.

Patricia Hill Collins (2000, p. 5) informs us that Western white and liberal feminisms have also contributed to the suppression of the ideas of black women who have a 'distinctive African-influenced and feminist sensibility about how race and class intersect in structuring gender'. Despite these sensibilities and unique perspectives, African-American, aboriginal and other women of color have historically been excluded from white feminist organizations (Giddings, 1984; Zinn et al., 1986; Caraway, 1991). In fact, traditionally, many US white feminist scholars have resisted the idea of including their black colleagues and their theories. The omission of black feminists from mainstream accounts and texts implied that all women share the same experience, namely that of cis-gender heterosexual middle class white woman. Therefore, this omission is another form of oppression (hooks, 1991).

Box 4.6

Patriarchy is the system that entrenches the rule of the father/male guardian as the dominant leader within a household, and/or in the broader (economic, political, social, and cultural) structures of society.

Patriarchy is not a separate moment in history. This means that patriarchy, as a system of oppression, has historically been interlinked and co-constituted by other systems of oppression such as colonialism, capitalism and Western imperialism. This does not mean, however, that patriarchy did not exist in pre-colonial, or pre-capitalist contexts, but rather that the current form of patriarchy – *heteronormative capitalist white supremacist patriarchy* – cannot be discussed or understood separately from capitalism, imperialism and colonialism. In addition, it is explicitly connected to ideas of production, reproduction, and value.

Box 4.7

Heteronormativity is the social ordering that accepts the complementarity between the sexes as normal and natural, hence privileging heterosexuality as natural and desirable while simultaneously denouncing sexual minorities as abnormal and unnatural. For example, when we look at our pop culture, whether in movies and television shows portraying heterosexual couples as the main characters, in pop songs and children's books and animated films, which almost exclusively focus on heterosexual nuclear families, we are bombarded by the notion of heterosexuality as the 'normal', 'natural' and most desirable form of sexuality.

Neoliberal globalization: a gendered and racialized process

If we examine the process of 'neoliberal globalization' as a gendered and racialized process, we can see that it is both a reflection and continuation of patriarchal cultural codes through economic and governance policies. These are evident when we examine what value is assigned comparatively to female and male labor, as well as in ongoing changes in the global/national economic architectures – the rise of informal and virtual labor, for example. Men, especially those who are economically, ethnically, racially and geopolitically privileged (i.e. white Western middle-class/elite men), continue to dominate institutions of power and authority worldwide, and characteristics seen as masculine, such as strength, rationality, objectivity, and autonomy continue to dominate economic policy and geopolitical thinking (Peterson, 2010).

Whitworth (2006, p. 88) argues that 'like mainstream IR before it, IPE [International Political Economy] had rarely acknowledged, much less analyzed, how female subordinations are created and sustained both nationally and internationally', and yet, gendered bodies and discourses have played a central role in shaping our understanding of economic practices, reproduction and labor (Peterson, 2010). What comes to be understood as masculine has gained more commodified value than what is constructed as feminine (dependent, emotional, volunteer and subjective). In contrast, women's work and feminized qualities are devalued, deemed economically irrelevant and characterized as subjective and unskilled – they are either poorly paid or not paid at all (Bakker and Gill, 2003). This highly gendered, or 'masculine' foundation of political practices (economic policy) is contradictory; it devalues reproduction and social reproduction – mostly unpaid labor such as cooking, cleaning, and care work, largely performed by women/women of color – while at the same time depending on this exploitation to reproduce the system. Adopting an intersectional lens highlights the fact that devalorization of labor across race and gender lines impacts women of color more harshly in the current global economy in domestic jobs, migration and global political economy of prostitution.

A great example of this devalorization would be the care/domestic work performed by migrant women/women of color. According to the ILO estimates, women make up 87 percent of domestic workers in general, and 73 percent of domestic migrant workers worldwide. This means that five in every six domestic workers are women (Simonovsky and Luebker, 2011, p. 6). In addition, female domestic workers make up '3.5% of all female employment and 7.5% of all female wage workers in the world – reflecting the importance of domestic work as a source of employment for women' (Tijdens et al., 2011, p. 7). These workers, 'often either belong to historically disadvantaged and despised communities such as minority ethnic groups, indigenous peoples, low-caste, low-income rural and urban groups, or are migrants' (Oelz qtd in Tijdens et al., 2011, p. 11). Abigail Bakan and Daiva Stasinlus argue that 'racialized images of womanhood play an important role in justifying to employers why non-white women of color are "naturally" suited for childcare and housework' (qtd in Whitworth, 2006, p. 94). Due to the feminized nature of domestic and care work, even paid domestic work is hardly visible in society and or regulated by governments; this situation leaves domestic workers, mostly women of color, vulnerable to unfair and abusive treatments and unequal/minimum wages (ILO, 2010, para 4). Although, in constructing the language around migrant workers one should stay away from victimization discourses, employing the language of 'choice', renders invisible the structural constraints and the powerful economic dynamics that provoke female migration. This is a good example of how patriarchy linked to other historical forms of oppression (such as neoliberal capitalism) creates a 'seamless web of economy, polity, and ideology' (Collins, 2000, p. 5) allowing an effective system of social control to keep women of color in a socially, intellectually and economically subordinate position.

Box 4.8

Social reproduction refers to both biological reproduction (i.e. childbirth and rearing), and to the reproduction of social relations that aim to create and maintain the unequal processes of exploitation that are central to the functioning of capitalism. Therefore, social reproduction has a crucial role in the international political economy as it involves institutions whose ethos is in direct collusion with neoliberal policies and values. Institutions such as education, healthcare, and other social services, create and recreate neoliberal/sexual/racial subjectivities and class relations. The labor power and reproductive capacity of women has long been central to systems of commodity exchange and capitalism.

Black and postcolonial feminisms

Postcolonial and black feminisms adopt a critical lens while investigating the interrelation of race, class, and gender within the broader scope of imperialism and global capitalism. They also seek to account for the long lasting gendered and racial consequences of colonialism and slavery on the current socio–politico–economic structures and systems. 'Who can speak?' and 'who is being listened to?' become important questions in postcolonial feminism as they challenge the centrality accorded to white middle class heterosexual woman and her experience. By doing so postcolonial and black feminists reflect and take into account the multiplicity/diversity of experiences and different forms of oppression produced and reproduced since the colonial encounter (Collins, 2000). In addition, postcolonial theory acknowledges that by imposing Eurocentric forms of knowledge, we risk devaluating other forms of knowing the world and the critical insights and offerings of marginalized groups (Collins, 2000).

What do we see and discover when we include these silenced and exiled voices and perspectives back into our feminist IR theory? What happens when we interrogate the history that is written from the andro-eurocentric perspective, through gendered and racialized analytical standpoints? (Chowdhry, 2007). In order to know the answer to these questions, let us put on our critical analytical lens and look into the mainstream discourses of development in IR. Looking through such critical/intersectional lens, one realizes that the Third World has been constructed by the West as perverse, passive, abnormal and feminine. Hence, its socio–cultural values and institutions are usually depicted as irrational and effeminate with its economic developments always needing a mature and masculine/rational guardian (usually the West).

Indeed, as many postcolonial theorists such as Ilan Kapoor have argued, colonial projects were often justified through sexism, racism and homophobia. By emphasizing the hegemonic heterosexual masculinity and rational (scientific) methodology, the West has justified its civilizing missions against the 'feminized' and 'irrational' locals who have long been represented in early colonial reports and European popular culture as emasculated, sexual deviants and degenerates, in need of a European civilizing intervention (Kapoor, 2015). Reports from sixteenth- and seventeenth-century European travel journals, such as Edward Long's *History of Jamaica*, refer to Africans as licentious and ill-tempered who lack self-control and cognitive maturity to deal with their bodily desires (quoted in Young, 1995, p. 151). Encountering 'Africans', indigenous people, and the racialized 'unknown' others and their cultures, European colonizers used simple categories to fit/reduce these 'different' and 'unknown' others in order to make them 'known'/'same' for the sake of colonizers' own internal anxieties. Unknown and different are scary categories. Unknown and different can challenge one's self-centric perception of the world and show them another way of being. Knowing something, on the other hand, is a type of mastery. It gives one an illusion of power over the 'known'.

Therefore, in order for the colonizers to claim power over the colonized others, the first step was to reduce them to categories that were already known to Europeans, categories such as effeminate, irrational, passive, and docile – terms that were already in existence in European discourse and consciousness. However, it is important to remind that these categories were not uniquely constructed to represent the colonized; these were/are the projection of the West's internal misogyny and lack of trust against the internal other – the women – especially poor women. The West's internal mistrust of women and anything feminine was projected onto the racialized and sexualized non-West allowing its colonial and imperial interventions (Kapoor, 2015). Anne McClintock (1995, p. 22) shows us how lands were labeled as 'virgin territories' to rationalize 'penetration' and 'rape' while at the same time presenting their inhabitants as effeminate, who did not know how to penetrate the 'land' and take advantage of it. In this regard, masculine/feminine was/is intertwined with known/unknown and rational/emotional binaries so that the West's self-image of undisputed masculinity could be secured and its continued presence justified in the colonies (Chowdhry, 2007).

From unveiling Algerian women (Fanon, 1965) to saving Afghan women (Agathangelou and Ling, 2004a), colored woman's body has always been the site of contestation, colonial negotiation and exploitation. The myth of the 'erotic East' constantly repeated in European writings and travelogues by geographers, travelers and anthropologists depicted Arab and Muslim cultures as irrational, mysterious and sexually promiscuous (Kapoor, 2015, p. 1614). This construction, explicitly named by Edward Said as 'Orientalism', has much less to do with the 'Orient' than it did with the projection of West's misogynist, homophobic and masculine anxieties on the colonized/East (Said, 1978). The bodies of these mysterious 'oriental' women, who were/are hidden under their veils awaiting freedom, has justified/still justifies the aggressive interventions taken by the West to save these women from their either hyper-masculine or effeminate men (in both cases these men lack the right version and dosage of masculinity). More recently, the so-called war on terror has also formulated the enemy in ways that continue to project colonial tropes. US President George W. Bush, for instance, restructures the war on terrorism within gendered and racial discourses to meet its patriarchal needs. However, these discourses of saving and unveiling oppressed Muslim women are not a new phenomenon. In *A Dying Colonialism*, Fanon (1965) illustrates how Algerian women's veil revealed the profound sexist and racist notions of the French colonizer. Depictions of veiled Algerian women as passive victims of their 'backward' patriarchal societies worked as a convenient justification for the continuation of colonialism as these women needed to be 'rescued' by their white masters.

As the 'natural order' allowed the patriarch to discipline and punish his wife for disobedience within Europe, many of the West's racist, sexist and homophobic assumptions informed the violence against the colonized in the name of colonial control, desire and discipline – enshrining colonial racial-gender power hierarchies in the process. Some scholars such as Robert Young (1995, p. 19), refer to colonial projects as 'desiring machines' deployed to control colored women's bodies, as well as natural resources. Through a reading of nineteenth-century scientific texts on miscegenation, race, and identity, Young demonstrates how the underlying desire for inter-racial sex was a prime motivator in Victorian colonialism and capitalist expansion. Young argues that English identity was contradictory, fixed by a desire for hybridity defined as intra-racial fertility (polygenism and monogenism) between races, rationalized for both accumulation and exploitation of indigenous 'foreign' bodies. While simultaneously exhibiting revulsion toward this 'mixing' of races, 'theories of race were thus also covert theories of desire' (Young, 1995, p. 9). Homoerotic and passionate sexual desires for wealth, power, colored women's bodies, and resources were manifested through discourses of race and racial mixing. For Young, this problematic of interracial sexuality at the core of race and culture is fundamental to conceptions of Englishness during this period, and was in constant tension with hierarchical racism and the disgust for perceived 'inferior races'. Within this context, Young (1995, p. 181) re-defines colonialism as a 'desiring machine', one which centers on both 'capitalism's desire for control of wealth, bodies, and resources', and the resultant creolizations – mixing of race and culture – that provide the 'hybrid' foundations for globalizing practice of European colonization.

Box 4.9

In Postcolonial Studies and Gramscian theories, *subaltern* refers to populations that are socio-politico-economically marginalized by hegemonic power, and are subordinated within its power structures.

Feminist theory versus practice

'It is not easy to name our pain, to make it a location for theorizing.'

(hooks, 1991, p. 11)

Some critics argue that in the era of neoliberalism and white supremacist patriarchy, feminism has become the 'new vogue' among some academics in ivory towers that are disconnected from everyday experiences of women, men and children (hooks, 1991; MacKinnon, 1991). Within white supremacist capitalist patriarchy, commodification of feminism and marketplace empowerments, such as using feminist ideology in Cover Girl and Dove advertisements, is on the rise as if one can drop the name feminism without understanding what profoundly radical and 'transformative politics and practice' feminism is supposed to offer (hooks, 1991).

What types of feminist theories and writings are transformative then? In the previous section, it was argued that in order for a feminist theory to be able to capture the everyday realities of individuals, it should do more than merely focus on isolated categories; rather it should theorize the interconnections between gender, race, sexuality, ableism, colonialism and capitalism. In addition, for a theory to be transformative it also needs to be socially lived, humble in its scope and approach and require grassroots participation (hooks, 1991). According to bell hooks (1991, p. 5), 'any theory that cannot be shared in everyday conversation cannot be used to educate the public'. Feminist theory for hooks should deeply connect to radical progressive activist roots in order to be liberating, and this is only possible if theory links itself directly to the everyday life of individuals and attempts to speak to their daily struggles. Hence, the inclusion of 'personal testimony and personal experience' to theory-making processes in IR is necessary for creating a link between feminist theory and activism, a kind of feminism from below.

What makes feminist radical transformation possible is integrating feminist thinking and practices into our daily life. Feminist theories should have the ability to speak to the widest public audience; this can be manifested through feminist writing and public engagement/activism. In addition, theories should be capable of including the voices and experiences of marginalized groups into IR, not in forms of isolated and independent voices, but in a form that these voices of the marginalized and the *subaltern* complement each other and illustrate an interdependency similar to African-American women's quilting techniques (Brown, 1989). The non-uniform but nonetheless connected pieces of quilts sown by African-American women 'are capable of telling different stories to different audiences' (Chowdhry, 2007, p. 105). Feminist theories in IR must include different voices into their theorization so that theories be reflective of the different social, political and epistemological contexts from which these voices have emerged. If this multiplicity of theories is avoided in our feminist theorizations, then we might fall into the trap of universalizing and essentializing an individual's experience over the other many different experiences. As Chowdhry (2007, p. 106) mentions, storytellers, like the African-American women quilters, provide a counterpoint to the managers of order and homogeneity by narrating a story of difference, 'of a just community', 'in which all people are represented and none left out, no matter how small or seemingly insignificant the individual scrap of fabric'. But are all stories welcome in our collective feminist quilting of the world? What types of stories will be seen and/or included in our feminist theorization/quilting?

Gayatri Spivak's famous question 'can the subaltern speak?' investigates the problem of whether marginalized people, including women of color, can actually speak even when feminist IR theories are opening a space for them to do so. For Spivak (1988), the subaltern cannot by definition recover her voice. Spivak claims that there is no escape from these power structures, therefore it is impossible for the subaltern to speak in a way that she can be understood or heard. In addition, IR as a colonized field always runs the risk of re-colonizing the voices of the subaltern as they attempt to enter the field. However, Spivak's position on the absolute silence of the subaltern can be seen as problematic.

Box 4.10

Each piece in the *traditional African-American quilt pattern* inhabits a unique color and form without necessarily adopting an uninformative pattern. However non-uniform, a beautiful pattern created of pieces of fabric demonstrates that membership in pattern does not require blending with other scraps. According to Brown, African-American women quilters 'often place in juxtaposition odd-sized scraps of fabric that appear to clash with one another. Uniform size is not a criterion for membership in the quilt, nor is blending with all other scraps…viewers of such quilts who evaluate aesthetic beauty in terms of sameness, repetitive patterns, and overall homogeneity are often disoriented' (Brown qtd in Chowdhry, 2007, p. 105).

The problem is with Spivak's claim of 'deafness to the native voice where it can be heard [..] attributes an absolute power to the white dominant discourse' (Kilomba, 2010, p. 26). Historically, the colonial project has assumed that every language and every word out of the subaltern's mouth is for the consumption of the colonizer rather than for the subaltern's own name and community.

This process itself, if continued, can render the subaltern a forever slave of white imagination. Hence, one should not assume that marginalized people, including women of color, have to always position their speech as a confrontation or a response to white masculine consciousness. Doing so, as argued by Kilomba (2010), would re-affirm the position of white masculinity as the dominating power and the main consumer of ideas. Collins (2000) also demonstrates that the above-mentioned claims see the colonized as incapable of speaking in their own name and designate their speeches as unsatisfactory or inadequate – therefore soundless, inaudible.

'It is not easy to name our pain, to theorize from that location', hooks (1991, p. 11) says as she reminds us that 'to create theory from the location of pain and struggle' takes a lot for courage as they who tend to speak from the location of pain and exposed wounds will give us their experience as a teaching and guidance, 'as a means to chart new theoretical journeys' (ibid.). Theorizing from the location of pain can be liberating as it enables us to remember our journeys and to recover ourselves, 'it charges and challenges us to renew our commitment to an active, inclusive feminist struggle' (ibid.). It is also important to remember that the task of transformative feminism and its theorization is not to 'solve' the problems of inequality, gender/racial hierarchies, or global violence; rather it is to open up spaces and create platforms within which we can hear one another against the backdrop of the various power struggles that pit us against each other. This transformative feminism allows us to find theoretical and material ways of connecting to one another's struggle through sharing, listening, and negotiating.

Box 4.11: Key points

- Gender should be seen beyond biological difference and physical anatomy and rather as implicated in relations of power which intersect with race and racisms.
- Intersecting of different social identities and systems of oppression and domination such as race, class, gender, sexual orientation, and culture illustrate how International Relations silences and dismisses the voices that do not fit within its masculine and Eurocentric framework.
- Patriarchy is not a separate moment within history, but it is historically constituted and co-constituted by other systems of oppression, therefore it cannot be fully grasped without contextualizing it within the histories of colonialism, capitalism and Western imperialism.
- Postcolonial and black feminisms adopt a critical lens while investigating the interrelation of race, class, and gender within the broader scope of imperialism and global capitalism.
- From a postcolonial perspective, masculinity and femininity are intertwined with other categories such as civilized/uncivilized, known/unknown, and rational/emotional through which Western empire's self-image of undisputed masculinity has been secured and its continued presence has been justified in the colonies.
- What makes feminist radical transformation possible is integrating feminist thinking and practices into our daily life. Feminist theories should have the ability to speak to the widest public audience; this can be manifested through feminist writing and public engagement/activism. In addition, theories should be capable of including the voices and experiences of marginalized groups into IR; this can be done not through isolated and independent voices, but in a way that these marginalized and subaltern voices complement each other and illustrate their interdependency.

Suggested readings

Chowdhry, G., and Nair, S. (2004). (Eds.). *Power, postcolonialism, and international relations: Reading race, gender, and class*. London and New York: Routledge. Using a wide range of postcolonial and critical readings, *Power, Postcolonialism, and International Relations* investigates the implications of race, class and gender relations for the structuring of world politics.

Collins, P.H. (2000). *Black feminist thought: Knowledge, consciousness, and the politics of empowerment* (2nd edition). New York: Routledge. *Black Feminist Thought* not only investigates the ideas of Black feminist intellectuals, but also pays close attention to the lived experiences of African-American women outside academia in order to provide an account of the importance of community-based and self-defined knowledge.

hooks, b. (1981). *Ain't I a woman: Black women and feminism*. Boston: South End Press. Looking through a feminist lens, hooks examines here the implications of the politics of racism and sexism for African-American women's experience and their relationship with current society.

Kilomba, G. (2010). *Plantation memories: Episodes of everyday racism*. Munster: Unrast-Verlag Publications. *Plantation Memories* describes the psychological reality of everyday racism based on personal accounts and biographical narratives, and deconstructs the normality of racism towards black women's bodies. It asks: What does it mean and what is it like to live in a body that has historically been constructed as 'the other'? What is it like to be silenced?

Whitworth, S. (2004). *Men, militarism and UN peacekeeping: A gendered analysis*. Boulder: Lynne Rienner Publishers. Written from a feminist perspective, Whitworth's book criticizes the UN's peacekeeping operation highlighting the racial and gendered dimension of its missions. This book also investigates the contradiction between how peacekeepers and peacekeeping missions have been portrayed by the UN as peaceful and benign, and the militarized masculinity that underpins the peacekeepers' group identity.

Bibliography

Agathangelou, A.M., and Ling, L.H.M. (2004a). Power, borders, security, wealth: Lessons of violence and desire from September 11. *International Studies Quarterly*, 48, 517–538.

Agathangelou, A.M., and Ling, L.H.M. (2004b). The house of IR: From family power politics to the poisies of worldism. *International Studies Review*, 6, 21–50.

Agathangelou, A.M., and Turcotte, H.M. (2010). Postcolonial theories and challenges to 'first world-ism'. In L. Shepherd (Ed.). *Gender matters in global politics: A feminist introduction to international relations* (pp. 44–58). New York: Routledge.

Bakker, I., and Gill, S. (2003). Ontology, method & hypotheses. In I. Bakker and S. Gill (Eds.). *Power, production and social reproduction* (pp. 17–41). London: Palgrave.

Bogin, R., and Loewnberg, B.J. (1976). *Black women in nineteenth-century American life: Their words, their thoughts, their feelings*. University Park, Pennsylvania: Pennsylvania State University Press.

Brown, E.B. (1989). African-American women's quilting: A framework for conceptualizing and teaching African-American women's history. *Signs*, 14, 921–929.

Caraway, N. (1991). *Segregated sisterhood: Racism and the politics of American feminism*. Knoxville, TN: The University of Tennessee Press.

Chowdhry, G. (2007). Edward Said and contrapuntal reading: Implications for critical interventions in international relations. *Millennium*, 36, 101–116.

Chowdhry, G., and Nair, S. (2004). (Eds.). *Power, postcolonialism, and international relations: Reading race, gender, and class*. London and New York: Routledge.

Clough, P.T. (1994). *Feminist thought*. Cambridge: Blackwell Publishers.

Cohn, C. (1987). Sex and death in the rational world of defense intellectuals. *Signs*, 12, 687–718.

Collins, P.H. (2000). *Black feminist thought: Knowledge, consciousness, and the politics of empowerment* (2nd edition). New York: Routledge.

Crenshaw, K. (1991). Mapping the margins: Intersectionality, identity politics, and violence against women of color. *Stanford Law Review*, 43, 1241–1299.

Dalla Costa, M., and James, S. (1975). *The power of women and the subversion of the community*. Bristol, UK: Falling Wall Press.

Fanon, F. (1965). *A dying colonialism.* New York: Grove Press.

Giddings, P. (1984). *When and where I enter: The impact of black women on race and sex in america.* New York: W. Morrow.

Gilmore, S. (2017). The Canada most people don't see. *Globe and Mail.* Published on June 5, 2017, 1–3.

Hartsock, N.M. (1983). The feminist standpoint. In S. Harding and M.B. Hintikka (Eds.). *Discovering reality* (pp. 283–310). Boston: D. Reidel.

Hansen, L. (2010). Ontologies, epistemologies, methodologies. In L.J. Shepherd (Ed.). *Gender matters in global politics: A feminist introduction to international relations* (pp. 17–27). New York: Routledge.

hooks, b. (1991). Theory as liberatory practice. *Yale Journal of Law & Feminism,* 4, 1–12.

International Labour Organization. (2004). *Towards a fair deal for migrant workers in the global economy.* Session 92, report 6. Geneva: ILO.

Kapoor, I. (2015). The queer third world. *Third World Quarterly,* 36, 1611–1628.

Kilomba, G. (2010). *Plantations memories: Episodes of everyday racism.* 2nd edition. Munster: Unrast-Verlag Publications.

Kollontai, A. (1977). *Selected writings of Alesandra Kollontai.* Trans. by Alix Holt. London: Allison and Busby.

Krishna, S. (2001). Race, amnesia and the education of international relations. *Alternatives,* 26, 401–424.

Loewenberg, B., and Bogin, R. (1976). (Eds.). *Black women in nineteenth-century American life: Their words, their thoughts, their feelings.* University Park: Pennsylvania State University Press.

Lopez, K. (2013). *Chinese Cubans: A transnational history.* Chapel Hills: University of North Carolina Press.

Lorde, Audre. (1984). *Sister outsider: Essays and speeches.* Trumansburg, NY: Crossing Press.

McClintock, A. (1995). *Imperial leather: Race, gender and sexuality in the colonial contest.* New York: Routledge.

MacKinnon, C.A. (1991). From practice to theory, or what is a white woman anyway? *Yale Journal of Law & Feminism,* 13–22.

Newman, J., and White, L.A. (2006). *Women, politics, and public policy: The political struggles of Canadian women.* Toronto: Oxford University Press.

Oelz, M. (2011). *Remuneration in domestic work.* Geneva: ILO, Domestic work policy brief 1.

Peterson, V.S. (1992). Security and sovereign states: What is at stake in taking feminism seriously? In *Gendered states: Feminist (re)visions of international relations theory* (pp. 31–64). Boulder, CO: Lynne Rienner Press.

Peterson, V.S. (1999). Sexting political identity: Nationalism as heterosexism. *International Feminist Journal of Politics,* 1, 21–52.

Peterson, V.S. (2010). International/global political economy. In L. Shepherd (Ed.). *Gender matters in global politics: A feminist introduction to international relations* (pp. 204–217). New York: Routledge.

Putnam, L. (2013). *Radical moves: Caribbean migrants and the politics of race in the jazz age.* North Carolina: University of North Carolina Press.

Said, E. (1978). *Orientalism.* New York: Pantheon Books.

Siebler, K. (2010). Teaching the politics of Sojourner Truth's 'Ain't I a woman?'. *Pedagogy,* 10, 511–533.

Shepherd, L.J. (2010). *Gender matters in global politics: A feminist introduction to international relations.* New York: Routledge.

Simonovsky, Y., and Luebker, M. (2011). *Global and regional estimates on domestic workers*. Geneva, ILO: Domestic work policy brief 4.

Smith, S., Booth, K., and Zalewski, M. (1996). (Eds.). *International theory: Positivism and beyond*. Cambridge: Cambridge University Press.

Spivak, G.C. (1988). Can the subaltern speak?. In C. Nelson and L. Grossberg (Eds.). *Marxism and the interpretation of culture* (pp. 271–313). Urbana: University of Illinois Press.

Terborg-Penn, R. (1998). *African American women in the struggle for the vote, 1850–1920*. Bloomington: Indiana University Press.

Tickner, J.A. (1997). You just don't understand: Troubled engagements between feminists and IR theories. *International Studies Quarterly*, 41, 611–632.

Tickner, J.A. (2005). What is your research program? Some feminist answers to international relations methodological questions. *International Studies Quarterly*, 49, 1–21.

Tijdens, K., and van Klaveren, M. (2011). *Domestic workers: Their wages and work in 12 countries*. Report. Amsterdam: University of Amsterdam.

Whitworth, S. (2004). *Men, militarism and UN peacekeeping: A gendered analysis*. Boulder: Lynne Rienner.

Whitworth, S. (2006). Theory and exclusion: Gender, masculinity, and international political economy. In R. Stubbs and G. Underhill (Eds.). *Political economy and the changing global order* (pp. 88–99). Third Edition. Don Mills: Oxford University Press.

Young, R. (1995). *Colonial desire: Hybridity in theory, culture, and race*. London and New York: Routledge.

Zalewski, M. (2010). Feminist international relations: Making sense…In L. Shepherd (Ed.). *Gender matters in global politics: A feminist introduction to international relations* (pp. 28–43). New York: Routledge.

Zinn, M.B., Weber, L., Higginbotham, E., and Thornton Dill, B. (1986). The cost of exclusionary practices in women's studies. *Signs: Journal of women in culture and society* 11, 290–303.

5 Gender, nation, and nationalism

Nivi Manchanda and Leah de Haan

Introduction	80
Nation and nationalism	81
The state	83
Postcolonial voices	85
Feminism, gender and the femininity/masculinity binary	87
Nationalism and gender	91
Conclusion	94

Introduction

This chapter explores the relationship between gender and nation. Both these concepts have long and complex histories as key terms in International Relations (IR) and cognate disciplines. Whilst they are both core concepts, they are only occasionally entered into a dialogue with each other; they are mostly dealt with as disparate and unrelated notions (Thapar-Björkert 2013). Moreover, both these concepts themselves rely on discourses and discussions which have until recently taken place in, and been confined to, separate rather than overlapping domains. Such discussions have in turn produced and engaged a vast array of other complex concepts, such as the state, nationalism, feminism, femininity, and masculinity to name a few. In order to properly examine the relationship between gender and nation and how both of these are researched, interpreted, and critiqued, it is imperative to first interrogate their respective academic trajectories.

Nationalism and the nation, and gender and feminism are crucial components in the lexicon of political theory, but they are also part of our mundane, everyday lives (Sok Kuam Fung 2016). Nationalism is frequently evoked in films (even if not labelled as such), most recently for instance in Dunkirk (2017), and experienced routinely in sports, such as at football (soccer) games. These very same things – films and football – also rely on and propagate certain understandings of gender through scenes of warfare or of soldiers returning home, or indeed through the figure of the masculine footballer, even if those are not explicitly stated.

This chapter will start by discussing nation, nationalism and the state. It will then proceed to analyse feminism, gender, and the femininity/masculinity binary. Finally, it will bring these two concepts together to see how they relate to each other, what they reveal about each other and what questions they raise in the context of International Relations. The chapter will thus mainly focus on answering the following question and the further questions it raises: Why is the nation conceived as feminine? What does this mean for the relation between the state and the nation? What does this mean for the relationship between woman and the state? What is the relation between militarization, the masculine hegemonic state, and other feminized nations?

Nation and nationalism

Discussions of nation, nationalism and the state have been key to political science and International Relations theorizing since the inception of these disciplines. States are political arrangements in which all of the world's land and population have been subdivided. Nationalism appears to be one of the main driving forces which mobilizes people. The 'nation' is often seen as the main source of identity, identification, and unity for those people contained within the defined territory of a state. Without the nation and the state, it would be impossible to grasp our social, economic, and political realities. We now turn our attention to the ways in which the nation is conceptualized, then present the debate around the origin of nationhood and nationalism, and also identify the different understandings of what the state is and how it relates to the nation.

Given the importance attached to the nation, it is perhaps unsurprising that what *exactly* the concept refers to is somewhat contested. Most foundational political concepts have a myriad of interpretations and meanings attached to them. The stakes are high, especially when differentiating between cohesive ethnic groupings and 'nations' (Smith 2010, 5–14). Although some degree of arbitrariness is unavoidable, there is a consensus on a number of counts (Özkirimli 2000). First, the nation requires a defined group of people. Secondly, these people need to feel that they have shared cultural characteristics which unite them, such as norms, myths, social practices, and symbols (Jeffery 2014; Özkirimli 2000). Thirdly, over and above the social connection among these people, there must be a belief that this group has a right to *territorial self-determination*. That they are entitled to a space, a state, which is theirs to govern and inhabit (Barrington 1997). Although a nation does not require, it frequently coincides with, shared ethnic heritage and entails a pursuit of self-governance, even if the pursuit is ongoing and/or deemed to be unsuccessful.

Whilst there is thus some consensus on the abovementioned key characteristics of a nation, scholars occupy distinct and often contradictory positions when it comes to the finer details. In order to examine these differences, we will now turn to a few key theorists who embody the main perspectives in theoretical discussions of the nation. In mainstream political theory, there are three main approaches or streams of thought on what nations are and how they have developed over time: namely *primordialism* (Shills; Geertz), *modernism* (Hobsbawn; Anderson; Hroch) and *ethno-symbolism* (Smith; Armstrong) (Özkirimli 2000). Before we turn to these different streams of understanding nationalism, it should be stressed that these are not specific theories in and of themselves, but rather are best understood as 'outlooks' or 'viewpoints', that converge on specific key characteristics of nationness (Özkirimli 2000). Within these perspectives there is often a significant amount of diversity and contradiction. However, comprehending the broad similarities within these schematic streams will aid in conceptualizing the different views on the nation and its emergence and development.

First, the primordial position on the nature of nations is largely centered on two facets. First, it posits that nations are the product of processes and developments dating back to antiquity and, secondly, nations and the bonds among people of the same nation are considered as 'real' and 'natural' (Ichijo and Uzelac 2005, 51–55). According to Edward Shills, who coined the term primordial in relation to the nation, the nation as a unit is analogous to the family. He argued that families are not created over time through association but that there is some innate kinship, connection, and bond among family members (Özkirimli 2000). The family then, like the nation is in some ways an innative and pregiven grouping. According to the primordial view, nations are similarly 'as natural as speech, sight or smell' (Özkirimli 2000, 64). For primordialists, nationalism comes after the nation, and thus it is the idea or belief which grows out of the nation and is what mobilizes an already existing nation to push for self-determination.

Modernism then emerged as a theory reacting against the older, primordial understanding of the nation. As with primordialism, there are a variety of positions within the modernist conceptualization of the nation but modernist theorists, too, share common themes. The main tenet of the modernist understanding of nations is that it is a product of modernity and it was an entity created by various modern trends and processes (Gellner 2006). These processes can be traced back to the French Revolution and include the development of the global, capitalist economy, industrial production methods, the development of bureaucracy, migration from rural into urban spaces, and secularism. Thus according to this perspective, the processes of modernity produced nationalism, which in turn created the nation. In this manner, modernism attacks both of the founding pillars of primordialism: (i) it contests the antiquity of nations and (ii) subverts the notion that nations are inherent to the human condition. For modernists, it is the notion or idea of nationalism which produces the nation, and not the other way around, in stark contrast to the primordialist. Within modernism, different authors and positions have attached different priorities to particular processes of modernity in order to explain the production of nationalism. Özkirimli divides modernists' priorities into three categories: those focused on economic transformations (Nairn 2003; Hechter 1975), those focused on political transformations (Breuilly 1982; Hobsbawn 1992), and those focused on social transformations (Gellner 2006; Anderson 2006) (Özkirimli 2000).

Following this, ethno-symbolism emerged as the third position, occupying the 'middle-ground' when it comes to theorizing the nation; it contends that both modernist and primordialist theses are too extreme and that the two views should be softened and combined. Ethno-symbolists feel that the shared myths, mores and symbols which predate the formation of nations cannot be ignored as held by the modernists, but also that the manner in which the primordialists dismiss the effects of the processes of modernity on the formation of nations is equally flawed (Smith 2005, 94–112). Two leading ethno-symbolists – Armstrong and Smith – maintain that the nation existed before nationalism. Armstrong is firmer on this, but Smith's definition of nationalism as being 'a social and a political movement to achieve the goals of the nation and realize the national will' (Smith 1991, 72) suggests that he concurs with the suggestion that the nation is the source of nationalism, not the reverse.

The state

Having now briefly discussed the different ways that the nation is apprehended in political theory, it is of foremost importance to stress that the nation is not the same as the state. Although these concepts are regularly conflated, they are not synonyms. Their conflation is not altogether unexpected, because these two concepts are closely related; however, they must be subject to a deeper analysis and understood in their proper contexts and relation to each other for us to have a more nuanced understanding of these crucial building blocks of politics and IR.

First, the state is frequently characterized by four distinct factors: it requires a population; it needs clear and defined territorial borders; it must have an established government which regulates order, legislation, and enforcement and is recognized as the body in charge of the state beyond its borders; and finally it must possess sovereignty (the definition of which is also contested), but for our purposes here is best described as international autonomy regarding decision-making, the realities within the state, and independence from direct influence (Ioannidis 2014). In this way, the state is not simply defined by internal characteristics, but also by the way it relates to other states and the wider network of international relations.

One of the most regularly invoked, even ubiquitous, definitions of the state is Max Weber's, who characterizes the state as a 'community that successfully claims the monopoly of the legitimate use of physical force within a given territory' (Weber 2004). Whilst this is a more sophisticated way to describe the state, and one which is more focused on authority and legitimacy, it is clear that it does also incorporate the previously described four characteristics of the state. The work on democratic states focuses on the contracts between citizens and governments – where people enter into a reciprocal arrangement with their government; they pay taxes to the state and it ensures their security. In addition, prominent Western political theorists through the ages including Thomas Hobbes, John Locke and Charles Tilly all see the state as a guarantor of cooperation amongst individuals, facilitating a peace that would be impossible without an overarching structure. Hobbes famously stressed that life without a state would be 'nasty, brutish, and short' (Hobbes 1651) because only a state could ensure that people are not concerned solely with their own short-term survival.

There are other theorists, however, within the critical traditions of Marxism, feminism and postcolonialism that highlight the ways in which the state is more aptly conceived as an institutionalized political structure of power that maintains social relations, which are complicit in actively oppressing and subordinating certain groups of people. Scholars working in these critical traditions do not necessarily contest the four characteristics of the state listed above, but stress the need to view the state as both a conduit and the embodiment of systems of domination such as patriarchy, class oppression and racism (Mackinnon 1982; Mitchell 1991).

This discussion should adequately highlight that the state is clearly different from the 'nation' but the reason the state and the nation get conflated, despite the fact that one appears to be a socio-political structure and the other a community, is because of their development within Europe. The coterminous manner in which statehood and nationhood developed has largely resulted in an overlap of nations and states in Western Europe (Lansford 2000). Whilst there are naturally exceptions, such as Catalonia in Spain, this means that in Europe most nations successfully formed their state and most states fostered a coterminous nationalism (Jeffery 2014). Self-determination was achieved relatively easily in the European experience. Nonetheless, a state does not require a nation and a nation does not always fulfil its requirement for a state. There are states with multiple nations (South Africa) and there are nations without a state (Palestine, Kurdistan).

Having clearly presented the mainstream discussion on what exactly a nation is, how it is different from the state and what the main understanding of it is, it is also important to stress that there are a whole host of positions, perspectives, and concerns which are not discussed in such a conventional conceptualization of what the nation, nationalism and the state are. Before we turn to gender as a thematic that problematizes these limited mainstream interpretations of state- and nation-hood, we will highlight some obvious shortcomings and suggest some alternate, postcolonial voices.

One aspect that these three mainstream theories on the nation and nationalism have in common is that they appear to see the nation and culture as relatively static and homogenous. Though they might disagree on the nature of communities or how they were created, they accept their uniformity or character as commonsense. These accounts dismiss the fact that there are certain mores, traditions, morals, symbols and practices which are coopted to form the national narrative and others which are actively suppressed or simply sidelined. Equally, these approaches ignore the fact that any identification with a nation is also based on an exclusion. For there to be a unitary nation (an 'us'), there must always be something against which this is pitted (a 'them'). This idea is most compellingly explored by Edward Said in his *Orientalism* (Said 1978). This can be seen at play in border controls, strict immigration regimes and gruelling 'citizenship tests'.

The rather superficial understanding of the nation is also owed to the macro-level and top-down perspectives on which it is built. Peoples' lived experiences are hardly ever taken into account, and the ways in which national identities are manifested, reproduced, navigated, contested, and embodied are not paid much heed when dealing with definitions of the nation (Sok Kuam Fung 2016). How do banal, mundane, and everyday events and experiences stand in relation to the nation and nationalism and what role do they play in their power and their reproduction? In order to even begin answering this question, one must look beyond the three traditional understandings (primordialism, modernism and ethno-symbolism) of what a nation is and where it came from.

Another major limitation of the manner in which the nation is apprehended and represented by mainstream accounts is their *Eurocentrism*. This Eurocentrism is evident, even foundational, in these discussions on a number of counts. First, the nation-state is a particular and peculiar Western construct, as discussed above. Secondly, the Western, and even more the Anglo-Saxon, experience is granted primacy, often to the detriment of the experience of other nations. And thirdly, the Western nation and experience is held up as the superior, even the ideal type. It is often alleged that there is a *correct* type of nationalism and a perverse type; the one that founded and buttressed the European nation-state, and the other outside of it that is a perversion of it – for instance, in reference to Arab nationalism (Özkirimli 2000, 5). The paramountcy of the European experience does gross injustice to the multiple nations and nationalisms that exist around the world. Moreover, it does a disservice even to countries in Europe and the Western hemisphere by homogenizing their experience and flattening their diverse and manifold experiences.

Postcolonial voices

Frantz Fanon, an early voice in postcolonial and Marxist thinking, discusses both the strengths and weaknesses of nationalism in his seminal *The Wretched of the Earth*. His writing speaks to Third World national liberation movements, and is directed against colonial rule and oppression. He is often seen as a 'Third World nationalist and revolutionary' and thus provides us with an alternative conceptualization from the mainstream discussion highlighted in this chapter.

First, Fanon stresses the importance of 'national identity' in the fight against colonial rule, but maintains that the relationship between these two forces is complex. Colonial rule and the conditions that come with it present a narrative, a story, of Western exceptionalism, which discredits and dismisses any suggestion of a national culture, consciousness or power with regard to the colonized (Fanon 1963a). However, this suppression of a unified colonial identity actually leads to countermovement where 'the native intellectuals...decided to go back further and to delve deeper down; and…with the greatest delight that they discovered that there was nothing to be ashamed of in the past, but rather dignity, glory, and solemnity' (Fanon 1963a, 210). Thus, for Fanon, nationhood is key in dismantling the shackles of colonial suppression, even as the colonizers' rhetoric and practice chips away at national, ethnic, and community identities and tries to portray it as a culture of 'barbarity'.

But Fanon was not a straightforward nationalist, for he also argued that a national consciousness is not sufficient to bring down a colonial regime and can indeed exacerbate problems. Ideas of the nation rely on ideas of community and connectedness; however, in practice there are always inequalities and discrepancies inherent within narratives which stress homogony and interconnectivity. There are always 'national middle classes' who have benefitted from colonial rule and this not only highlights the heterogeneity present within a nation and within national identity, but also shows that nationhood does not mean that everyone's perspectives and interests align (Fanon 1963a). Moreover, it is frequently the elite middle classes or the *bourgeoisie* that take over once a nation or country has shed its colonial rulers, and continue capitalist exploitation under the rubric of nationalism (Fanon 1963b).

Another crucial postcolonial perspective on the nation and its perceived homogeneity is Homi Bhabha. Bhabha as a literary critic and postcolonial theorist also engages with the previously mentioned debate concerning the antiquity or modernity of nations, albeit with a different perspective. He discusses Anderson's notion of imagined communities (recall: modernism) and how the nation draws on both ideas of timelessness and modernity, of being socially constructed and drawing on history (Bhabha 1990, 1). In this sense one can see how he raises similar concerns about the ambiguity of nations as those raised by ethno–symbolists.

But crucially, Bhabha also highlights the ambivalent relationship the nation has with inclusion and exclusion, as it actively requires both to perpetuate it. Nationalism creates both a feeling of unity within the nation and feelings of difference between the nation and the outside. Furthermore, Bhabha, much like Fanon, emphasizes the heterogeneity over the homogeneity of nations. More concretely, Bhabha writes of the *Others* within the nation (Bhabha 1990, 4). Not all members of a nation chime with its ideas, and these 'others' often challenge the nation's ideational structure. The fierce and acrimonious debate currently raging in India about whether it is a Hindu nation or a secular one is an example of the ways in which the nation excludes some of its own, and how these others try to carve a space for themselves and mount a challenge to the nation's identity.

The nation is both constrictive and productive: 'The nation, as a form of cultural elaboration…is an agency of ambivalent narration that holds culture and its most productive position, as a force for subordination, fracturing, diffusing, and reproducing, as much as producing, creating, forcing and guiding' (Bhabha 1990, 3–4). Though Bhabha may not be directly speaking of the intersection between gender and nationhood, it is a similar exclusion and bleeds into our discussion of how gender, femininity and women are influenced by nationhood and nationalism.

Feminism, gender and the femininity/masculinity binary

We now address the core of this chapter: the relation between gender and the nation. In order to do this, it is important to note that feminism, the main (but not only) school of thought that deals with gender, has a long and rich history. Despite this, the discipline of IR has largely dismissed feminist and gender considerations and feminist IR has long been a marginalized part of the discipline. This has meant that whilst there has been much noteworthy feminist IR, it has not had much effect on how the mainstream conceptualizes core concerns for IR nor how these issues should be understood. Thus most concepts within IR are developed and seen solely from a male perspective and are thus masculinized (Youngs 2004, 76). Postcolonial feminism, and feminism in general, reject IR's masculinist tendencies.

First and foremost, feminism is defined by its normative and ethical commitment to ending the political, economic, social, ideological, and cultural subordination of women. Feminism does this by examining the workings, reproduction, and experiences caused by patriarchy, and in social structures in which masculinity is hegemonic. Secondly, feminism can be applied as an overarching strategy to conducting academic research in an ethical manner as it highlights the problems within society in the way research is conducted. Ackerly and True (2008) demonstrate how feminist theory is useful in showing that the ideas and opinions of the researcher subconsciously make their way into research, the issues caused by inequalities between the researcher and the subjects, and what information, knowledge, and concerns are included in the research. Thirdly, it investigates other power hierarchies by examining their gendered nature and the way these relate to power disparities. In order to discuss how exactly power hierarchies can be gendered and the nature of the masculinity–femininity binary, let us first move on to what feminists mean when they refer to 'gender'.

In order to discuss the concept of 'gender', it is important to differentiate it from 'sex'. In the eighteenth century, the understanding was that there was only one sex (Laqueur 1990). Women and men were considered the same sex, with women simply possessing 'inverted male genitalia' and the differences between men and women were explained away by suggesting that women simply have less perfect versions of the same genitalia (Hawkesworth 2013). Due to political and scientific changes throughout the nineteenth century, males and females began to be conceptualized as two different sexes and this binary was used to justify a growing trend, which excluded women from accessing the political opportunities that started becoming available to ordinary citizens in Europe (Hawkesworth 2013). Although feminists over the years have fought for space for women in the public domain, even the idea that there are only two sexes (or three) has come under attack. Feminist theorists previously argued that sex was a natural given binary but that gender was a socially constructed understanding that was attached to it. Feminists such as Judith Butler have categorically challenged biological accounts of binary sex, claiming that it is not just gender but also sex that is socially and culturally constructed and that in order to move beyond binary conceptions of gender, we must also do away with binary conceptions of sex (Butler 1990, 10–36).

Furthermore, research indicates that there is no connection between biological sex and behavior, skills, and affinity (Hawkesworth 2013). This means that not only is an understanding of people based on an arbitrary binary of male and female misleading, but that 'masculine' and 'feminine' do not correspond with the categories of 'male' and 'female'. Thus, *gender* highlights both the artificial nature of characteristics or behavior ascribed to individuals who are considered men or to individuals who are considered women, and the normative dimension of this ascription (Butler 1990, 10–14). It is not simply that the female sex is considered to behave in a certain way, but there is an expectation that women will and should behave in a certain manner. Gender is thus artificial, normative, and socialized, and not 'natural'.

The so-called biological opposition between males and females has been mobilized to oppress women, by claiming that they were naturally less capable and were pre-determined for certain social roles. Most societies still view men and women differently, and have different expectations attached to male and female persons. At the most basic level, man is considered superior and expected to be 'masculine' and woman viewed as inferior and expected to be 'feminine'. It is due to this, feminists argue, that women are treated worse than men in social, economic, political, and ideological terms and that anything that is considered feminine is undervalued. By analysing power hierarchies and asymmetries, feminist theory looks at the ways in which facets and aspects of society deemed 'feminine' are attached less value and authority than those that are considered masculine. To take one example from our everyday lives, 'official' labor is considered superior and more important than unpaid, unofficial labor. The former is 'masculine' whilst the latter tends to be considered feminine. Housework or childcare is viewed as less important, less fulfilling, and easier, it is associated with women and femininity, and is accorded less power and less worth.

This binary construction of gender, where the 'feminine' gender is exemplified by gentleness, being connected to nature, irrationality, weakness and simplicity is all pervasive. In similar fashion, the 'masculine' gender is associated with rationality, culture, strength, ambition, and complexity in most spheres of life. The self/other binary we saw in reference to nationalism rears its head again. In a practical sense this has resulted in women being relegated to the private sphere, considered less able than men, and requiring guidance or supervision from men.

In addition to the basic concepts and discussion on which the feminist academic tradition is founded, there are a number of key debates which characterize the direction feminist thought is currently moving in. A short analysis of these debates will help us understand gender, feminism, and their relation to the nation better.

First, for eminent scholar Judith Butler, the coherence of gender is produced through repetitive and stylized acts that over time get coded as 'normal' (1990; 2009). Gender is performed by everyone based on 'reiteration, recognition, and authority' (Hansen 2000, 303). Thus, we reproduce a gendered performance we have been socialized into. This is in turn recognized within our society's wider understanding of gender and the type of gender someone should be performing. This performance is authoritative due to social convention and expectation, which in turn influences its reiteration. Those individuals who do not perform gender in a way that makes them comprehensible and recognizable are in danger because it can result in them being marginalized and ostracized. Boys are required to dress in a certain way from a young age, and girls are likewise socialized into liking pink. Boys play with action heroes and girls with Barbie dolls. These recognizable performances of gender are not always easy for or desired by the performer, 'and the reproduction of gender is thus always a negotiation with power' (Butler 2009, i). Performativity thus goes a long way in explaining the tenacity of gender in the face of all its shortcomings.

Another key discussion occurring within feminism is the fact that most understandings on feminism, gender, and women are developed from a singular location, the *Global North*. Chandra Mohanty (1988, 65), a prominent postcolonial scholar, has highlighted that feminist scholarship tends to discuss Third World women as a 'homogeneous group' which is based on a perceived dependency and thus reifies a supposed victimhood. The cause of this characterization is that the type of feminist writing which receives the most attention is written by a relatively similar type of author: white, middle-class, Global-Northern (Mohanty 1988). Whilst this is in itself an issue that needs addressing, it leads to a number of problematic side-effects. First, this type of feminist writing is presented as representative of women's struggles, experiences, and situation more generally, although it actually ends up eliding and erasing the experience of most women in the Third World. Secondly, it gives the idea that the writing of these authors can be liberating and emancipatory for all women, and actually ends up feeding colonial savior narratives – where the white man is joined by white women to save brown and black bodies (Spivak 1987).

Abu-Lughod stresses how this type of *savior* narrative can be incredibly problematic by highlighting three aspects that this *saving* would include. First, it suggests that one is capable of saving and that saving needs to occur. Secondly, and possibly most crucial to emphasize, is the fact that there is an unacknowledged violence in the revolutionary act of 'saving her *to* something' (Abu-Lughod 2002, 788). It does not only reinstate existing structures of subjugation but creates new ones. Thirdly, constructing oneself as a *savior* means one takes up a position of superiority and overconfidence which is precisely the type of attitude and perspective which postcolonial feminism attempts to combat (Abu-Lughod 2002, 786–789).

In her seminal essay, "Can the Subaltern Speak?" (1987), Spivak highlights how complex and loaded the relationship between any *Global Northern* and *Global Southern* woman is (in terms of academic research) and how hard it is for a dialogue between the two to be conducted. Kapoor draws on Spivak to highlight methods which can be applied, such as acknowledging one's privileged position and applying the same analytical tools to make a research *encounter* as ethical as possible (Kapoor 2004). Kapoor and Spivak are attempting to both conduct postcolonial feminist research themselves and provide a blueprint for both human sciences and society for addressing the concerns raised by postcolonial feminism. Problems of diversity and representation are increasingly being addressed by postcolonial feminist scholars, such as Mohanty, Spivak, and Abu-Lughod, and this is indispensable because a white unrepresentative feminism significantly detracts from its ability to create a more equal world.

Whilst postcolonial feminist thought is reshaping the assumptions that feminism has been based on for many decades within IR through combining different modes of thinking, wider intersectionality is also becoming increasingly important to feminism. Thus one of the recent developments is seeing gendered hierarchies and the subordination of women as connected to a range of forms of subordinations including race, sexuality, class, disability, and age (Cho, Crenshaw, and McCall 2013; Collins and Chepp 2013). The core contention of this framework is that systems of subordination are interconnected, inter-dependent, and mutually constitutive. They reinforce each other's existence, help their reproduction (continuation), and rely on similar social processes of exclusions, asymmetries, othering, and hierarchies. Within this framework, attempting to understand one type of subordination without discussing the others to which it is related would not only be reductionist, but counter-productive. One of feminism's biggest strengths is the fact that it lends itself to intersectionality and aids one in understanding exactly how discrimination, subordination, and scapegoating function in society.

One of the aspects of individuals' experiences which intersectional feminism includes is thus sexuality, and it is this new-found focus on sexuality which has led to a recent development in political theorizing, which utilizes feminist concepts, namely *queer theory*. Whilst it agrees with feminism that gender is a social production, it critiques feminism for not challenging 'heteronormativity' enough. It places heteronormativity, the normative preference for heterosexual relationships and inclinations over any others, alongside patriarchy as a social structure that is violent and exclusive. Queer theorists propagate a closer look at sexuality and identities – including LGBT, gender ambiguous and intersex peoples – as a first step in the effort to do away with straitjacketing binaries and reductionist understandings of concepts such as gender, sex, and sexuality

(Hagen 2016). In this way, queer theory stresses that neither gender, nor sex should be seen as a binary but as fluid spectrums and that identities and physical characteristics can fall anywhere on that spectrum without political, social, or economic repercussions. According to queer theory, such concepts are far more fluid than traditional feminist thought sees them as being, and rely on notions of the 'normatively good' (the CIS[1] white male) and the 'normatively bad' (the deviant transsexual black woman).

Nationalism and gender

How exactly do nationalism and gender intersect? What do they mean for each other? Although gender and nationalism are mutually reinforcing and co-constitutive, only a handful of scholars of nationalism and the nation reference gender, and likewise, most discussions within feminist thought sidestep a discussion of the nation. These problems deserve sustained attention.

First, given the conventional wisdom that women are inferior to men, it should come as no surprise that discussions of nationalism and the state rarely discuss women. Whilst this is slowly improving, Thapar-Björkert (2013) identifies three other reasons for this dismissal within discussions centering on the nation. First, there has been a tacit assumption that the experiences of nationhood and its processes were identical for men and women. If this is the case, then naturally there would not seem to be any push to an analysis of the specific experiences of women and non-male persons. Secondly, men are largely considered responsible for producing both the structures of the state and the ideological underpinnings of the nation and thus women's relationship to their development was seen as less than important. Indeed, some feminists also believe that nationalism, especially in its militaristic and jingoistic variations, is primarily a masculine domain. For instance, Cynthia Enloe espouses this view by stating that 'nationalism has typically sprung from masculinised memory, masculinised humiliation and masculinised hope' (Enloe 1989, 43). Thirdly, Western political theory is strongly committed to the notion that there is a divide between the private and the public and that the public is what politics is concerned with. Women have historically been relegated to the private sphere, and therefore not featured in discussions pertaining to nationalism. These gendered and myopic assumptions have come under fierce attack by feminist and queer scholars. They have convincingly shown how not only is the dichotomy between 'private' and 'public' false, but also that women have occupied and continue to shape discourses of nationalism in a variety of ways. Most curiously, this is witnessed in the strange gendering of the 'nation' as 'feminine'.

Thus, on the one hand then, women are hardly ever placed at the center of discussions on nationalism; on the other hand, rather ironically the nation is understood and represented as feminine. How and why is this the case? As highlighted in the discussion on the femininity and masculinity binaries above, aspects of society that are seen as feminine are considered to be weaker, irrational, natural, and passive. The nation – in contrast to the state – is also attributed these qualities, especially as something needing protection. The nation is conceived 'as a loved woman in danger or as a mother who lost her sons in battles]…[and] men are called to fight "for the sake of our women and children" or to "defend their honour"' (Yuval-Davis and Anthias, 1989, 9–10). Additionally, the nation is frequently equated to the home because they invoke similar emotional connections. Both nations and homes comfort people and make them feel safe – like children in the womb. It is no coincidence then, that in many languages one's native country is fondly described as the 'motherland'. It is also no coincidence that whilst 'motherland' is evocative of nurturing, love and fertility and most often deployed in fond and protective contexts, fatherland is redolent of wartime propaganda and 'harsher' patriotic rhetoric. This romanticizing of the 'home' is also fraught because the home is one of the spaces where masculine domination is enacted, and thus the making of the nation concurrently involves the violent expulsion of groups that are rendered unfit or incompatible with the claims and propositions of nationhood that are embedded in the mobilizing rhetoric of nationalists.

Through conceptualizations of the nation as feminine and the state as masculine, the state can be mobilized and militarized in protection of the nation. Militarization is the social, political, and economic mobilization of resources to both enhance the military and its importance and make it pervasive throughout society (Bickford 2015). This militarization is of course not just material, but also happens to identities and it is this way that masculinity is militarized in order to protect the femininity of the state. It should be stressed such militarized masculinity should also not be considered *normal*, but simply a development through which the state and society can be mobilized: 'the link between masculinity and the military is constructed and maintained for the purpose of waging war' (Eichler 2014, 81). This militarization is one of the aspects of the state which highlights not only the perceived masculinity of the state and its institutions, but also reinforces the gender stereotypes (Enloe 1989).

One of the reasons this is critical, is not simply because it solidifies the type of relationship and influence the state has on society but also highlights the relationship between one state and another nation, or how nationalism is mobilized towards the *Other*. Often nations are strategically characterized as feminine, sometimes whole 'enemy' populations are feminized to sanction invasion and war. In the so-called 'War against Terror,' we can see how Afghanistan has been depicted as weak and its populace feminized to justify intervention (Manchanda 2015). It is due to this feminized characterization of the enemy, that rape in wartime remains such a pervasive crime (Thapar-Björkert 2013). Rape is a way of dominating an entire nation, because it reaffirms the dominance of the masculine invader and re-inscribes the weakness and passivity of the feminine *Othered* nation: 'Rape constitutes an instrument of militarized, masculinized nationalism' (Thapar-Björkert 2013).

Box 5.1: The exclusivity of nationalism

It is July 11, 2010. There is a palpable nervous tension in the air. But also camaraderie. Strangers helping each other unload their crates of beer; giving each other high fives. Mostly though, there is orange everywhere. Orange clothes. Orange flags. Even orange wigs. I think if you don't know the Dutch, this would look very strange. But it's the final of the FIFA World Cup and they really want that cup. Hours before kick-off it is all over the television. As the time draws closer people get more and more excited, they are watching it on big screens in public and small screens at home.

But there are only men on the field warming up and only men's voices heard discussing from the studios. During the ads the women appear – selling cars, cologne, looking very pretty and being largely silent. Even in pubs and in homes, there doesn't seem much space for the women. They get asked to fetch beers, to grab more snacks from the kitchen, to clean up the spills. Somehow, in this moment of pride reverberating in the Netherlands, there isn't space for everyone. Some are more Dutch than others.

Women's roles are often circumscribed both within and because of nations. Yuval-Davis and Anthias note that women are seen as biologically reproducing the nation and being responsible for its survival. This is reinforced through 'using national and religious discourses about the duty of women to produce more children' (Yuval–Davis and Anthias 1989, 8). Moreover, due to their perceived importance in ensuring the nation's survival, there are restrictions on who women can have sex with and marry, and in this way, they maintain the barriers of the nation by conserving its perceived genetic *purity*. A good example of this is Judaism, and specifically Israel, as one is only considered Jewish if one's mother is Jewish. This way women are directed in a way which will maintain a certain image of the nation; an image which ensures the nation can be conceived of as being homogenous. Both of these roles for women within the nation are solely based on their ability to bear children and highlight how the (masculine) state exercises a particular control over women to maintain the *purity* of the nation. In order to maintain such purity, the state controls, directs, and sustains the type of reproductive behavior which will promote it. An extreme and ghastly example of the maintenance of the purity of the nation was the Holocaust, but similar dynamics have been at play in the wiping out of aboriginal populations in Australia, for example.

Women are also assigned the role of the 'carriers' and 'bearers' of a nation's culture. This is due to assumptions about women's location in the private sphere

---

Box 5.2: Key points

- Nationalism and feminism are important terms both in everyday life and in the discipline of International Relations (IR)
- IR's theorizing on nationhood, nationalism and the state is Eurocentric, i.e. IR accords the Western experience of statehood and nationhood primacy, often neglecting their diverse manifestations in other parts of the world.
- Both 'gender' and 'sex' are social constructs. 'Men' and the characteristics associated with 'masculinity' have more economic, social, cultural and political power than 'women' and 'femininity'.
- The nation is frequently constructed as feminine, whereas the state is considered masculine; the nation is thus seen as needing protection, whereas the state is accorded the role of protector.
- The best way to understand the relationship between gender and nationalism is through an 'intersectional' lens – this is a perspective that stresses the need to look at the ways in which systems of oppression interact on the basis of race, gender, sexuality, age, disability, etc.

---

and as 'naturally' more prone to childcare, which make them the ideal figures for socializing children into their nation. Here, again, women are not considered to be shaping understandings of the nation and the culture of nationhood over time. Rather, they are simply vessels conveying the national identity fostered and upheld by men, onto the next generation. Lastly, although there is an understanding that women are involved in political, economic, military, and social struggles, their roles in these struggles are largely secondary and in capacities reduced to 'supportive and nurturing' variants (Yuval-Davis and Anthias 1989, 10). These final two roles for women with regard to the nation are more about the types of tasks they can and should be performing. Both require them to be nurturing, whether to children who need be told about their nation or to the men they are supporting within struggles. The assumptions highlighted about women's place being in the private sphere is re-inscribed in this discussion of what roles they play within the creation and reproduction of the nation: they are at home having children, looking after children, and supporting their husbands, fathers, and brothers. They are mostly invisible and their identity is derivative.

Conclusion

There is a great demand for more understanding of the manner in which the nation and gender interact and with the growing nationalist movements across the globe and this demand will become even more urgent. First, it is vital that IR and the human sciences more generally stop relying on simplistic, white-washed understanding of both the nation and gender. Whilst the myriad of theorizing are produced globally by individuals such as Mohanty, Butler, Crenshaw, to name a few incredibly influential names, the mainstream conceptualization of nation and gender within human sciences remains largely untouched. As McLaughlin Mitchell, Lange, and Brus (2013, 490) stress, IR remains a male-dominated and rather traditional field, and this is a continuing and viscous trend due to the fact that 'male scholars are significantly less likely to cite work by female scholars' – citations which in turn influence both promotions and tenure decision-making. Secondly, if one wants to truly grasp the relationship between nationhood and gender, then gender must be understood intersectionally. Sexuality, race, age, disability, class must all be taken into account, because all of these are interactional at the level of experience.

Thirdly, it may be worth thinking about whether 'gender' and 'nationalism' as social constructs (and lived experiences) do more harm than good. By reifying binaries and 'othering' some sections of the population, both gender and nationalism, albeit in different ways, end up exacerbating discord and asymmetry. We tentatively suggest that doing away with these concepts, hard as it may be given how prevalent and institutionalized they are, would lead to fewer divisions and a more egalitarian world.

Note

1 Where *Trans* refers to individuals who do not identify with their socially prescribed gender or sex, CIS refers to individuals who, regardless to what extent, do.

Suggested readings

Abu-Lughod, L. (2002). Do Muslim women really need saving? Anthropological reflections on cultural relativism and its others. *American Anthropologist*, 104, 783–790. Taking its cue from Gayatri Spivak, this article convincingly debunks the popular myth that Muslim women in Iraq and Afghanistan are desperately in need of Western intervention and 'saving'. It neatly brings together the themes of race, gender, and imperialism.

Anderson, B. (2006). *Imagined communities: Reflections on the origins and spread of Nationalism*. London: Verso. A bit dated but still one of the best treatises on the origins of nationalism and why it continues to be such a powerful driving force in contemporary world politics.

Butler, J. (1990). *Gender trouble: Feminism and the subversion of identity*. New York: Routledge. An excellent if complex book that complicates conventional understandings of 'sex' as rigid biological truths and mounts a challenge against natural and essentialized accounts of the 'female'. Butler also enunciates the performative aspects of gender.

Mohanty, C. (2003). *Feminism without borders: Decolonizing theory, practicing solidarity*. Durham NC: Duke University Press. An excellent book that interrogates the extent to which feminism can be used as a global and transnational movement to forge solidarity around the world against exploitative states and capitalist systems. Mohanty deftly grapples with some of the most pressing issues confronting feminist theory and praxis today.

Puar, J. (2007). *Terrorist assemblages: Homonationalism in queer times*. Durham: Duke University Press. An essential read that delineates the ways in which modalities of power – race, sexuality, class, ethnicity, and nation – are working to bolster the contemporary forces of securitization, nationalism, and counter-terrorism. Puar examines how certain subjectivities (such as gay CIS white men) are brought into the fold of liberal politics to the detriment and exclusion of certain other (usually racialized 'Eastern') bodies from the remit of nationalism, security, and politics.

Bibliography

Abu-Lughod, L. (2002). Do Muslim women really need saving? Anthropological reflections on cultural relativism and its others. *American Anthropologist*, 104, 783–790.

Ackerly, B. and True, J. (2008). Reflexivity in practice: Power and ethics in feminist research on International Relations, *International Studies Review*, Vol. 10, No. 4, pp. 693–707.

Anderson, B. (2006). *Imagined communities: Reflections on the origins and spread of Nationalism*, London and New York: Verso.

Barrington, L.W. (1997). 'Nation' and 'Nationalism': The misuse of key concepts in political science, *PS: Political Science and Politics*, Vol. 30, No. 4, pp. 712–716.

Bhabha, H.K. (1990). Introduction: narrating the nation, in H.K. Bhabha (Ed.) *Nation and Narration*. London: Routledge, pp. 1–8.

Bickford, A. (2015). Militaries and militarization, Anthropology of. In J.D. Wright (Ed.). *International encyclopaedia of the social & behavioral sciences* (2nd edition), London: Elsevier.

Breuilly, J. (1982). *Nationalism and the state*, Manchester: Manchester University Press.

Browne, K. and Nash, C.J. (Eds.) (2010). *Queer methods and methodologies: Intersecting queer theories and social science research*, Farnham and Burlington: Ashgate Publishing Company.

Butler, J. (1990). *Gender trouble*. New York and Abingdon: Routledge.

Butler, J. (2009). Performativity, precarity and sexual politics, *AIBR: Revista de Antropología Iberoamericana*, Vol. 4, No. 3, pp. i–xiii.

Chatterjee, P. (2012). Nationalism today, *Rethinking Marxism*, Vol. 24, No. 1, pp. 9–25.

Cho, S., Crenshaw, K., and McCall, L. (2013). Toward a field of intersectionality studies: Theory, applications, and praxis, *Signs: Journal of Women in Culture and Society*, Vol. 38, No. 4, pp. 785–810.

Collins, P.H. and Chepp, V. (2013). 'Intersectionality', in G. Waylen, K. Celis, J. Kantola and S.L. Weldon (Eds.). *The Oxford handbook for gender and politics*. Oxford: Oxford University Press, pp. 57–87.

Eichler, M. (2014). Militarized masculinities in International Relations, *Brown Journal of World Affairs*, Vol. 11, No. 1, pp. 81–93.

Enloe, C. (1989). *Bananas, beaches and bases: Making feminist sense of international politics*, London: Pandora.

Fanon, F. (1963a). On national culture, in *The wretched of the earth*, Translated from French by C. Farrington. New York: Grove Weidenfeld, pp. 206–248.

Fanon, F. (1963b). The pitfalls of national consciousness, in *The wretched of the earth*, Translated from French by C. Farrington. New York: Grove Weidenfeld, pp. 148–205.

Gellner, E. (2006). *Nations and nationalism* (2nd edition), Oxford: Blackwell Publishing.

Hagen, J.J. (2016). Queering women, peace and security, *International Affairs*, Vol. 92, No. 2, pp. 313–332.

Hansen, L. (2000). The little mermaid's silent security dilemma and the absence of gender in the Copenhagen school, *Millennium: Journal of International Studies*, Vol. 29, No. 2, pp. 285–306.

Hawkesworth, M. (2013). Sex, gender, and sexuality: From naturalized presumption to analytical categories, in G. Waylen, K. Celis, J. Kantola and S.L. Weldon (Eds.). *The Oxford handbook for gender and politics*, 31–56.

Hechter, M. (1975). *Internal colonialism: The Celtic fringe in British national development*, London and New York: Routledge.

Hobbes, T. (1651). *Leviathan*, London: Andrew Crooke.

Hobsbawm, E.J. (1992). *Nations and nationalism since 1780* (2nd edition), Cambridge: Cambridge University Press.

Ichijo, A. and Uzelac, G. (Eds.). (2005). *When is the nation?: Towards an understanding of theories of nationalism*, London: Routledge.

Ioannidis, C. (2014). Are the conditions of statehood sufficient? An argument in favour of popular sovereignty as an additional condition of statehood, *Jurisprudencija*, Vol. 21, No. 4, pp. 974–987.

Jeffery, C. (2014). Introduction: Regional public attitudes beyond methodological Nationalism, in A. Henderson, C. Jeffery and D. Wincott (Eds.) *Citizenship after the Nation-State. The comparative territorial politics series*, London: Palgrave Macmillan.

Kapoor, I. (2004). Hyper-self-reflexive development? Spivak on representing the Third World 'Other', *Third World Quarterly*, Vol. 25, No. 4, pp. 627–647.

Lansford, T. (2000). Post-Westphalian Europe? Sovereignty and the modern nation-state, *International Studies*, Vol. 37, No. 1, pp. 1–15.

Laqueur, T. (1990). *Making sex: Body and gender from the Greeks to Freud*, Cambridge: Harvard University Press.

McClintock, A. (1991). No longer in a future heaven: Women and nationalism in South Africa, *Transition*, Vol. 51, pp. 104–123.

MacKinnon, C. (1982). Feminism, Marxism, method, and the state: An agenda for theory. *Signs: Journal of Women in Culture and Society*, Vol. 7, No. 3, pp. 515–544.

McLaughlin Mitchell, S., Lange, S., and Brus, H. (2013). Gendered citation patterns in international relations journals, *International Studies Perspectives*, Vol. 14, pp. 485–492.

Manchanda, N. (2015). Queering the Pashtun: Afghan sexuality in the Homonationalist imaginary, *Third World Quarterly*, Vol. 36, No. 1, pp. 30–45.

Mitchell, T. (1991). The limits of the state: Beyond statist approaches and their critics, *American Political Science Review*, Vol. 85, No. 1, pp. 77–96.

Mohanty, C. (1988). Under Western eyes: Feminist scholarship and colonial discourses, *Feminist Review*, Vol. 30, pp. 61–88.

Mohanty, C. (2003). *Feminism without borders: Decolonizing theory, practicing solidarity*, Durham NC: Duke University Press.

Nairn, T. (2003). *The break-up of Britain: Crisis and neo-nationalism* (3rd edition), Altona Vic: Common Ground Publishing.

Özkirimli, U. (2000). *Theories of nationalism: A critical introduction*, Basingstoke and New York: Palgrave.

Puar, J. (2007). *Terrorist assemblages: Homonationalism in queer times*, Durham: Duke University Press.

Rao, S. (1999). Women-as-symbols: The intersection of identity politics, gender, and Indian nationalism, *Women's Studies International Forum*, Vol. 22, No. 3, pp. 317–328.

Said, E. (1978). *Orientalism*, London: Penguin.

Smith, A.D. (1995). *Nations and nationalism in a global era*, Cambridge: Polity Press.

Smith, A.D. (2000). *The nation in history: Historiographical debates about ethnicity and nationalism*, Hanover: University Press of New England.

Smith, A.D. (2005). The genealogy of nations: an ethno-symbolic approach, in A. Ichijo, and G. Uzelac (Eds.) *When is the nation?: Towards an understanding of theories of nationalism*, pp. 94–112.

Sok Kuam Fung, A. (2016). Identity and politics: Reflections of a diasporic hybrid, *Journal of Narrative Politics*, Vol. 3, No. 1, pp. 56–64.

Spivak, G.C. (1987). Can the subaltern speak?, in C. Nelson and L. Grossberg (Eds.) *Marxism and the interpretation of culture*, Champaign: University of Illinois Press.

Thapar-Björkert, S. (2013). Gender, nations, and nationalisms, in G. Waylen, K. Celis, J. Kantola and S.L. Weldon (Eds.) *The Oxford handbook for gender and politics*, Oxford: Oxford University Press, pp. 803–827.

Weber, M. (2004). Politics as a vocation, in D. Owen and T.B. Strong (Eds.) *The vocational lectures*, pp. 32–94.

Youngs, G. (2004). Feminist international relations: A contradiction in terms? Or: Why women and gender are essential to understanding the world 'we' live in, *International Affairs*, Vol. 80, No. 1, pp. 75–87.

Yuval-Davis, N. and Anthias, F. (Eds.) (1989). *Woman-Nation-State*, Basingstoke and London: The Macmillan Press Ltd.

6 Postcolonialism and International Relations

Intersections of sexuality, religion, and race

Momin Rahman

Introduction   99
The recent internationalization of LGBT politics
   and consequent resistance   100
Thinking beyond 'freedom' and 'oppression' by understanding
   LGBT identities in the context of modernity   102
Case study on LGBT politics and Muslim cultures:
   The triangulation of homocolonialism   105
Conclusion   113

Introduction

In this chapter, the experience of LGBT Muslims is used to explore the complexities of the internationalization of LGBT politics. The analysis begins with the current wave of IGO proposals on the rights of LGBT people and also discusses the resistance that these attempts have faced. There is also focus on how the resistance is framed as a lack of modernization in specific nations, regions and cultures, and that this is a simplistic model that assumes a linear and universal progress in history and thus ignores the full socio–historical context of *modernity*. Specifically, a focus on modernization as a coherent linear process positions the West as a superior 'civilization' since this is where modernization has occurred first. Furthermore, it contains inaccurate assumptions about the universality of cultural understandings of gender and sexuality and it ignores the role that colonialism, racism, orientalism, *Islamophobia* and *heteronormativity* play in structuring sexual diversity during the era of modernity. The chapter explores these concepts in relation to the opposition between LGBT and Muslim cultures and argues that a model of *homocolonialism* more accurately describes the intersecting processes and conditions in which LGBT politics is being drawn into International Relations. It is then argued that we need a more empirically based intersectional understanding of cultural differences in sexual diversity in order to usefully promote LGBT politics and security internationally. The focus on LGBT Muslims demonstrates how understanding their identities challenges the negative consequences of homocolonialism and leads us to explore more effective strategies for LGBT freedom in the context of contemporary International Relations.

The recent internationalization of LGBT politics and consequent resistance

While the European Union (EU) is the largest IGO to include protections for LGBT rights in its policies (since 2000), other IGOs are still debating these issues, but there has been some notable recent progress. In November of 2016, the UN Human Rights Council approved the appointment of its first Independent Expert on violence and discrimination against LGBT[1] people on the basis of their sexual orientations or gender identities (SOGI). This new position is a result of a process that began in 2011 when the Human Rights Council made its first ever statement on the importance of LGBT issues and called for a report on global homophobic discrimination.[2] There is a similar debate on SOGI rights underway in the Commonwealth, which is the world's third largest IGO (Lennox & Waites 2013). Moreover, the protection and promotion of LGBT rights has become part of the official foreign policies of countries where these rights are domestically established, such as the United States, the United Kingdom, Canada, and the Netherlands. These policies have included both the promotion of LGBT rights within IGO forums such as the Commonwealth and UN by these governments, and integration of LGBT rights within their individual international development policies.[3]

This recent emergence of the international promotion of LGBT equality is a distinct historical phenomenon, not seen before in world politics. It is taken by some to be the inevitable next stage in the expansion of LGBT rights and peoples and it is logical, therefore, to view this new focus on LGBT rights in international politics through a 'progress' narrative. This assumption of inevitable and desirable progress is shared by both LGBT and mainstream political organizations as well as IGOs including the UN and the recently established Equal Rights Coalition (ERC). The 2012 UN report, *Born Free and Equal*,[4] overwhelmingly supports the idea that SOGI rights are a core component of human rights, undoubtedly strengthening the 'progressive' side of the debate that sees the expansion of LGBT rights as inevitable.

There is also widespread resistance to these attempts at 'progress', both at IGOs such as the UN and Commonwealth, particularly from countries where LGBT issues remain criminalized and/or at the margins of citizenship. Moreover, the resistance is increasingly organized trans-nationally, through what Weiss and Bosia have described as an emergent 'global homophobia' (2013), often drawing together religious groups and governing elites in strategic mobilizations of anti-LGBT politics ranging across the global north and south. Resistance to progress on SOGI issues is, therefore, both domestic in the states that criminalize and oppress such behavior, and international, when these states engage in world politics.[5] It is important to understand the rationale behind this resistance. For example, the Organization of Islamic Co-operation (the

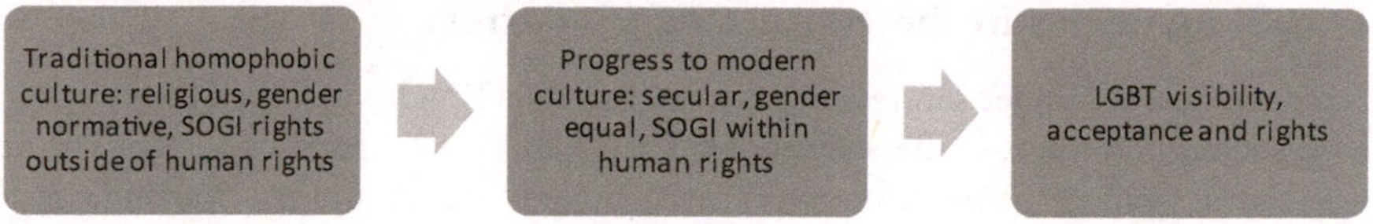

Traditional homophobic culture: religious, gender normative, SOGI rights outside of human rights	→	Progress to modern culture: secular, gender equal, SOGI within human rights	→	LGBT visibility, acceptance and rights

Figure 6.1 The modernization progress model of LGBT identities and rights

second largest government level IGO) has protested the appointment of the UN Independent Expert, as did many countries in sub-Saharan Africa, citing the lack of sensitivity to cultural differences in approaches to sexuality.[6] These discourses of cultural traditionalism rely on a gendered heterosexual traditionalism that defines LGBT identities as perversions of a 'natural' order and they are often combined with a religious framework of gender and sexual 'naturalness'. As shown in Figure 6.1, in these cases, SOGI rights are not seen as part of universal human rights but as outside of 'normal' human rights.

There is increasing evidence that the movement towards 'modern' societies, both culturally and economically, is the main correlation for the success of LGBT politics. For example, the Pew Research Center's global comparison of national attitudes to homosexuality shows that there is a global divide, with more secular and economically developed countries leading the acceptance of homosexuality and, conversely, poorer and more religious countries showing the least acceptance, clustered mainly in sub-Saharan Africa, the Middle East, South and East Asia.[7] This 'progress' model for LGBT rights is sociological rather than political, but its assumptions underlie much of the political framing of why LGBT rights are a sign of cultural advancement, and conversely why those who resist such rights are stuck in 'traditional', unmodernized, cultures.

At a more analytic level, this dialectic of progress versus oppression ignores the complexities of sexuality and its social and historical significance. Specifically, the human rights framing of SOGI issues claims LGBT as historically and culturally universal identities, which ignores the emergence of our contemporary understanding of LGBT in Western societies during a specific socio-historical context over the last 150 years or so. The assumption of universal, trans-historical sexual identities also results in a lack of interrogation of the links between sexuality and ethnicities during the era of Western colonialism, and therefore a lack of understanding of the links between colonialism and contemporary resistance from postcolonial nations. This criticism of the dominance of Western understandings of sexuality is not, however, a defense of the resistance against progressing LGBT rights around the world, but rather the reasoning is that a simplistic understanding of these rights as historically and culturally universal actually *reduces* the likelihood of successful global progress because it does not address the underlying causes of contemporary resistance. Understanding the complexity of resistance is a better basis through which to achieve meaningful progress.

Thinking beyond 'freedom' and 'oppression' by understanding LGBT identities in the context of modernity

A commonsense understanding of progress for LGBT rights as linked to modernized societies, reinforces the assumption that 'traditional' nations and immigrant populations will become more tolerant as they get richer and more secularized. Given the current state of the world economy and the disparities between the global north and south, and the fact that socio-economic opportunities are usually limited for immigrants to the West from 'traditional' cultures, the assumption that making societies and/or immigrant populations richer in order to erase homophobia would seem to be a long-term waiting game. Furthermore, simply waiting for this kind of economic modernization offers no immediate support to those LGBT populations in homophobic countries who are being oppressed or to LGBT in minority immigrant populations that remain culturally homophobic. Furthermore, the current strategy from many LGBT NGOs and supportive governments to bypass this sociological understanding and simply frame LGBT as universal human rights is not a convincing or successful strategy to engage in as we see from the organized resistance to this move.

For example, a brief search of news sites or social media news feeds will show how governments of countries such as Russia or Uganda argue against LGBT rights, both as impositions from Western cultures and as a threat to their traditional culture of gender organization and/or religion. The homophobia used by this resistance characterizes LGBT as non-human or less than normal humans and so de-legitimizes the equation of LGBT people with human rights. This often resonates with the populations because the social formations that led to *publicly visible* LGBT lives and identities in the West *do not exist* in these cultures.

A first step in moving beyond this current framing and its seemingly impossible oppositions is to recognize some of the sociological realities that underlie the progress model and how this requires a more nuanced political strategy.

First, the model of 'progress' for LGBT rights is based on *Western* experience – those societies that were first to adopt a capitalist economy and, with the related impact of rational scientific thought, move first towards a secularization of their governance and culture from the seventeenth century onwards. It is these societies that are most 'modernized' in the sense of being the most affluent and secularized and this is a result of their position within *modernity*. Sociologically, modernity refers to the period of Western colonialism from the sixteenth century onwards, the related industrialization of the West with the advent of modern rational capitalism, and the foundational shift towards rational scientific, fact-based, explanations of the natural and social worlds. These interrelated transformations have been and continue to be significant in their impacts on the organization of sexuality.

Modernity entailed new conceptualizations of gender, often based on emerging understandings of biology and psychology, and related to the division of labor that came with modern capitalism. These new ideas legitimized the notion of women as ideally suited to the domestic realm with a passive sexuality under the control of the male husband (Weeks 1989). This created an ideology of *heteronormativity*; a normalization of rigid binary gender divisions, that required an increased policing of 'deviant' gendered and sexual behavior. The contemporary political identities of 'lesbian' and 'gay' have their origin in nineteenth-century scientific categorization and subsequent regulation of non-normative identities. Indeed, it is in the early stages of modernity that we first see the use of the term homosexuality, and it is a term of stigma, associated with mental and physical degeneracy and resulting in increasing medical and legal regulation, reworking existing religious sanctions into new or enhanced laws that punished 'the abominable vice of buggery' (Weeks 1989, 99). The emergence of sexual identities in the modern age is therefore only the 'tip' of the iceberg, based on the social formations indicated below in Figure 6.2.

This social structure of sexual identity is only gradually broken down in the more recent era of modernity. Progressive gender and sexual politics only emerges in the later stages of modernity in the West, after the 1960s, and is produced by the increasing educational and economic independence of women, breaking the binary divides of gender and associated sexual behaviors (Weeks 2007). Moreover, it has taken until the last two decades or so to see full citizenship being achieved by LGBT individuals in Western countries, with trans rights still lagging behind (Hildebrandt 2014). It is therefore important to understand that current sexual diversity politics has emerged within the specific sociological context of Western modernity in two major and distinct ways. First,

Figure 6.2 The social structure of heteronormativity

the impact on the regulation of gender and sexuality in enshrining a capitalist and male-dominated or patriarchal heteronormativity which created institutionalized homophobia and oppressed LGBT identities for most of modernity. Secondly, in the very recent stages of modernity, we have witnessed the movements towards progress based on the increasing wealth of Western societies that permits some equalization of gender divisions through access to women's economic independence, leading to an associated challenge to heteronormativity and homophobia, consequently allowing for the emergence of LGBT politics.

Another political problem with the progress model is that it ignores the sociological impact of Western *colonialism* during modernity and the consequences this had for how ethnic hierarchies are related to the organization of gender and sexuality. The physical practices of colonialism were justified by ideological frameworks of imperialism and one major dimension of that ideology was the assumption that Western cultures had a more 'civilized' treatment of women and sexual behavior. The colonized 'other' was often represented as sexually promiscuous or immoral, and therefore uncivilized and in need of Western 'improvement' (McClintock 1995; Said 1979). But, remember that in this period of colonialism, it was the newly rigid male-dominated or patriarchal heteronormativity that was the Western model and this resulted in narrower versions of appropriate sexuality for women and increased regulation of non-heterosexual behaviors. This increasing legal and social regulation of women and non-heterosexuals was apparent in the home imperial nations (McClintock 1995; Weeks 1989) and was also applied to colonized areas and nations, both in settler and military colonialism, resulting in the imposition of laws against homosexuality in particular, in many colonized countries (Lennox & Waites 2013). Ideas of *racial hierarchies* developed during this time and, as with gender divisions, they were based on emerging biological 'science' (Fenton 2010) and these were intertwined with the patriarchal and homophobic framework of Western heteronormativity.

Thinking historically and sociologically about modernity is important because it forces a recognition that sexuality is not simply a 'natural' aspect of individuals, but has been subject to re-organization and re-conceptualization in socio-historical context. Contemporary LGBT politics has emerged in the West during modernity because of specific, primarily *oppressive*, consequences of modernity that first entailed the identification of homosexuality as a stigmatized, deviant identity and also connected these ideas to racial hierarchies. The move towards 'progress' is both *very* recent and dependent upon new social transformations around gender in the Western countries that have benefitted most from their position of control within modernity as a capitalist, colonialist and racial set of global transformations.

The historical formation of modernity as a Euro-centric capitalist, colonial enterprise continues to play out in contemporary times, with economic inequalities mapped onto geographical areas that correlate with the era of Western colonialism, and these areas broadly correlating with regions that oppose or resist LGBT rights (Pew 2013). Furthermore, there are complications in that contemporary modernity is globalized through travel and the digital age in a way that is historically distinct. Thus, ideas and experiences of 'liberated' Western LGBT identities circulate in a way that was not the case in the initial period of Western gay liberation and, in terms of International Relations, issues of LGBT rights as part of IGO activity is similarly a context that Western LGBT organizations and populations did not contend with. With this more complex understanding, we can now see that the underlying assumption that the rest of the world will simply follow Western versions of LGBT progress is fundamentally flawed because it ignores the specific context that Western societies have enjoyed in modernity and, conversely, ignores both the historical and contemporary distinctions in context for non-Western societies in dealing with LGBT. Specifically, the current framing of LGBT rights as universal human rights is based on a long-term and complex social development in the *West* and so when it is presented as an ahistorical universal principle, it ignores the complexities of the 'progress' model (not least in the West itself) and fails to take account of the distinctive contemporary political and social contexts of those countries that resist LGBT rights.

Case study on LGBT politics and Muslim cultures: The triangulation of homocolonialism

Islam is often seen as an extreme example of the opposition between LGBT rights and non-Western cultures, with Muslim states at the forefront of resistance to international human rights of SOGI and enforcers of some of the most oppressive laws against LGBT people. Furthermore, Muslim religious leaders often reiterate extremely negative views on sexual and gender diversity, influencing both minority and majority Muslim populations who express some of the most negative attitudes towards homosexuality in national and global comparison (Pew 2013). At first glance, it is easy to slot this opposition between LGBT and Muslim cultures into the progress model, but we already know that this is too simplistic because it does not take account of the contexts of modernity for the formation of sexualities, ethnicities and racism and the intersection of these with contemporary International Relations. Accordingly, a more complex model is appropriate: one that acknowledges that LGBT politics, Muslim homophobia and Western modernity are part of a triangulated process of *homocolonialism*, illustrated in Figure 6.3 below.

This process of homocolonialism is primarily one of political positioning that produces a negative political process. It begins with LGBT politics deployed as the vanguard of Western civilization's development and progress, something that has occurred only in the last decade or so as Western governments and LGBT NGOs who have advanced LGBT citizenship have turned their attention to non-Western cultural and state homophobias. This normalization of LGBT rights in many Western countries has been usefully conceptualized by Puar as 'homonationalism' (2007). Homocolonialism extends this insight into the realm of International Relations, recognizing that the homonationalist tendencies of many Western societies have led to the 'pinktesting' of Muslim majority nations for their attitudes to SOGI rights, as well as testing Muslim immigrants and refugee Muslim populations for their 'tolerance'

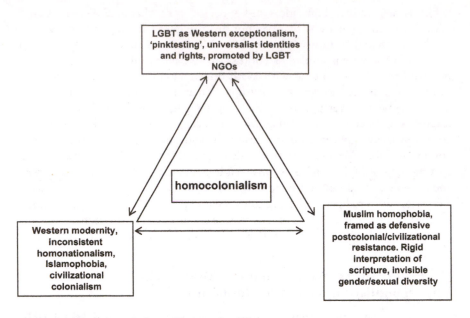

Figure 6.3 The triangulation of homocolonialism

towards homosexuality (Rahman 2014). It is important to note two points here: first, that this discourse assumes a universalist, transcultural and trans-historical idea of what it means to be gay, lesbian, bi or trans even though it is based on Western experiences.

Secondly, this equation of LGBT rights with Western societies validates the *exceptionalism* of Western modernity by suggesting that the best examples of Western civilization embrace SOGI rights and implies that these rights and identities are possible *only* in Western social and political formations. Even though the embrace of LGBT is inconsistent across the West, it is that very inconsistency which requires LGBT politics to be understood both as outside of the 'core' West, and as illustrative of its best version. At this point of the triangulation, LGBT rights are not just human rights but come to symbolize Western exceptionalism, projected outwards from the West, which is another point of the triangulation. SOGI rights have therefore come to share a space with ideas of Western superiority deriving from the West's privileged position within modernity. In the current context, this means that LGBT politics shares a space in a range of Western civilizational criteria that includes Islamophobia and the West's economic superiority over the Global South.

The third position is Muslim culture and populations are seen as distinctly outside of the West and its modernity, even when those populations are immigrant minorities *physically* within the West. These populations are uniformly characterized in opposition to the vanguard position of LGBT identities. There is ample survey evidence (Pew 2013; Rahman 2014), and the recent organized resistance at the UN is but the latest example of international condemnation of LGBT by Muslim nations. The point to understand, however, is not that the combination of Islamophobia and the LGBT criteria excuses Muslim homophobia, but instead that this discursive framing of homocolonialism increasingly provokes Muslim homophobia and, by doing so, legitimizes repressive Muslim governance. Homocolonialism *suits* repressive and patriarchal Muslims leaderships in governments and religious communities because they can claim cultural or national legitimacy by resisting LGBT rights as a Western imposition and continuation of attempts to colonize non-Western cultures. Thus, Muslim leaderships are not passive 'dupes' of homocolonialism; they have agency in how they participate in this positioning. This resistance also depends upon rigid interpretations of Islam as a religion and renders invisible historical and contemporary forms of sexual and gender diversity in Muslim cultures. In turn, this resistance confirms the irredeemable characterization of Islam as a conservative religion and Muslim adherents as consequently too 'traditional' for the modern world. In this closed loop of triangulation, we can see how *both* LGBT rights and Muslim homophobia are drawn into confirming Islamophobia, and confirming that LGBT rights are only possible in the West.

An important point to remember is that the process of homocolonialism can be both intentional and unintentional. Many activists and policy makers working for LGBT IGOs and governments are genuinely committed to the security and well-being of LGBT peoples, but their actions may unintentionally contribute to and reinforce homocolonialism. A major issue here is that, despite nods to cultural variations, most policy defaults into assuming that Western identities and outcomes of equality are the ultimate policy aim. On the Muslim side, there is also perhaps unintentionality, although this may seem less obvious given the evidence of widespread Muslim homophobia, but there is also evidence that Muslims value equality, human rights and, in some cases, see LGBT as part of this framework (Environics 2016; Pew 2013).

Prioritizing LGBT Muslims to disrupt homocolonialism

The triangulated process described above means that both Muslim postcolonial/religious resistance and Western universalist LGBT politics compound the assumption that there is *only one possible form* of sexual diversity, which has already been achieved in the West and is fundamentally incompatible with Muslim cultures and societies. This means that both the subject of LGBT Muslims and the possibilities of LGBT Muslims being and belonging are rendered invisible. First and foremost, we must recognize the dangers of assuming that Western LGBT identity and politics are the only possible form of existing and living sexual diversity and thus avoid an unintended homocolonialism. Think for a moment if we positioned LGBT Muslims in the center of Figure 6.3 (p. 106): the recognition that there are, and always have been, people from Muslim cultures who have sexual and gender diversity renders the structure and flows of the triangulation illogical and unworkable. In this sense, LGBT Muslims are an *intersectional* social

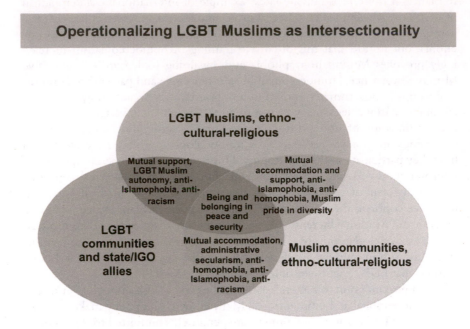

Operationalizing LGBT Muslims as Intersectionality

Figure 6.4 Muslim LGBT as intersectionality

and political identity – showing the connections and overlaps between apparently dichotomous cultures and peoples. This is a challenge to *both* Western/international LGBT groups *and* to Muslim cultures because an intersectional perspective demands that we recognize that the experiences of an intersectional identity are not 'minority' experiences within a dominant identity category, but are *fundamentally different* and *equally legitimate ways of being* that dominant identity (Rahman 2010). In Figure 6.4, we see an alternative to the triangulation of homocolonialism, that asks us to consider how the lives of LGBT Muslims can be bettered by recognizing the assumptions of modernity, colonialism, racism and sexuality that underpin homocolonialism.

The analytical requirements of an intersectional approach: anti–essentialist understandings of sexualities, ethnicities and cultures to move towards LGBT Muslim freedom

The politics of trying to legitimize LGBT Muslim identities and rights are incredibly complex, varying by nation and international political relationships. However, there are some steps that can be taken to help us to build a terrain of dialogue, and if we are to move from the triangulation of homocolonialism to the operationalization of intersectionality, then we need to think more critically about sexualities, ethnicities and cultures in both West and East.

The first problematic issue is the conceptualization of sexuality because if we can only think of sexuality as another term for an innate or biological sexual identity, we cannot begin to understand the social significance and regulation of the issue. In contrast to this biological view, it is important to consider what sexual acts mean in the cultural and political context in which they occur, including how they signify social identities and social hierarchies and how we as individuals use these cultural and political meanings to develop our own identities and behaviors. As argued in the section on modernity above, gender structures are fundamental to understanding how sexuality is regulated and experienced. Categories of gender have expectations of sexual behavior and identity associated with them, most obviously in the essentialist biological understanding of gender as a binary structure of man and woman, defined by their reproductive capacities. This assumption of heterosexuality is present in all cultures and is often the basis of social regulation of non-conforming gender identities and sexualities, validating 'naturalist' heterosexual sexualities over all others, thus creating sexuality as a hierarchy both within heterosexuality and across the range of sexual identities. Framing LGBT rights as human rights ignores this fundamental significance of sexuality as a marker of gender normativity and hence miscalculates the resistance that is aimed at preserving patriarchal *gender* norms. For example, when the OIC argued against the appointment of the Independent Expert on SOGI rights, they framed part of their resistance as a defense of 'traditional' roles for men and women, similar to the ongoing (predominantly Christian) religious and conservative arguments against trans rights in the United States. Any possible dialogue on LGBT Muslims needs to begin with a recognition that all cultures are patriarchal, across West and East, and so both that Muslim homophobia is not unusual when viewed in these terms, and that a human rights framework does *not* address this underlying significance of sexuality.

Secondly, this equation of gender with sexuality is a *naturalist* one, based on biological and spiritual and psychological definitions of what is 'normal' and 'naturally' part of our human 'essence'. Feminists and LGBT theorists have characterized these ways of thinking as 'essentialist' and critiqued their patriarchal, trans-cultural and often ahistorical justifications. In our example, anti-essentialist understandings of sexuality are needed because of historical and cultural specificity. We must recognize that the Western way of being LGBT is not necessarily the same across time and cultures and, as argued earlier, derives from the Western experience of modernity. So while individuals experience sexuality as a biological act, it is also a form of social identification, but the meaning and conceptualization of the social identity varies across culture and history.

For example, there is a large and growing body of academic research on Muslim sexual diversity, and this contributes to raising contemporary visibility, as well as rendering visible histories of sexual diversity from Muslim cultures.[8] This evidence shows both experiences of being LGBT that are both distinct from Western versions and, importantly, some similarities in those experiences in the contemporary world of globally circulating media. LGBT politics must, therefore, adopt a more rigorous anti-naturalist understanding of sexuality that is open to understanding that sexual diversity will come in different forms in different cultures, even if the principle of non-discrimination remains a universal goal. Moreover, this understanding is not just needed in the context of external Muslim cultures but also in the West, since we know that there are established LGBT organizations in the West that have yet to fully consider the distinct needs and oppressions of racialized minorities, including LGBT Muslims.

Of course, the specificity of LGBT Muslims also demands that we understand that sexuality, is not constituted by gender alone but that ethnicity is a significant dimension. Similarly, this means that we need an anti-naturalist understanding of ethnicity in the sense that we do not equate ethnic identity with innate and unchanging cultural values. Fenton describes the way in which '*ethnicity*' has displaced 'race' as an analytical term, largely because the latter contained essentialist assumptions of biological differences that were operationalized in an oppressive way in the nineteenth and early twentieth centuries, particularly by equating the white Caucasian 'race' with superior moral and cultural capabilities (2010, 17–19). Ethnicity, by contrast, is more commonly understood to refer to identity groupings that may derive from common biological descent but are primarily marked by cultural practices and values rather than by physical biological differences. Most contemporary academic work therefore rejects essentialist characterizations of race but, as Meer and Modood argue (2012), everyday conceptualizations of ethnicity can still be reductive to a biological understanding of race in the case of Muslims. They argue that we must understand racism as not just referring to a 'race' or group of people with biological characteristics inherited through descent, but that, in practice, these groups often have associated distinct cultural practices, with religion a primary one amongst these. Therefore, in practice, racism is aimed at ethnic groups that have both biological and cultural characteristics in common. This is more relevant to our example because we see reductive essentialist characterizations of cultural values associated with Muslim ethnicities. This can have problematic consequences for LGBT Muslims, who can suffer from a reductive association of Muslim culture with homophobia and an assumption that they must abandon their culture in order to be fully LGBT (Abraham 2009, 2010).

Thus far, the implications of an anti-essentialist understanding have been illustrated with a focus on Western LGBT groups and the ways they can benefit LGBT Muslims by thinking more analytically about sexuality and ethnicity. However, these points also apply to Muslim groups and cultures as well. One of the negative consequences of the Muslim investments in homocolonialism is a narrowing of Muslim interpretations of religion, particularly in the realm of gender and sexuality with the extreme wing of fundamentalist interpretations illustrating an unyielding essentialism around scripture, culture, and sexual diversity. And yet we have increasing evidence that there has been a range of gender and sexual diversity in various Muslim cultures, as referenced in the various collections above. In the current political climate, the research being done on Muslim homoeroticism and gender diversity is primarily possible in the West, as is the activism necessary to force visibility and political change but, ultimately, we will also need to see Muslim communities resist essentialist characterizations of their own culture in terms of both race and sexuality, both minority groups in the West, and majority cultures internationally.

Further requirements of intersectionality: challenging Islamophobia to undermine Muslim homophobia

We have seen above how LGBT Muslims are an intersectional identity and thus how they force a recognition of anti-essentialist understandings of sexuality and ethnicity. This analysis also requires a recognition of the intersecting formation of the negative reductive contexts that LGBT Muslims face, namely racism and homophobia. While the research evidence suggests that LGBT Muslims do encounter racism, many of them perceive this or experience it directly as Islamophobia.

The Runnymede Trust research and policy group in the United Kingdom is credited with an early influential report on Islamophobia (1997). The EU has published various reports and the Organization of Islamic Cooperation has published an annual report on Islamophobia since 2008[9] and academic analysis of Islamophobia is a growing field (Kunst et al. 2013). Islam describes a religion, and Muslims are the people who are its followers, but Islamophobia conflates the two, referring overwhelmingly to a prejudice against populations. Meer and Modood (2012, 50) argue that we must understand contemporary Islamophobia as a form of racism since it is based on a form of cultural antipathy to Muslim identities and practices as an ethnic group rather than an exclusively religious one. The issue for us is that LGBT rights are being drawn into a more general Islamophobic discourse and that this, in the triangulation model, reinforces a homophobic response from Muslim cultures as a legitimate defense of their culture against Islamophobia, thus reinforcing essentialist understandings of Muslim sexuality and ethnicity.

LGBT rights must be divorced from Islamophobic discourses as one component of any broader movement away from Muslim homophobia and this will not be possible unless we recognize that Islamophobia is not simply a contemporary form of racism, but that it has a longer history in modernity that intersects with the myth of LGBT rights as evidence of Western exceptionalism. We need to decolonize our understandings of modernity and sexuality and the concept of Orientalism is useful to help us achieve this end.

Edward Said conceptualized Orientalism in his 1979 study of the military and economic dominance of the West from the eighteenth century onwards. As Bhambra (2007) argues, most Western explanations of modernity proceed as if colonialism was not a central aspect of the West's 'development' during this period. Shared cultural assumptions in the West in both academic and public life have become used to the idea that the West is more developed, more successful, than the rest of the world, and its colonial past is not implicated in its own successes or the failures of the 'under-development' of non-Western societies (Bhambra 2007). Said shifted this kind of assumption by illustrating that Western colonialism during modernity produced new ways of thinking and understanding the world that legitimized colonialism. Specifically, public and academic knowledge of the time created the idea of the colonized 'East' or the 'Orient', as inferior and traditional and thus ripe for a 'progressive' or 'civilizing' control by the more 'advanced' nations of the West. Orientalism thus legitimizes Western control as *beneficial* to the colonized.

The interrelated ideas or discourses of Orientalism reflect the power of the West and its economic and military subjugation of Asian empires and their peoples. Orientalist thinking is both an expression and form of power and has a social dominance or hegemonic status, always prioritizing Western cultures, societies and peoples. Said's (1981) study of media representations of Islam and Muslims bears this out and is confirmed by the huge amount of further study that confirms biased and stereotypical methods of representing Muslims. For more recent evidence, see Karim's (2003) study of negative representations of Islamic 'others' by Western media covering the two decades before 9/11, supported by Poynting and Mason's (2007) study that points out that anti-Muslim media representations had been consistent in the United Kingdom and Australia prior to 9/11, though such particular events do provide a spike effect. Here we can see how it legitimizes racism as Islamophobia because Orientalism maps ethnicities of the colonizer and colonized onto a hierarchy of power according to culture and race.

We can immediately see the connection here with the contemporary international politics of LGBT rights, whereby Western governments are leading the charge to 'civilize' traditional homophobic nations and cultures. We need to recognize the ways in which LGBT rights are being drawn into this homocolonialism and recognize the intersectional nature of this relationship. Understandably, many LGBT organizations in the West have focused on challenging heteronormativity within their own political jurisdictions, and have not been engaged in an intersectional politics of anti-racism or, more recently, anti-Islamophobia. However, in the contemporary world of migration and expanding LGBT visibility, these issues demand acknowledgement and action from mainstream LGBT groups, particularly if their aim is to support LGBT Muslims who want to exist within the mainstream LGBT community.

The benefit of addressing these issues more directly is that they also support a potential dialogue between LGBT groups and mainstream Muslim communities, both in national contexts and in international political forums. This may seem an impossible task right now, but there are areas of common experience between Muslims and LGBT groups, not least of which is discrimination, either through Islamophobia or homophobia. Rights of non-discrimination are a fundamental part of the expansion of liberal equality towards social justice that feminism, gay liberation and ethnic politics have all helped to shape and there should be more discussion of the commonalities in political structures and policies that prevent homophobia *and* racism or Islamophobia. Recognizing the colonial Orientalist inheritance of Islamophobia is a first step towards creating a dialogue that may help to reduce the defensive cultural essentialism of Muslim communities on issues of religion and sexuality. For example, LGBT groups in the West could adopt a more principled engagement with intersectional oppressions of ethnicity and sexuality by resisting the 'pinktesting' of immigrants and refugees for their attitudes to LGBT rights, and by asking their governments to resist Islamophobic foreign policies. These interventions would not silence our ability to critique Muslim homophobia, but allow us more credibility to confront specific instances of Muslim antipathy to sexual diversity by illustrating that we refuse to allow LGBT rights to be deployed as part of Islamophobia.

Conclusion

As Said argued, Orientalism is symbiotic, producing a subordinate that reassures the superiority of the dominant. Moreover, this operates not only at the level of cultures or civilizations, but also at the level of identities, creating a dialectic of the 'norm' and the 'other'. The first point about understanding the 'other' sociologically is that it is *relational*, acquiring social stigma because a dominant group labels it as deviant (Goffman 1986). Orientalism draws our attention to the process of othering by demonstrating how culturally dominant forms of hierarchical thinking about racialized groups and historical civilizations produce a direct characterization of subordinate individuals as 'others'. Combine this with the understanding that Muslim cultures are seen as 'Other' to the successes of Western modernity, and you have a deeper understanding of contemporary Islamophobia. The contemporary internationalization of LGBT politics is problematic because it is reinforcing Islamophobia and thus provoking Muslim homophobia. This process has been identified through a model of the triangulation of homocolonialism, and an alternative understanding of the opposition between LGBT and Muslims that places LGBT Muslims at the center of our focus has been suggested. Such an understanding requires anti-essentialist and intersectional understandings of sexuality, ethnicity, Islamophobia and modernity.

Notes

1 I am using LGBT (lesbian, gay, bisexual, transgender) throughout as most policy documents use this formulation, although most LGBT organizations recognize that this is limited and often have extended formulations.
2 See the UN website at for the Independent Expert's first statement, and links to the UN's current campaign activities and reports on LGBT issues, framed as SOGI issues (sexual orientation and gender identity), www.ohchr.org/EN/NewsEvents/Pages/DisplayNews.aspx?NewsID=20954&LangID=E, accessed December 1, 2016.
3 See, for example, the UK's range of policies and resources at their Department for International Development, www.spl.ids.ac.uk/sexuality-gender-faith, accessed December 2, 2016.

4   See www.ohchr.org/EN/Issues/Discrimination/Pages/BornFreeEqualBooklet.aspx, accessed December 2, 2016.

5   See the various interactive maps at the UN sites mentioned in notes above, or the annual survey of laws by the International Lesbian and Gay Association at http://ilga.org/downloads/02_ILGA_State_Sponsored_Homophobia_2016_ENG_WEB_150516.pdf, accessed October 6, 2016.

6   For a full account of this specific vote and its context, see http://arc-international.net/global-advocacy/human-rights-council/32nd-session-of-the-human-rights-council/appointing-an-independent-expert-on-sexual-orientation-and-gender-identity-an-analysis-of-process-results-and-implications/annex-ii-description-of-the-vote-on-the-sogi-resolution/, accessed December 2, 2016.

7   See www.pewglobal.org/2013/06/04/the-global-divide-on-homosexuality/, accessed January 6, 2017.

8   See, for example, historical evidence in Babayan and Najmabadi (2008), Murray and Roscoe (1997); for more contemporary evidence, see Habib (2010) and Rahman (2014).

9   See their website at www.oic-oci.org/oicv2/page/?p_id=182&p_ref=61&lan=en#).

Further readings

Puar, J.K. (2007). *Terrorist assemblages: Homonationalism in queer times*. Durham and London: Duke University Press. Punar's Conceputalization of homonationalism in *Terrorist Assemblages* has become an influential concept in the normalization of LGBT within Western exceptionalism.

Rahman, M. (2014). *Homosexualities, Muslim cultures and modernity*. Basingstoke: Palgrave Macmillan. Rahman provides a comprehensive overview of theoretical and empirical work on LGBT Muslims.

Weeks, J. (1989). *Sex, politics and society*. London: Longman. This books remains a foundational text in understanding the regulation of homosexuality in the context of Western modernity.

Weeks, J. (2007). *The world we have won: The remaking of erotic and intimate life*. New York: Routledge. Provides a useful summary of the changes in the contexts that led to the contemporary LGBT movements in the West.

Weiss, M.L. and Bosia, M.J. (Eds.). (2013). *Global homophobia: States, movements and the politics of oppression*. Chicago: University of Illinois Press. A collection of essays that is an important early intervention in the contemporary internationalization of LGBT politics.

Bibliography

Abraham, I. (2009). 'Out to get us': Queer Muslims and the clash of sexual civilization in Australia. *Contemporary Islam*, 3, 79–97.

Abraham, I. (2010). 'Everywhere you turn you have to jump into another closet': Hegemony, hybridity, and queer Australian Muslims. In S. Habib (Ed.). *Islam and homosexuality, Vols 1 and 2* (pp. 395–418). Santa Barbara, CA: Praeger.

Babayan, K. and Najmabadi, A. (2008). *Islamicate sexualities: Translations across temporal geographies of desire*. Cambridge, MA: Harvard University Press.

Bhambra, G. (2007). *Rethinking modernity: Postcolonialism and the sociological imagination*. Basingstoke: Palgrave Macmillan.

Environics (2016). *Survey of Muslims in Canada* 2016, www.environicsinstitute.org/uploads/institute-projects/survey%20of%20muslims%20in%20canada%202016%20-%20final%20report.pdf, accessed May 1, 2016.

Fenton, S. (2010). *Ethnicity*. Cambridge: Polity Press.

Goffman, E. (1986). *Stigma: Notes on the management of spoiled identity*. New York: Touchstone.

Habib, S. (Ed.). (2010). *Islam and homosexuality. Vols 1 and 2*. Santa Barbara, CA: Praeger.

Hildebrandt, A. (2014). Routes to decriminalization: A comparative analysis of the legalization of same-sex sexual acts. *Sexualities*, 17, 230–253.

Karim, H.K. (2003). *Islamic peril: Media and global violence*. Montreal: Black Rose Books.

Kunst, J.R., Sam, D.L. and Ulleberg, P. (2013). Perceived Islamophobia: Scale development and validation. *International Journal of Intercultural Relations*, 37, 225–237.

Lennox, C. and Waites, M. (Ed.). (2013). *Human rights, sexual orientation and gender identity in the commonwealth: Struggles for decriminalisation and change*. London: School of Advanced Study.

McClintock, A. (1995). *Imperial leather: Race, gender and sexuality in the colonial context*. London: Routledge.

Meer, N. and Modood, T. (2012). For 'Jewish' read 'Muslim'? Islamophobia as a form of racialisation of ethno-religious groups in Britain today. *Islamophobia Studies Journal*, 1, 34–33.

Murray, S. and Roscoe, W. (Eds.). (1997). *Islamic homosexualities: Culture, history and literature*. New York: New York University Press.

Pew Research Center (2013). *The Global Divide on Homosexuality*. Available at www.pewglobal.org/2013/06/04/the-global-divide-on-homosexuality/. Accessed March 28, 2015.

Poynting, S. and Mason, V. (2007). The resistible rise of Islamophobia: Anti-Muslim racism in the UK and Australia before 11 September 2001. *Journal of Sociology*, 43, 61–86.

Puar, J.K. (2007). *Terrorist assemblages: Homonationalism in queer times*. Durham and London: Duke University Press.

Rahman, M. (2010). Queer as intersectionality: Theorizing gay Muslim identities. *Sociology*, 44, 1–18.

Rahman, M. (2014). *Homosexualities, Muslim cultures and modernity*. Basingstoke: Palgrave Macmillan.

Runnymede Trust (1997). Islamophobia: a challenge for us all [online]. Available at www.runnymedetrust.org/uploads/publications/pdfs/islamophobia.pdf, accessed March 2, 2016.

Said, E. (1979). *Orientalism*. New York: Vintage Books.

Said, E. (1981). *Covering Islam*. New York: Vintage Books.

Weeks, J. (1989). *Sex, politics and society* (2nd edition). Harrow: Longman.

Weeks, J. (2007). *The world we have won: The remaking of erotic and intimate life*. New York: Routledge.

Weiss, M.L. and Bosia, M.J. (Eds.). (2013). *Global homophobia: States, movements and the politics of oppression*. Chicago: University of Illinois Press.

7 Race and global inequality

Naeem Inayatullah and David L. Blaney

Introduction	116
Inequalities	117
Colonization, racialization, and development	119
Capitalism, wealth, and sacrifice	122
Global inequality, IR, and the racialization of units	125
Conclusion	130

Introduction

We moderns pride ourselves on our commitment to equality. Yet this commitment co-exists with great inequality in power, income, wealth, and status, creating vast disparities between individuals, countries, and racialized groups. For some, nothing can justify these inequalities. But most of us accept *some* justifications for inequality, especially those that rely on individual achievement and merit. These justifications seem consistent with our ideas of individual freedom. Inequalities that result from coercion violate our commitment to individual freedom and we do not use them to justify inequality. Likewise, we reject justifications for inequality that suggest a permanent inferiority of those who command less power or wealth. These seem at odds with our assumption of human equality.

We explore how merit and inequality are linked to the role of markets in modern society in the first section. Markets, it is argued, are sites for the exercise of human freedom and since market competition rewards individuals for their contribution, not only are differential outcomes justified, they also provide incentives for individuals to develop their talents for the benefit of society as a whole. But we accept these unequal results as just only if market competition is fair. Markets must operate according to fair rules and everyone must have the opportunity to cultivate talents that they bring to the market.

In the second section, we observe that the assumption that modern thought is definitively egalitarian falls apart when we see how key modern thinkers give highly racialized accounts of human history. Kant, for example, poses the question of why people who do not progress exist at all. Hegel suggests that

Northern Europeans assume a leading role in creating the modern world while history renders a monstrous verdict on others: Amerindians extinguished; Africans enslaved; and Asian civilizations defeated and colonized.

A third section draws on the great analysts of capitalism: Adam Smith and Karl Marx. Both attach immense importance to capitalism's revolutionary wealth production which allows higher levels of human creativity and great advances in civilization. But each sees that some must be sacrificed to this engine of human ennoblement. For Smith, wealth production requires that laborers are locked into a role that procures only bare subsistence. Marx similarly condemns capitalism's brutal exploitation of labor, though he concedes that capitalism's historically progressive role justifies its violent colonial relations and its destruction of backward ways of life.

In the fourth section, we show that the ethical claim that rewards in markets follow from individual talents and efforts is racialized. In International Relations, unit-level explanations are privileged to the exclusion of those who examine the whole of the system. The preference for the former means that global inequality cannot but be a product of differences in unit-level traits and actions. This preference erases evidence of violent colonial processes that confine individuals, groups, or countries to limited positions within a capitalist global division of labor. An unacknowledged ethical judgment is exercised. The gap between rich and poor, development and underdevelopment is seen as emerging naturally. The gap results when individual units employ different levels of skill and effort. Some may thrive. But others may not be able to develop at all. Here we show the racialized judgments of Kant, Hegel, and even Marx.

Finally, once we understand that global inequalities are not simply earned but shaped by a history of violence and the structural processes of capitalism, we can imagine alternative and more democratic principles of wealth acquisition and distribution.

Inequalities

The most popular contemporary justification for inequality in income and wealth argues that inequalities are the result of differences in *merit* – in talent or effort. Markets and other competitions are thought to assess, judge, and reward individuals according to their effort or skill.

Markets legitimate inequality through three separable, but usually linked arguments. First, unequal outcomes are justified because they result from the free choices of individuals, usually exchanges in the market (Nozick 1974). *Individual freedom* is so highly valued that unequal outcomes resulting from individual choices must be accepted as the unfortunate result of our commitment to freedom. The market is valued precisely because it is claimed to be a sphere in which individual freedom reigns, despite the inequalities of income and wealth that result.

Secondly, unequal outcomes are seen as just because they reflect the *unequal contributions* of individuals (Hayek 1960, 1976; Friedman 1962). This is a commutative sense of justice, where individuals receive what they are owed or what is their due. Again, markets are seen as important, here as key instruments for providing what individuals are owed. The unequal rewards achieved by individuals in markets directly reflect (it is supposed) individual differences in contribution – of skill, knowledge, effort, or resources.

Thirdly, and usually intertwined with the others, unequal rewards are thought to provide information and *create incentives* (Hayek 1967, 1976; Friedman 1962). Again, the market mediates this process. It provides information for individuals, telling them where to increase their effort, develop their talents, and augment their knowledge. And it tells them where to remove such effort. Following these incentives allows individuals to maximize their rewards through market competition. The market efficiently and smoothly aligns these individual contributions of effort, skill, and knowledge to the needs of other people, including firms, and thereby produces a social good.

These three claims tie market results to effort and merit. This allows them to be remarkably effective in justifying the inequalities of income and wealth created and sustained by markets. That differences in effort and merit explain and justify inequalities across individuals, groups, and countries depends on a crucial additional condition of *fairness*: that the competition is fair (Nozick 1974). If competitive processes are rigged in some way, we find it hard to claim that unequal outcomes are just rewards. Various forms of cheating or arbitrary exclusion might challenge the fairness of outcomes. To assure this is not the case, competitions are governed by rules that assure the connection between results and competitors' efforts, knowledge, or skills. We know that competitions are and have been unfair. But this is no real challenge to this position. The response is swift and easy: we must therefore make markets more fair.

A second condition appears more intractable and continuously casts doubt on the justness of inequalities in income and wealth. Inequality can be acceptable and justified if everyone has a fair chance to compete in what Issac Kraminick (1981) calls the 'race of life'. If everyone has opportunities to compete, and if the competitive process is fair, than the result can be seen to be fair and acceptable – even if there are losers. This condition requires that the initial opportunities for success prior to the competition are fairly distributed. We need to believe that everyone had a fair chance to develop their talents, cultivate knowledge or had assets adequate to enter into market competition. This condition is much more difficult to sustain than fair rules, especially if the unequal rewards of market processes are cumulative across generations. Where the rules of market society allow advantages or disadvantages gained by families to be passed onto later generations, unequal life chances and unfair opportunities become prevalent. Intergenerational cumulative success or failure puts different levels of resources in the hands of competitors that significantly influence their capacity to develop their talents and acquire knowledge or bring assets to the market. The idea that reward matches merit is undermined when prior success shapes life chances and future opportunities to compete.

This problem is magnified when we ask: how do individuals, groups, or countries acquire their initial assets prior to their entry into market competition?

This pre-history of market society is usually bracketed or treated as irrelevant to our thinking about the justness of market outcomes. But doing so covers many problems. Inheritance from wealthy ancestors shapes people's life chances, apart from their own merit. The opposite is also true. It is difficult to rise above an inheritance that provides few resources or opportunities. These patterns of inheritance for individuals, groups, and countries include the results of past violence – conquest, enslavement, or systematic exclusion based on class, race or gender. We find our belief in the justice of the market strained when the market produces unequal rewards tied to such inheritance. They begin to offend our sense of human equality (Pogge 2002).

Yet, these seemingly unjustified inequalities persist. We appear to accept their inevitability. However great the inequality or the depth of poverty and despair into which some individuals, groups and countries fall, we act as if these conditions are the result of the inability to compete successfully in modern market conditions. We are able to act as if these conditions result from fair competitions because we overlook the histories that have shaped the modern world. Or, we might openly or covertly share racialized explanations of why some fail and others succeed. Such racialized explanations have a prominent place in the architecture of modern consciousness forged alongside European colonization.

Colonization, racialization, and development

We can date the beginnings of European colonization with the 'discovery' and conquest of the Americas. And, we can trace practices of racialization to this encounter of the European self and Amerindian other. Lewis Hanke, in *Aristotle and the American Indians* (1959, ix), writes, 'Generally speaking, there was no true racial prejudice before the fifteenth century, for mankind was divided not so much into antagonistic races as into Christians and infidels.' Religious or cultural differences exhibited by Amerindians were treated as grave errors or deficiencies, but also as malleable. Since the Indians were equally God's children, they might be educated and converted to European beliefs and ways of life (Todorov 1984). These religious or cultural differences also were racialized. *Racialization* involves degrading a group beyond the possibility of the 'promise of equality'. A racialized group is claimed to exhibit 'indelible and insurmountable' deficiencies that place its members apart from and below full humanness. They can be marginalized and even exterminated because they exhibit few human traits and produce shallow accomplishments (Fredrickson 2002, 12–13, 19). Race and racialization appear, then, not as biologically based or a fixed feature of human social life, but as a cultural project with a particular history, deployed for particular purposes.

As religious differentiation and prejudice gave way to racialization in the sixteenth and seventeenth centuries, both social thought and folk beliefs increasingly turned to environmental and biological factors to explain the firm differences between Europeans and others. Even when Europeans saw all peoples as deriving from a single creation and therefore part of a single human family, an often-disputed point, they characterized African, American, and Asian races as intrinsically deficient in character or biological endowments. These differences might be due to effects of the isolation of some races from the centers of European Christian civilization, an isolation that magnified and hardened differences. But this line of reasoning was gradually supplemented and supplanted by explanations rooted in climate and environment favored by the emerging human sciences. Some regions were either too hot or too cold to allow proper human development. Only temperate zones, such as those occupied by Europeans, were conducive to human progress. A racial science begins to take recognizable form in the late-eighteenth century, reaching its heights in the nineteenth and early twentieth centuries (Fredrickson 2002).

Some still took a more optimistic view. For example, Adam Smith and most of his eighteenth-century Scottish Enlightenment colleagues thought of the differences between 'peoples', 'tribes', 'nations', or 'races' as principally cultural. They were confident therefore that a European cultural makeover brought about by the global extension of commercial relations could lead all peoples to a civilized state (Berry 1997, 93–99; Blaney and Inaytullah 2010, chapter 1). Other thinkers, more disposed to harden differences between peoples as 'indelible and insurmountable', took as evidence of racial inferiority the fact that many non-European peoples resisted European tutelage and clung to their own beliefs and ways of life. These peoples appeared unable to see the truths and advantages offered by European civilization. We might rightly wonder if this resistance was a response to toppling existing civilizations, political subjugation, and forced labor. Nevertheless, violent treatment was justified because of these peoples' apparent permanent deficiencies in material achievement and cultural understanding.

That such *theories of racial inferiority* thrive in the modern era casts doubt on the strength of the modern commitment to equality. Two key European thinkers, Immanuel Kant and Georg Hegel, who are often celebrated for their theorization of and commitment to freedom and equality, illustrate the precarious place of human equality in the construction of modern thought.

Kant shows his cards when, in his *Philosophy of the History of Mankind* (1785), he asks European philosophers to think about societies that were cut off from material and intellectual world circuits and which seemed unconcerned to produce social and technological progress. He wondered what purpose, for example, the Tahitians served in human history: 'why they bothered to exist at all, and whether it would not have been just as well that this island should have been occupied by happy sheep and cattle as by happy men engaged in mere pleasure?' (quoted in Serequeberhan 1996, p. 341; see also Bernansconi 2002).

Hegel answers Kant's question within his *philosophy of history*. For Hegel, history moves towards the realization of human freedom but not always in ways that humans immediately understand. History's forces may be creative and kind, but they also are violent and cruel. The complex machinations of world history – including genocide, slavery, colonialism, and capitalism – cannot be assessed according to the prevailing morality of the times or as specified by a particular nation (Hegel 1991, sections 340–343; 1953). Rather, in Hegel's narrative what is done *to* some (who are mostly non-Europeans), and done *by* others (mostly Europeans) must be assessed according to their role in history's deeper purpose – purposes that perhaps only scholars and philosophers come to know.

Hegel's account racializes the actors who perform these roles in this world historical drama (Hegel 1975, 152–155; see also Bernasconi 2000). He follows the emerging racial science in mapping racial categories onto continents, so that now racialized non-Europeans are given only secondary relevance to producing the flow of 'world history'. Europeans chart and shape this flow in which non-Europeans are condemned to the 'slaughter-bench': extinction, enslavement, or colonization. Such 'monstrous sacrifices' have meaning, he insists. They are 'the means for realizing the essential destiny, the absolute final purpose...and true result of history' (Hegel 1953, 20–27). History achieves its ends through conflict, war, suffering, and death.

Hegel (1975, 52, 163–5) is specific in describing how racial differences map onto historical destiny. For example, *Amerindians* exhibit no physical vigor. Nor do they exhibit a capacity to learn. Hegel asserts that 'America has always shown itself physically and spiritually impotent'. Even its flora and fauna are inferior. Amerindians are 'like unenlightened children, living from one day to the next, and untouched by higher thoughts and aspirations'. The 'erosion' of 'nearly seven million have been wiped out' from the 'breath of European activity'. Hegel refers to the number (quite low by contemporary estimates) as evidence of the necessary historical fate of America's native populations.

Africans, on the other hand, retain a vital energy. They can be taught. Nevertheless, Africa, he tells us, has 'no historical interest of its own...[they] live in barbarism and savagery' and without the achievements of culture. Hegel recommends that Europeans take in Africans as slaves. He writes, 'To become free...to acquire the capacity for self-control, all nations must...undergo the severe discipline of subjugation to the master'. Slavery and colonialism, for Hegel, lift lower races, like Africans, to culture, progress, and freedom (Hegel 1975, 177–190; see also Hoffheimer 1993 and 2001).

Asians, by contrast, were once the vanguard of humanity. But that historical leadership has passed from them and into new hands. Their civilizations are moribund and easily toppled by Europeans who now assume the role of historical leadership (Hegel 1975, Part I).

There is an undeniably monstrous realism here. Modern European philosophers' celebration of the achievements of freedom and equality occur alongside Europe's rise to domination, the Atlantic slave trade, the Amerindian genocide, and massive degradation of non-European ways of life. We might be tempted to ignore any such connection but Hegel is clear eyed. He racializes non-European peoples to give this European slaughter bench a causal and ethical necessity. He explains and justifies relations of superiority and subordination, despite the modern presumption of human equality. Hegel's division of races into the historically victorious and defeated builds on a recognizable principle.

The pivotal issue is whether certain 'nations' or 'races' have the capacity to effectively manipulate nature for their own purposes. Their historical role is determined and merited by their capacity to produce. The ability to change and reorder nature distinguishes the only *seemingly* human, like Kant's Tahitians who are equivalent to happy sheep, from the *actual* humans who recreate nature to meet their own needs. Hegel shares this principle with Marx, as we shall see below, even if they differ in their attitude towards those cultures headed for the slaughter bench of history.

Capitalism, wealth, and sacrifice

We often treat our ideas about merit and inequality as a description or, perhaps, as an idealization of *capitalism*. Capitalism, we think, is about organizing social life around markets. Markets are where we realize our freedom and have our merit tested and rewarded proportionally. And, if we think about history at all, we may think that markets help to break down social orders organized around fixed hierarchies. In these hierarchical societies, inequality seems normal or 'natural' and equality is anathema because it collapses ranks that are believed necessary to sustain the natural order – for example between lord and servant, king and commoner, citizen and slave. Liberated from these fixed hierarchies, a capitalist order frees us to place ourselves in society based on our own talents and efforts. A society organized around markets should be indifferent or even opposed to practices of racialization, and therefore supportive of greater equality. But, consistent with our story about inequality and merit, economic theorists such as Friedrich Hayek (1960, 1976) and Milton Friedman (1962) tell us that income differentials, even vast differentials, are the consequence of modern freedoms, they indicate a healthy and robust society at work.

We are often told that Adam Smith is the founding father of such thinking and his authority is used to justify organizing society in capitalist terms. But closer reading suggests Smith's views are more complicated (Blaney and Inayatullah 2010, chapter 2). He does claim that a 'system of natural liberty' offers a path to wealth that makes civilized life possible. Many societies, including those hierarchical orders of earlier eras, restrict how individuals use or exchange their own property, violating natural liberty and limiting wealth production. Where natural liberty flourishes, where all individuals are free to seek beneficial exchanges or investments, there is constant inducement to technical innovation and improvements in labor productivity that allow greater wealth production (Smith 1976, Book I, chapters i–iii, Books III and IV). Nevertheless, in Smith's account of *wealth production* these improvements do not correspond to widespread social mobility. A commercial society is organized into three great *ranks or classes* – owners of capital, landowners, and workers – each locked into its essential role in wealth production (Smith 1976, Book I, chapters vi–ix). To simplify, we will consider only the first and the third.

Those who possess capital can exercise command of the necessary components of production. Owners put forward money, renting land, buying tools and raw materials, and hiring labor, in order to produce goods for sale, but only in expectation of a return well beyond what they initially risk (Smith 1976, Book I, chapters ix–x). What is crucial in Smith's account is that concentration of money in the hands of owners is a precondition of wealth production, not its result. Without this pre-existing concentration, this class cannot fulfill its role in the production of wealth.

Labor enters into the production of wealth much differently (Smith 1976, Book I, chapter viii; see also Montag 2005). Because laborers possess almost no accumulated money, they are unable to support themselves or their families without working for owners of capital. Modern wealth production has labor's dependence as a precondition since goods cannot be produced without labor and owners of wealth cannot command labor unless laborers are dependent on wages for their livelihood. In mirror opposition to owners of wealth, labor's lack of money must pre-exist modern wealth production, instead of being a result of differential returns to effort or talent.

And if owners of capital invest with the expectation of a return beyond their initial investment, laborers can expect only physical subsistence or a little bit more if high growth rates can be sustained for some time. Owners of capital normally attempt to push wages below the level of subsistence, but they are checked only because such low wages reduce the supply of labor over time. Since laborers are unable to voluntarily withhold their labor from the market, the supply of labor is controlled by population dynamics, including infant mortality rates, so that more children die when wages fall below subsistence. This shrinks the population of available labor and forces owners of capital to increase wages to a rate that allows more children to survive and the population of workers to increase. In order to attain its 'natural' price and fulfill its role in wealth production, the children of workers must be allowed to live or die according to the needs of the owners of wealth.

On close inspection, Smith's account of wealth production in a commercial society allows little possibility for upward mobility, since each class or rank performs a particular structured role. Despite this, he *doesn't* racialize these different ranks as other thinkers did. In fact, Smith argues that placement in these classes does not much reflect some underlying difference in talent and effort among individuals or groups, though it may turn on access to education. He stresses, instead, that the different position of individuals in society, including, for example, between a philosopher and a street porter, are more the results of the emerging *division of labor*, than its cause. Even the differences in education that separate individuals are a product of the more extensive division of labor possible in a commercial society (Smith 1976, Book I, chapter i; see also Fleischacker 2004, 64–65). Thus, for Smith, we do not so much place ourselves or achieve our position in society by our merit. Rather, we are shaped to assume a rank and serve a role in a division of labor that makes expanded wealth production possible.

Marx is heir to Smith – though his stark portrait of capitalism is much better known than Smith's. Marx's account of a society is riven by class. For workers, capitalism involves the most complete subordination, the deepest exploitation, and the most abject misery known to history (Marx 1973, 452–4, 488, 612–3; 1977, 272, 291–92). Less well appreciated is that Marx also follows Smith in giving capitalism a transformational historical role (Blaney and Inayatullah 2010, chapter 5). The forces unleashed by capitalism will destroy all the *fixed* relations of earlier societies: capitalism undercuts inflexible social hierarchies, mobilizes inert and immobile populations, and enlivens stagnant productive forces.

For Marx, the major point of comparison was European feudalism (Marx and Engels 1970, 43–46; Marx 1973, 471–516). He insists that capitalism produces and requires *six* qualities that distinguish the modern era. Capitalism, in principle, puts equality in the place of fixed status differences (Marx 1973, 156, 241–243, 325, 496; 1977, 270, 280). Now all face each other as *formally equal property owners* in relations of exchange. This newfound equality as property owners supports the *freedom* to alter one's social position by allowing individuals to enter into new lines of production and wider circuits of exchange. Relative to traditional society's restricted social role in group, family, or village life, capitalism supports *individuality* by allowing movement from the village or the transformation of village social relations.

As cause and consequence of these three changes, capitalism produces unprecedented levels of *social wealth*. Human productive capacities are transformed where capitalists use their social power to bring vast armies of workers together with modern science and more efficient machines. Building this material infrastructure for wealth production makes possible and depends on humans *overcoming nature's indifference*. Transforming nature so that it gives up its capacities for human use also changes humans (Marx 1973, 152, 158, 325, 611, 704; 1977, chapters 14 and 15). It transforms the level and quality of our needs and the new scale of industrial production to meet those needs triggers a change in our very nature: we become more *self-consciously aware* of what it means to be humans living and producing together. Capitalism also brings humans closer together, hastening into contact the various cultures on our planet (Marx and Engels 1970, 72–78; 1978). And it generates that self-consciousness of humanity by providing some people the time and the means to study the human condition (see Bill Warren 1981, chapter 2).

We might think that bringing the planet together is no more than breaking down barriers, like, say, 'Chinese walls', to global communication and exchange (Marx and Engels 1978, 474–7). But Marx (1977, Part 8) is clear that capitalism extends itself across the globe by destroying pre-capitalist ways of life. He delivers his judgment upon the backwardness of non-European ways of life with the vehemence common to Kant and Hegel and colonial powers themselves. Marx reports that England's destruction of Indian crafts was producing 'the only *social* revolution ever heard of in Asia' (Marx 2001a, 65). In a highly racialized account, Asia offers examples only of despotism, superstition, cruelty, and, worst of all perhaps, a stagnation that left human beings subject to nature's unchanged paltriness. Through English colonialism,

India is unified, subject to uniform rule, including modern property rights, and connected internally and globally by the telegraph, the railway and the steamship. Indians are brought into the modern world via education and the inculcation of a scientific outlook (2001a 65–66; 2001b, 70–71). Though suffering no illusions about colonial violence and cruelty, Marx (2001b, 73–75) nevertheless believes that it provides the spark that brings backward peoples into the theatre of human history. Marx, unlike Hegel, exhibits a sense of lament and loss, but his evaluation of the historical role of capitalism trumps such concerns.

Marx provides no remedy for the violence and subjugation wrought by capitalism, except in the future. The energies of capitalism require exploiting workers and this exploitation must be endured until capitalism has prepared the world for a post-capitalist future. The burden of this necessary preparation of material conditions and human consciousness fall upon people across the globe: workers, perhaps implicitly racialized as white or treated as of a lesser European stock, who already perform their subordinate role in capitalist production, and those racialized and colonized figures that must still be subsumed fully into capital's logic. In this respect, capitalism seems largely indifferent to culture and race. All must be subjected in the present for a genuine human history to be born.

Both Smith and Marx warn us that capitalism's great historical purposes of wealth creation and the transformation of human society require deeper costs than economists usually admit. These greatest of our political economists also cast doubt on the idea that modern inequalities bear a clear and close relationship to merit or that they can be characterized simply as a product of voluntary market exchanges, mediated by rule of law within a framework of legal equality. Rather, the operation and extension of capitalism depends on compulsion, whether by the threat of physical and social deprivation enforced by the market or by the whip and sword of colonization. We might wonder how we continue to sustain the idea of a virtuous link between freedom, merit, and inequality.

Global inequality, IR, and the racialization of units

We begin this section with two stories. The first comes from Jeffrey Sachs' *The End of Poverty* (2005), a work he hopes will inspire richer societies to come to the aid of those that have fallen behind. His story is that once, a few centuries ago, all the countries of the world lived in roughly the same level of poverty. But with the rise of capitalism in certain parts of Europe, these few European areas pulled away from all other countries because they were able to harness human labor and knowledge to the project of creating wealth. Smith, Hegel, and Marx would agree. We see clearly, Sachs suggests, that different degrees of success in implementing capitalist wealth production result in unequal levels of development that explain today's differential levels of national incomes and rates of poverty. The conclusion is right in front of our noses. We can increase incomes and reduce poverty by extending market competition to the entire globe. But poverty will shrink only if we give a small boost to those at the bottom who otherwise would be unable to successfully enter markets. Sachs recognizes that inequalities, perhaps even vast inequalities, are justified only when all have a genuine opportunity to enter market competition. Otherwise, it would hardly seem fair. The contours of Sachs' story are familiar. We hear it again and again in beginning courses in economics and from figures traveling in the most respected policy circles.

The second story comes from books like L.S. Stavrianos's *Global Rift* (1981), Eric Wolf's *Europe and the People without History* (1982), and Alexander Anievas and Kerem Nişancioğlu's *How the West Came to Rule: The Geopolitical Origins of Capitalism* (2015). These authors organize the narrative differently. Stavrianos (1981, 23, 26) rejects the idea that we can explain development from 'individual national viewpoints' since the prospects for *development* and systematic *underdevelopment* of regions have been conditioned by being 'tightly integrated' as 'components of the international market economy'. Wolf (1982, 3, 18) describes a world not of autonomous and self-creating units, but of global processes interconnected into a 'totality'. A 'methodological internalism', that constructs a story of the 'autonomous and endogenous "rise of the West"' ignores, as Anievas and Nişancioğlu (2015, 4–5) show, the 'intersocietal' connection and processes involved in creating the modern world.

Though their accounts vary in detail, they converge in describing the terrain of the fourteenth to sixteenth centuries as politically, culturally, and economically wildly variegated, a feature of our past Sachs ignores. In fact, this is a story not so much of countries, as we would now think of them and Sachs would have it, but of kingdoms, empires, city-states, towns, and villages. Political borders are porous and effective governance disappears the further one moves from the seat of rule. And rulers are usually satisfied with tribute, leaving localized authority structures and economic practices in place. It is difficult to identify any political or social space comparable to today's nation-states that could be treated as developing (or not).

Nor does the world exist in some *initial state* of poverty. Some old empires in Asia are quite advanced technologically, combining extensive manufacturing and highly productive agriculture to produce levels of income and wealth not seen in Western Europe until at least the eighteenth century. The empires of pre-colonial America are as developed as the European invaders, but for firearms and resistance to disease. Various African kingdoms display levels of development comparable to Europe before the depredations of the slave trade. In short, some regions and localities are richer and some poorer, peoples operating with different technologies and living in quite varied social systems and cultural beliefs, but there is no initial state of poverty to be found. And, with only a few exceptions, these localities and regions are not isolated; they are connected by flows of goods, people, and ideas that bring new influences, gradually altering existing social practices.

But nothing ties their fates together like the forces unleashed by European colonization and the spread of capitalism. Rulers are displaced by joint-stock companies and new colonial governors. The tight connections of agricultural production to local needs and purposes are dismantled, local land and labor now harnessed to the needs of the colonial power. Existing industries that served local needs and fed into circuits of long-distance trade are destroyed to clear the way for colonial monopolies that help fuel industrial development in the colonial centers. Lands seized and old livelihoods destroyed, people are exposed to starvation and disease, perhaps enslaved or otherwise coerced into toiling long hours on plantations, producing goods not destined for their stomachs, or building roads to move those goods to Europe. And even where put to work by capitalists as free labor, the masses of the world's workers find themselves locked into a subordinate position in this new capitalist world. The state of 'initial' poverty and eventual uneven development with which Sachs begins his book has its own story told by Stavrianos, Wolf, and Anievas and Nişancioğlu: it is product of colonialism and the violent spread of capitalism.

We might not be surprised that books such as these are not to be found alongside Sachs' on the shelves of the World Bank's bookstore. Nor would we expect such authors to be invited to share the dais with Sachs for a discussion of global development policy. But we can ask ourselves why the stories told by Stavrianos, Wolf, and Anievas and Nişancioğlu are not central to our discussions. Why does our official account of global inequality not begin with colonialism? Why does it begin with the idea of countries in an equal state of poverty that then develop unevenly according to their own resources and efforts?

We have two answers that draw on the work done in earlier sections. The first answer parallels our discussion in the first section, where inequality is understood and justified as a consequence of differences in individual talents and efforts. Our discussion here starts, as does the field of International Relations (IR), with *states as the units*. We show how the idea that global inequality reflects the merit of states as individuated units excludes from view the history of violence and the *structured social relationships* that produce and sustain global inequalities.

IR organizes the world as does a conventional map. Except for the poles, maps divide land areas into differently colored and bounded spaces identified by the name of a state. When reading a map, we take these boundaries to mean that each state is independent and legally governs the territory and the population contained within its borders and acts on behalf of that population in relations with other states. This is equivalent to saying that states are sovereign and that the world can be thought of as an international society of independent states.

This claim is at once ethical and explanatory. As the site of political community and the good life, a positive value is placed on the state's ability and freedom to act – to exercise sovereignty. The state-level is also privileged as the 'unit of analysis' for a science of IR. Since the state is treated as *the* locus of action and traits, explanation proceeds *from* the units *to* the outcomes of their interactions. Even if the outcomes of unit-level interaction may constrain actors in some fashion or appear as a structure that conditions the individual actors, explanatory or causal emphasis is placed on the actions or traits of the units as opposed to the determining effects of the structuring of the whole. We look at the world *as if* we can understand it primarily from 'below' unit-level actions and traits, erasing the possibility of a perspective from above – from the logic of the system as a whole (Singer 1961, 80–81).

We can see how this explanatory privileging works when we think of states as economic units – as *national economies*. What the state's population produces for itself is supplemented by exchanging some of its goods in international markets for the goods produced by other countries that it cannot produce for itself. In this way, international trade comes to be seen as an extension or outcome of the actions of the national unit. Though seen as an interaction of independent units, international trade does constrain and condition the units themselves. International trade is a market competition that differentially rewards actors for their varying contributions, leading countries to choose to specialize in certain efforts or talents. The national economy will gradually be restructured to favor the production of goods that it is relatively efficient in producing, creating a different set of capacities and traits that are the basis for future action and future rewards. Markets might be global but the rule of unequal outcomes still would be 'you get according to what you produce'. And because all outcomes are explained as the result of the free interactions of independent, sovereign units, global inequality is taken as *evidence of* the underlying inequality of countries' contributions to the international market.

So, we get the great modern story of European advance, which follows, in some respects at least, the accounts of Smith and Marx. Europe's great wealth results from its internal traits: rule of law, legal equality, property rights, free markets, scientific and technological innovation, and individual initiative. That the industrial revolution begins in Europe is proof of the superiority of its institutions and efforts. Economic development 'takes-off' first in European countries, making them the most competitive actors and they garner rewards proportional to their superior contributions. Inversely, the presence of poverty and underdevelopment in the Third World reflects these societies' inability or unwillingness to establish the institutions, the inventiveness, and the drive necessary to earn much in the way of rewards from the international market. To the extent that we are concerned about the social consequences of this failure to compete, we might call for interventions from the industrialized countries or international institutions to help remake the internal traits of Third World countries. Or, we might rely on the voluntary offices of civil society who travel in missions to teach others how to change and adjust their cultures and institutions.

Some things prominent for Smith, Hegel, and Marx are missing in this stylized but recognizable account. There is no colonial violence and no capitalist division of labor that structures the role of actors in wealth production. Though the advent of the modern age may herald an international society of states, arguably realized only with decolonization, it has also heralded colonialism and the spread of capitalism, binding the world into global system of production and exchange. We have here more than just an international society of independent states. We have a *global society*: a giant productive enterprise, each element – workers, occupational groups, capitalists, industrial sectors, regions, or states – part of an overall system. Each part is functionally differentiated and subordinated to a global production process and to the general purpose of producing wealth. If so, we may say that in a global division of labor wealth creation and wealth acquisition occurs independently of the will of its elements. It makes no sense, then, to give unit-level traits and actions such explanatory or causal privilege. The competition wasn't and isn't fair. Outcomes that were rigged by violence and inequalities are not only cumulative but also structural, so those at the bottom can hardly expect to improve their position.

An IR committed to unit-level explanations obstructs our ability to see this unfairness and mutes our ability to call it an injustice. It cannot read global inequality any other way than as reflecting underlying differences, as individual failures to compete. Nor can it allow itself to understand inequality in another way. The story of autonomous development seems to vindicate the sense that the West's wealth and power, and our own relative comfort and position, resulted from a (fair) market competition. It also offers consolation and hope to those who have fallen behind that they, with a little help, also might develop on their own.

A second answer harkens back to Kant and Hegel. Recalling that discussion, we cannot be confident that bringing colonial violence and domination back into view challenges the legitimacy of global inequality for most people. For Kant and Hegel, history dispenses its judgment upon various races' merits or historical contributions though violence, conquest, and colonial domination. To fall prey to those who lead history is simply evidence of a limited ability to master nature and, therefore, being naturally fitted to a subordinate role, or even extinction. Here, the unit-level traits of a country or people are racialized. As we mentioned, for Western consciousness, religious or cultural differences that were initially seen as remedied by conversion, eventually hardened into differences that were seen as 'indelible and insurmountable'. So also, protracted inequalities in development outcomes have come to be seen as reflecting a naturally unequal grading of Western and non-Western peoples.

The non-West's failure to keep up with the West serves as 'evidence' that reveals and confirms an underlying hierarchy of capacities and potentialities. The idea of a civilizational hierarchy merely names this underlying differential in the capacity of the autonomous units. Given the causal privileging of individual traits and efforts that rules out thinking, this hierarchy can only re-enforce the continuing 'evidence' of the relative failure of the non-West to develop or live up to civilized standards of governance. And it is not such a great leap from seeing global inequality as reflecting unit-level traits and actions to seeing these differences as natural deficiencies. This racializing move is built into the very methods by which we study global political economy.

Conclusion

The complicated texture of modern consciousness shapes not only what inequalities we can accept as justified, but also which accounts of inequality we are allowed to take seriously. Thus inequalities are explained and justified as the results of differences in merit, regardless of the violence that shaped their creation and however much they are shaped by structures over which individuals have little control. It is individual differences in traits and in effort that do all the ethical and explanatory work. Given the limited terrain of our thinking, moderns are continually tempted to explain inequalities in income and wealth as the result of the 'indelible and insurmountable' deficiencies of some groups.

To crystallize the issue of inequality, we might want to draw a parallel with the predicament of individuals within a less than fully committed welfare state. How are we to regard the individual who cannot meet her own needs within capitalist society? Do we emphasize the individual's common humanity? If so, do we want to change the rules of the market or find some other way to protect individuals from the harsh indifference of competitive markets? Or, do we retain competitive market pressure thinking that it is important to push individuals into productive competition even at the cost of sacrificing the social safety net and causing biological and social death?

This predicament is central to how we think of Third World states. In so far as Third World states are assigned the status of formal sovereign entities, they are held responsible for creating their own wealth through their own resources. This expectation is meant to mirror all those things that First World states are supposed to have done to achieve their own position. However, no state is ever strictly sovereign. Once we consider the historical context, states are also functionally and hierarchically differentiated as colonizer and colonized, developed and underdeveloped.

If we want to overcome this tension, we seem to have two options: emphasize sovereignty and insist that Third World states sink or swim on their own. Or, emphasize the overlap between states and all peoples' structural participation in the global economy. The latter option moves us towards establishing democratic principles of wealth acquisition and distribution.

Box 7.1: Story box

Simran Khosla uses the *CIA World Factbook* to ascertain every country's highest valued export, that is, the commodity that the country sells on the global market that brings in the most money. Khosla presents the material visually in a set of maps (http://thumbnails.visually.netdna-cdn.com/world-commodities-map_536bebb20436a.png).

What stories do these maps tell? We read them to say that some 'countries' dominate in the production and export of 'capital goods' as well as 'Machinery, Equipment, chemicals, electrical and optical equipment'. Meanwhile, other countries' most valued source of income is derived from minerals, agricultural products, oil, textiles, apparel, and semiconductors.

Box 7.2: Key points

1. Contemporary thinking justifies global inequality by linking market outcomes to individual effort and individual skill.
2. Major Western thinkers such as Kant, Hegel, Smith, and Marx rationalize inequality by making racialized arguments.
3. Adam Smith and Karl Marx produced incisive critiques of how capitalism produces inequality. Nevertheless, this critique is coupled with their support of capitalism's progressive historical role. This historical role is used to explain and validate Western society's colonial violence.
4. Contemporary International Relations theory shows a clear preference for unit-level analysis over a more system-level investigation. This preference hides Western colonial violence. It also excuses inequality by stressing the connection between individual effort/skill and market reward.

The maps indicate that, on the whole, the world is divided into two types of 'countries': those that produce knowledge intensive goods at the cutting edge of the newest technology; and those that are left, as the Bible says, to be the 'hewers of wood and drawers of water' (Joshua 9:23). The dynamic and knowledge rich economies are, unsurprisingly, the United States, Canada, most of Europe, China, and Japan. The 'countries' that provide the raw materials are from Central and South America (with Brazil as the exception), Asia (with, as noted, China and Japan as the exceptions), the Middle East (with Israel as the exception) and Africa (with no exceptions). In broad brush strokes, there is a global rift between the First World and the Third World; the former are wealthy and dynamic while the latter are subordinate and relatively poor.

If we now examine the top exports of a sample of 'countries' we see the following:[1]

Cuba: petroleum, nickel, medical products, sugar, tobacco, fish, citrus, coffee
Guatemala: sugar, coffee, petroleum, apparel, bananas, fruits and vegetables, cardamom, manufacturing products, precious stones and metals, electricity
Chile: copper, fruit, fish products, paper and pulp, chemicals, wine
Malaysia: semiconductors and electronic equipment, palm oil, petroleum and liquefied natural gas, wood and wood products, palm oil, rubber, textiles, chemicals, solar panels
Iran: petroleum 80 percent, chemical and petrochemical products, fruits and nuts, carpets, cement, ore
Gambia: peanut products, fish, cotton lint, palm kernels

Congo (Democratic Republic of): diamonds, copper, gold, cobalt, wood products, crude oil, coffee

USA: capital goods (transistors, aircraft, motor vehicle parts, computers, telecommunications equipment) 49.0 percent, industrial supplies (organic chemicals) 26.8 percent, consumer goods (automobiles, medicines) 15.0 percent, agricultural products (soybeans, fruit, corn) 9.2 percent (2008 est.)

This sample substantiates our claims about the division of the world. Of course, the exceptions – Brazil, China, Japan, and Israel – need explanation. These, as well as others (e.g. why a European country – Portugal – primarily exports agricultural goods) complicate the story. Nevertheless, we were astounded by the stickiness of historical patterns when we recognized that the overwhelming majority of Third World locales produce the same products that their colonizers cultivated and extracted – often, hundreds of years ago.

Note

1 *Source*: CIA Factbook; Exports – commodities (%). ('This entry provides a listing of the highest valued exported products; it sometimes includes the percentage of the total dollar value') www.cia.gov/library/publications/the-world-factbook/docs/notesanddefs.html

Suggested readings

Isaac Kraminick short essay, 'Equal opportunity and the race of life', nicely summarizes the argument about merit.

Thomas Pogge's *World Poverty and Human Rights*, especially chapters 1 and 8, explores the central ethical and political justifications for redressing global inequality.

George Fredrickson's *Racism: A Short History*, is an excellent introduction to the debates about the emergence and character of racism.

Though we recommend students go back to original sources in the cases of Smith and Marx, the discussions of Kant and Hegel by Robert Bernasconi and Michael Hoffheimer do justice to their works and bring together texts difficult for students to locate.

Any one of the books by Anievas and Nişancioğlu, Wolf, or Stavrianos would expose students to the story of global interconnections as a counterpoint to claims of separate or independent development.

Bibliography

Anievas, A. and Nişancioğlu, K. (2015). *How the West came to rule: The geopolitical origins of capitalism*. London: Pluto Press.

Bernasconi, R. (2000). With what must the philosophy of world history begin? On the racial basis of Hegel's Eurocentrism. *Nineteenth-Century Contexts*, 22, 171–201.

Bernansco003, R. (2002). Kant as an unfamiliar source of racism. In J.K. Ward and T.L. Lott (Eds.). *Philosophers on race: Critical essays* (pp. 145–66). New York: Blackwell.

Berry, C. (1997). *Social theory of the Scottish enlightenment*. Edinburgh: University of Edinburgh Press.

Bhambra, G.K. (2010). Historical sociology, international relations and connected histories. *Cambridge Review of International Affairs, 23*, 127–143.

Blaney, D.L. and Inayatullah, N. (2010). *Savage economics: Wealth, poverty, and the temporal walls of capitalism*. London: Routledge.

CIA Factbook, www.cia.gov/library/publications/the-world-factbook/docs/note-sanddefs.html accessed, July 30, 2017.

Fleischacker, S. (2004). *A short history of distributive justice*. Cambridge, MA: Harvard University Press.

Fredrickson, G.M. (2002). *Racism: A short history*. Princeton: Princeton University Press.

Friedman, M. (1962). *Capitalism and freedom*. Chicago: University of Chicago Press.

Hanke, L. (1959). *Aristotle and the American Indians: A study in race prejudice in the modern world*. London: Hollis and Carter.

Hayek, F. (1960). *The constitution of liberty*. Chicago: University of Chicago Press.

Hayek, F. (1967). *Prices and production*. New York: Augustus M. Kelley.

Hayek, F. (1976). *Law, legislation, and liberty. Volume 2: The mirage of social justice*. Chicago: University of Chicago Press.

Hegel, G.W.F. (1953). *Reason in history: A general introduction to the philosophy of history*. New York: Bobbs-Merill.

Hegel, G.W.F. (1975). *Lectures in the philosophy of world history*. Cambridge: Cambridge University Press.

Hegel, G.W.F. (1991). *Elements of the philosophy of right*. Cambridge: Cambridge University Press.

Hoffheimer, M. (1993). Does Hegel justify slavery. *The Owl of Minerva*, 25, 118–119.

Hoffheimer, M. (2001). Hegel, race, and genocide. *The Southern Journal of Philosophy*, XXXIX: 35–62.

Inayatullah, N. and Blaney, D.L. (2004). *International relations and the problem of difference*. New York: Routledge.

Khosla, S. http://thumbnails.visually.netdna-cdn.com/world-commodities-map_536bebb20436a.png; and, www.pri.org/stories/2014-05-14/map-shows-which-export-makes-your-country-most-money Both accessed, July 30, 2017.

Kraminick, I. (1981). Equal opportunity and the race of life. *Dissent, 28*, 178–187.

Marx, K. and Engels, F. (1970). *The German ideology, part one*, edited by C.J. Arthur. New York: International Publishers.

Marx, K. (1973). *Grundrisse: foundations of the critique of political economy*. New York: Vintage.

Marx, K. (1977). *Capital: A critique of political economy. Volume I*. New York: Vintage.

Marx, K. (2001a) British rule in India. In A. Ahmad (Ed.). *On the national and colonial questions: Selected writings* (pp. 61–66). New Delhi: Left Word Book.

Marx, K. (2001b). The future results of the British rule in India. In A. Ahmad (Ed.). *On the national and colonial questions*. (pp. 70–75). New Delhi: Left Word Book.

Marx, K. and Engels, F. (1978). The manifesto of the communist party. In R.C. Tucker (Ed.). *The Marx-Engels reader* (2nd edition) (pp. 469–500). New York: W.W. Norton.

Montag, W. (2005). Necro-economics: Adam Smith and death in the life of the universal. *Radical Philosophy*, 134, 7–17.

Nozick, R. (1974). *Anarchy, state and utopia*. New York: Basic Books.

Pogge, T. (2002). *World poverty and human rights*. Cambridge: Polity.

Sachs, J. (2005). *The end of poverty: How we can make it happen in our lifetime*. New York: Penguin.

Serequeberhan, T. (1989). The idea of colonialism in Hegel's philosophy of right. *International Philosophical Quarterly*, XXIX: 301–318.

Serequeberhan, T. (1996). Eurocentrism in philosophy: The case of Immanuel Kant. *The Philosophical Forum*, 27, 333–356.

Singer, D.J. (1961). The levels of analysis problem in International Relations. *World Politics*, 14, 77–92.

Smith, A. (1976). *An inquiry into the nature and causes of the wealth of nations.* Chicago: University of Chicago Press.

Stavrianos, L. S. (1981). *Global rift: The third world comes of age.* New York: William Morrow.

Todorov, T. (1984). *The conquest of America: The question of the other.* New York: Harper and Row.

Warren, B. (1981). *Imperialism: pioneer of capitalism.* New York: Verso.

Wolf, E.R. (1982). *Europe and the people without history.* Berkeley: University of California Press.

8 Discourses of conquest and resistance

International Relations and Anishinaabe diplomacy

Hayden King

Introduction	135
The clash of Western civilizations	135
Orthodox IR's theoretical and practical exclusions	139
Anishinaabek international politics	141
Conclusion	150

Introduction

The story that unfolds in this chapter is one of Indigenous resistance. It is a counter-narrative to the one most students of International Relations (and political science generally) have been told throughout their training and really throughout their lives in places like Canada or the United States. The history of our relationship, as Indigenous people and non-Indigenous newcomers, has fundamentally been about inter-national politics, resistance and domination, clashing ontological and epistemological traditions. And yet it has received limited attention in the discipline of International Relations (IR). Indeed, today Indigenous nations have much to say about global politics, political community, power, war and peace, but these perspectives do not appear in our texts or classrooms. Attempting to address this puzzle, this chapter proceeds in two parts. The first begins by explaining IR's erasure of both contemporary settler colonialism and Indigenous politics, reaching back to first contact through popular culture narratives. The second part re-inserts Indigenous peoples into the disciplinary landscape and articulates an Indigenous – and specifically Anishinaabe – theory of inter-national politics by focusing on three core concepts to the study of IR: the state, sovereignty and anarchy. Considering these parts together, students will have the opportunity to critically reflect on IR's exclusions, and creatively imagine how to re-engage with Indigenous ideas on productive terms.

The clash of Western civilizations

In the sub-field of International Relations, the epistemological violence towards Indigenous peoples is often via exclusion. Absent from orthodox explanations of

global politics or prescriptions of peace, it appears infrequently in the vast majority of the critical variant of the discipline espousing alternative visions of global
order. Generally, there is simply a void of Indigenous presence, thought or action.
This misrepresentation and exclusion is a widespread phenomenon dating back
to some popular fifteenth- and sixteenth-century accounts of transatlantic contact. In order to understand this process, a brief chronology of this continuity is
required before considering who and what Indigenous peoples really are.

The question at the heart of the inquiry here, how to explain Indigenous
misrepresentation and erasure from IR, is actually common across many areas
of public discourse in North America. Whether the Washington Redskins or
Cleveland Indians logos, the endurance of the Indian in the Western film genre,
popular Indian Squaw Halloween costumes, and so on, students should ask why
these clearly offensive images are still acceptable and celebrated. While many
other communities suffer all manner of representation issues, Indigenous peoples are singled out as acceptable for public ridicule, despite very visible protests.
The answer to this question is rooted in some of the first images and descriptions of contact between Europeans and Indigenous peoples. Consider the
depictions of Columbus encountering the Taino and Arawaks or Champlain
and the Algonquin and Haudenosaunee. What do viewers see? The central,
noble figure of civilization surrounded by savages. This is the 'origin story' for
all that would follow. This trope, which emerged at various points in the early
contact relationship, demonstrates an important point about the continuity of
the misrepresentation of Indigenous peoples generally but also specific to IR.

A core and enduring theme in early accounts by European explorers is
the Indian appetite for human flesh. While the narratives are too many to
include here, Hans Staden's *True History: An Account of Cannibal Captivity
in Brazil* (1557) merits attention as the archetypal account. The *True History*
has numerous translations from the original German, multiple film adapta-
tions, works of analysis, even a children's book version (Jaurequi, 2010). The
account begins with Staden's capture by the Tupi, and follows his experiences
in the community as they live, work, and eat fingers and toes. Staden himself
was on the menu repeatedly only to escape by convincing the Chief he was
an emissary of God (i.e. magical). Staden writes that his predictions of the
future and manipulation of weather patterns convinced his captors to spare
him (Duffy and Metcalf 2011). Here is another dimension on travelogues: the
protagonist's ability to overcome their cannibal foes with their intelligence.
This is effectively an early incarnation of superiority discourse, the endurance
of which, with Indigenous peoples as the foil, is so prolific you can find it in
the most popular movie franchise in history. In *Star Wars: Return of the Jedi*,
just as the chanting, drumming Ewoks prepare to roast Hans Solo and Luke
Skywalker, they are tricked into believing C-3PO is God. And of course, they
then untie their captives, accept the newcomers' authority, and willingly join
in their war. While George Lucas is a self-conscious storyteller and Staden's
accounts have never been verified, the resulting consequences have been tremendously harmful.

There are a variety of explanations for these false narratives, wrapped up in the harms perpetuated by them. In his expansive account of the evolution of European legal orders in North America, Robert Williams (1990) describes the techniques of justification for the imposition of colonial laws onto Indigenous laws as 'discourses of conquest'. These are self-serving narratives designed to invalidate Indigenous laws and governance and thus create the appearance of a natural and necessary colonial expansion. In other words, crafting Indigenous inferiority through words and images were part and parcel of the effort to legitimize colonization. The discourses were so saturated they had, and continue to have, multiple sources. Missionaries, a large source of travelogues, would have been seeking to justify their own existence (without savages, who would Missionaries civilize?). Likewise, it was easier for merchants to legitimize their plunder if the previous owners of wealth were somehow unable to conceive of ownership. A more modern but nonetheless insidious articulation can be found in the games children play, like cowboys and Indians, or the Western film genre. Marshall Beier (2005, 14) writes that these iconic images 'valorized the violences of colonialism and, more particularly, each was allegorical in the sense that it rendered colonial conquest as natural, inevitable and desirable'. These are the 'hegemonic narratives of the colonial encounter'.

This explanation allowed people to observe Indigenous societies and see merely the primitive objects of their colonial inter-subjectivity that had been reinforced since first contact. Narratives and subsequent conclusions would be repeated with every new wave of settlers, effectively self-perpetuating the discourses of conquest, whether intentional or not, and spawning a racism, which has endured through time in legislation, policy, academia, and popular culture and caused untold subsequent harm to Indigenous peoples. Reflecting on the processes of colonization it becomes apparent that these distortions go beyond self-serving stories. Discourses of conquest are actually integral elements to settler colonization, and by extension, to international politics.

Settler colonialism and the application of conquest discourses

While there is not enough space in this chapter to describe the long and complex history of Indigenous–settler relations from the era of contact, to trade and reciprocity, to dispossession and colonization, students of IR are often denied an understanding of the process of settler colonization as a concept. The more commonly deployed term of colonization or colonialism does not describe well the experience of Indigenous people in North America or, for that matter, other settler British colonies such as New Zealand, Australia, and the United States. Traditional theories of colonization have generally asserted that imperial powers arrive, they exploit the land, resources and labor for as long as possible and then when administration of the colonies becomes more expensive than the wealth extracted, or colonizers are physically removed, colonization ends. The process of decolonization begins when the former colonial power leaves (Veracini, 2010; Hixson, 2013). Such was certainly the case in significant parts of Africa and Asia in the mid-twentieth century when European colonial powers withdrew from their former colonies, often only after years of revolt from the colonized. As a result, the immediate post-World War II period saw the creation of many newly independent states out of the ashes of European imperialism. Of course, while there are many post-colonial writers who insist that a form of economic colonization endured long after the war, Edward Said (1993, 9) had remarked that, 'in our time, direct colonialism has largely ended'.

The experiences of Indigenous peoples in North America, however, did not follow a similar contact-exploitation-colonization-decolonization trajectory (the debate about the efficacy of decolonization aside). Perhaps colonization in the Western Hemisphere initially followed the model, as the first European settlements in North America were set in motion by entities like the fur-seeking Hudson's Bay Company and the tobacco exporting Virginia Company. But the key difference in the North American context is that colonizers never left. While methods and focus of extraction have changed over time, the colonial presence has endured and multiplied. This is a reflection of the inadequacy of discussions of colonialism in places like North America, where it is ongoing. Commenting on the permanence of colonialism in contexts such as ours, Patrick Wolfe (2006) describes *settler* colonialism as a structural and permanent phenomenon, as opposed to merely an event or era. Resources and labor are not sufficient in this context. Land and territory are the overriding desire as settlement and long-term resource exploitation are the fundamental motivations of settler colonialism. In this pursuit, Indigenous political economies present an obstacle and must be liquidated, replaced with regimes that facilitate a different, contrasting type of economic activity. For Wolfe (2006, 388) this '*logic of elimination*' is undertaken violently or through assimilation, the forced adoption of children, and the breaking down of collective Aboriginal title into fee simple private lands ripe for the selling.

These processes are apparent to the casual observer of Indigenous–state relations in the North American context. There have been attempts of genocide via violence, forced removal, the removal of Indigenous children from communities to be placed in boarding schools, the legislative assaults on Indigenous culture and governance, and most recently the attempts to reconcile pre-existing Indigenous sovereignty with Crown sovereignty, as the Supreme Court of Canada puts it, through modern treaties and Aboriginal title extinguishment clauses, etc. Each of these efforts have part and parcel been reflected in the logic of elimination. From the euthanasia policy of the 1830s through the Gradual Civilization Acts of the 1850s and the 'protective' Indian Act still in place today, all premised on dispossessing and marginalizing Indigenous people (Miller, 2000). And while these are examples of settler state domestic policies, they must also be considered as the attempted domination of one distinct political community (or many, as is the case with Indigenous peoples) by imperial powers. International Relations makes these dynamics invisible, as demonstrated below.

A clearer case of the marginalization of Indigenous peoples from international politics on the basis of narratives of elimination comes from international law. The very first mention of Indigenous peoples in international law occurs soon after first contact as Spain and Portugal debate who gets to claim legitimate ownership of the new territories. The Pope intervened with the Doctrine of Discovery, effectively stating that if no Christians could be found, the first Christian nation coming upon these empty lands (*terra nullius*) could legally claim them (Henderson, 2008). From an international debate on the humanity of Indigenous peoples in 1555 organized by the King of Spain through to the first modern international rights mechanism on Indigenous peoples (UN Convention 107 in 1985), Indigenous peoples remained, at least in the realm of states and international institutions, those in need of civilization (Venne, 1999). This changed finally in 2007 with the adoption by the UN General Assembly of the Declaration on the Rights of Indigenous Peoples. This results in a five-hundred-year long struggle for accurate representation. This terse overview of Indigenous peoples in international law illustrates that conquest discourses are strategies in the logic of elimination, serving settler colonial interests. Narratives can have tangible consequences. This is true in the practice of international politics but also in our thinking and theorizing.

Orthodox IR's theoretical and practical exclusions

The above offers a partial explanation for the general lack of coverage and/or many instances of problematic engagements between Indigenous peoples and IR. Of course, a review of the discipline is also required. What kind of conclusions can we draw from IR's silence on Indigenous peoples beyond the discourse of conquest and/or settler amnesia? Of the brief and interspersed mentions of Indigenous peoples throughout the history of the discipline, references can be grouped by orthodox and critical interventions. In either case, Indigenous peoples and their philosophies are misrepresented, in the former, to justify core IR concepts such as anarchy and the state, and on the latter, to posit new and presumably better worlds or theories of the international, that ironically do not take Indigenous peoples seriously. Critical IR approaches such as post-modernism, Marxist traditions, and postcolonialism each perpetuate what Marshall Beier (2005) calls 'emancipatory violences'. The focus here, however, is on the harm perpetuated by IR's orthodox perspectives. The decision to focus on the 'traditional' theories of IR results from their dominance in the field. This led to the creation of foundational concepts in IR, which are primarily responsible for the erasure of Indigeneity from the literature. The survey below challenges those concepts in IR: the notions of the state, sovereignty, and anarchy.

The dominant unit of political analysis in IR is undoubtedly the state. While there is a vast literature critiquing the state as a normative political community and its effectiveness in promoting global peace, there is nonetheless a practical reality. The logic among orthodox IR's political theorists is relatively clear. Given anarchy as the guiding principle of political relationships between distinct peoples – that is, there are no overarching and compelling norms, rules or laws – international relations must then require elaborate, institutional arrangements to provide defense in a lawless world: strong states. These communities must also have 'government, sovereignty, territory, and population. Any unit which does not display these qualities…does not qualify' for participation in international relations. States are reified as the 'the supreme normative principle of the political organization of mankind' (Bull qtd in Shaw, 2002, 63). In other words, geographic containers with rigid borders, exclusive government powers, and exclusive sovereignty are necessary and desirable for political community among humans, and represent commonsense politics in an anarchic world. This reading of international law and society depicts an operation that first excluded Indigenous peoples from the legal conception of humanity by declaring them inhuman, primitive, and incapable of self-government and then used that construction of non-human savagery as the justification for the evolution of the state. Among philosophers, like Thomas Hobbes, Indigenous people were an example of the chaos that follows an anarchic world without mitigation (i.e. nasty, brutish, and short). This further alienated Indigenous peoples from European notions of community.

The state doubles-down on the exclusion of Indigenous peoples from humanity generally in ways at once straightforward and explicit, subversive and nuanced. This includes the concrete exercise of state power over Indigenous peoples, primarily through their absorption and assimilation. At the same time, the exclusive theorization of formal politics and governance through the historically specific, contingent body of the state is a discursive justification for marginalizing and excluding Indigenous peoples from international politics on their own terms. This exclusion is represented symbolically in European cartography, as Sa'ke'j James Youngblood Henderson (2008, 19) demonstrates in his deconstruction of the universally familiar geo-political map. He notes that 'humanity is viewed as a set of political states, with Europe at the center of the planet. The map does not reveal human or ecological diversity'. For Indigenous peoples who have never expressed political community as a geographic container with exclusive sovereignty historically or in contemporary times, the result is marginalization at best.

Beyond broad conceptual incompatibility over ideas as central to European political theories as the state and sovereignty, there are a number of related ideational and material challenges for Indigenous peoples in grappling with the state and sovereignty. With reference to Sham and Shohot (2012), six basic ways that Indigenous political communities contrast with the notion and realities of the state are elaborated. First, Indigenous governance pre-dates the emergence of states (of course, European states did not always exist either, but are themselves centuries-old contingent political development). Secondly, settler colonial states have crafted their images of states in opposition to Indigenous peoples, understood as threats or examples of undesirable difference. Thirdly, settler-states have only been possible through the theft of Indigenous territories, so that their existence is premised on the dispossession of Indigenous peoples. Fourthly, many Indigenous peoples reject the concept of a state to organize their societies, arguing that Indigenous self-determination implies radically different forms of governance. Fifthly, Indigenous territories often cross state borders, for example the Yanomami in Brazil and Venezuela or the Lakota, Salish, Blackfoot, and so on in Canada and the United States. Hence colonial states disrupt Indigenous governance and Indigenous political communities. Finally, settler colonialism has displaced peoples belonging to Indigenous nations throughout the globe, whether as the result of forcible relocations, dispossession through development 'projects' and processes or through adoptions into non-Indigenous families living outside of Indigenous homelands. Not only is the state antithetical to Indigenous peoples in its very constitution, but the existence of states then truncates Indigenous political relationships.

A final concept, and the one that underwrites strong states and exclusive sovereignty, is anarchy. While the various perspectives in orthodox IR vary on the precise nature of anarchy, if it can be manipulated or exploited, it nonetheless endures through realist and liberal thought. Constructivist thought, too, while suggesting that anarchy 'is what states make of it' (Wendt 1992, 391), nonetheless centers anarchy as a concept. All fundamentally return to the boundless power of states: the power to act under a condition of anarchy, to mitigate anarchy, or perhaps reject the notion altogether and construct something else. In other words, anarchy is used as an excuse for power politics. Indeed, anarchy permits and even requires states to restrain hostile entities (Indigenous peoples) in an anarchic world. Like the state and sovereignty, Indigenous conceptualizations are radical. While anarchy as a lack of coercive authority is desirable, anarchy permitting unbounded power is not. Indigenous people's international politics are not so arrogant as to assume humans, within or outside political communities, are not held accountable. There are indeed limits to action.

There is much to say about the isolation of Indigenous (and for that matter non-Indigenous racialized peoples) from the discipline of International Relations and the concepts that emerge from it. Interestingly the core foundational concepts, while divergent in content, share some similarities in scope. In other words, defining political communities, the nature of relationships between unique political communities and the limits (or lack thereof) on the exercise of power, are all of concern to Indigenous communities. This overview is not to dismiss outright the discipline and the practice of international politics, but to problematize and highlight the areas of incompatibility plus the links between IR and settler colonialism, and finally offer alternatives.

Anishinaabek international politics

Indigenous peoples have been practicing international politics long before the newcomers arrived. Settler colonialism came to dominate North America, and Indigenous peoples were reduced to novelty in the public imagination. Indeed, the great confederacies, conflicts, and peaceful resolutions to those conflicts were common phenomena among the Mi'kmaq, Haudenosaunee, Tsalagi,

Blackfeet, Dene, Salish, and so on. Diplomacy *via* treaties was a core feature of the relationship with Europeans when they arrived, and still structures that relationship. Moreover, Indigenous relationships with the land and neighboring communities today reflect a continuity of philosophy and practice of politics among distinct peoples and communities. In what follows, we isolate core values in the practice of Anishinaabe international politics through time (the Anishinaabe are described in detail below). The exercise, paired with the critique above, encourages students of IR to reflect on one Indigenous alternative to orthodox IR's vision of what politics can and should be. It considers Anishinaabe versions of the state, sovereignty and anarchy, but produces dramatically contrasting conclusions.

Odaenuah: a web of interconnected hearts

Anishinaabeg is a general term referring to the Indigenous individuals and communities of the Great Lakes and who share a language, culture, possess a common social-political history, similar legal orders, and economic activity. And yet, there is much that distinguishes those within this broad family. At the level of abstraction, the most general Anishinaabe are a handful of 'national' and or regional groups. The largest of these is the Ojibwe in the central Great Lakes, where there is also the Odawa and Pottawatomi to the east and west, respectively. These three groups are sometimes referred to as the Three Fires Confederacy (Benton-Banais, 1988). They occupy the intersection of Lakes Huron, Superior, and Michigan, and radiate outward into central and northwestern Ontario, and northern Michigan, Wisconsin, and Minnesota. To the west into Manitoba and Saskatchewan, the Anishinaabe are known as Saulteax, and in the east across Southern Ontario are the Chippewa (a colonial mischaracterization of Ojibwe) and Mississauga (who most closely resemble the Ojibwe). Into the Ottawa Valley, there are the Algonquin. And in northern Ontario, there are the related though largely distinct Mushkego, sometimes referred to as the Oji-Cree. Each of these political communities is tied loosely to a specific geographic area, and in that sense, conforms to a Euro-centric notion of political community (certainly reminiscent of a state). But closer consideration reveals much more nuance.

There have been Anishinaabe thinkers and leaders who have actually called for the creation of Indigenous states. In George Copway's infamous argument for assimilation, the vehicle through which that process could take hold would be an 'Indian state' (Ruoff and Smith, 2006). Even before Copway, the venerated Odawa leader Tecumseh tried to negotiate with the British for an Indian state west of the Great Lakes. This was the bargain struck for participation in the War of 1812 (Edmonds, 2006). Yet these examples are few and far between. In fact, there are no Anishinaabe thinkers calling for a state today. Instead, when we think and write about political community, and revitalizing political community, it is not the state we talk about, but the nation. Leanne Simpson (2011, 18–19) writes that, whether we are talking about self-determination or agency, it must be in a '*nation-based framework*'. Likewise, Dale Turner argues

Anishinaabeg (and Indigenous peoples generally) should be working towards 'defending the legal and political status of Indigenous nationhood'. This is in fact the contemporary discourse in the Canadian context: communities are called 'First Nations'. The regional political organization to which I belong is called the 'Anishinaabek Nation'. The Idle No More movement was simultaneously referred to as the 'Indigenous Nationhood Movement'. In fact, the current federal government in Canada is operating, at least nominally, on a 'nation-to-nation' basis with Indigenous partners.

So, it is with confusion that a review of Anishinaabe authors on the scope of political communities reveals uncertainty regarding the concept of the nation. Scott Lyons (2010, 115) writes that there has never been a 'nation' among the Anishinaabek, in fact, there is not even a 'word for nation in Ojibwemowin' (language of the Ojibwe). The very concept is European (and 'modern') and requires a host of related concepts (sovereignty, government, industry, etc.) that only came into indigenous conceptual lexicon through interaction with Europeans: 'what we now call an Indian nation was a modern invention born at the moment of treaty' (Lyons, 2012, 131). Gerald Vizenor (1984, 13) is likewise dismissive for some of the same reasons. For him, 'Anishinaabek' is merely a collective name referring to those speaking the same language, not 'an abstract concept of personal identities or national ideologies'. Vizenor (1993, 137) laments the construction of Anishinaabek tribes as cohesive 'nations' and sees the move as something akin to grotesque caricature implicated in settler colonialism: the 'political histories of the Anishinaabek were written in the language of those who invented the Indian, renamed tribes, allotted the land, divided ancestry by geometric degrees and categorized identity by colonial reservations'.

Heidi Stark and Michal Witgen separately offer an alternative of sorts. Indeed, the nation is constructed, they affirm, as all political communities are, but it was not forced upon Anishinaabek. As Stark (2012, 140) notes of the treaty-making era, 'some bands used (the notion of the nation) to their advantage, aligning their demands and presenting a unified front. Others sought separate treaties and refused to negotiate as one body'. Even earlier in Colonial New France, the French sought to 'constitute their native allies as nations, claim sovereignty over them as subjects, and incorporate their territory into the French empire' (Witgen 2007, 640). If these fictional nations could be absorbed, the French might convincingly construct a fictional empire using language that other Europeans could understand: sovereignty. For their part, the Anishinaabeg refused to simply fit into the parameters of a nation. They had a "capacity for transformation or shape-shifting" (Witgen, 2007, p. 646). This reveals a fluid and radically autonomous conception of the nation, one that underlies diplomacy, sovereignty and a theory of Anishinaabek politics generally and requires elaboration.

There are two metaphors to help explain this fluidity. Anthony Trueur (2010) describes our political communities as radiating from the heart outwards: 'ode' (the heart) is the center of the body. Odena (the village) is the center of the community, and doodem (the clan) is the center of spiritual (and sometimes economic) identity. Dewe'igan (the drum) is the center of the nation, or its heartbeat. Simpson (2011, 94) elaborates, interpreting Basil Johnson's use of Odaenuah to describe the nation as 'an interconnected web of hearts'. At any given time, in response to the nature of the situation, we might act at any of these radiating circles in the web – this is the shape-shifting Witgen describes. The second metaphor comes from Stark, who invokes the familiar fire metaphor. For her, communities are elemental but always changing, sometimes one inferno at other times smaller individual flames. In literal terms, sometimes we acted as a small grouping of families, usually in times of abundance and peace, and at other times expansive confederacies, like, of course, the Three Fires Confederacy (the Ojibwe, Odawa and Pottawatomi), or the vast treaty-making confederacies of the mid-1800s in Minnesota and Michigan. This fluidity is effectively a requirement because of the second core characteristic, autonomy.

In the early relationship between the French and the Innu, of the first to be welcomed into a community was Father La Juene, who remarked of his hosts' notions of autonomy that 'they ought by right of birth, to enjoy the liberty of wild ass colts, rendering no homage to anyone whatsoever, except when they like…they laugh at and make sport of their (leaders). All the authority of their chief is in his tongue's end; for he is powerful insofar as he is eloquent' (Sokolow, 2003, 210). In Indigenous society prior to settler colonialism, authority was based on effective oratory as opposed to coercion. A course of action had to be approved by those participating. There was no mechanism, for instance, to force individuals to fight in a conflict, unless they themselves chose to. This phenomenon was common among Anishinaabeg as well. As Basil Johnson writes of pre-contact Anishinaabeg:

> the sense of independence was…too deeply entrenched in the Anishinaabeg character to submit to a central government adherence to one set of laws as required by political and economic union. Nor did they feel that one community ought to submerge its wellbeing or commit its destiny to another. The individual must be free; so also his community. By having its own leaders, controlling the conduct of its own affairs, following customs of its own devisment, each community was free. No community dared presume to interfere in the affairs of another, even in times of war.
>
> (Johnson, 1976, 72)

In the contact era, this sense of independence was clear in numerous episodes, sometimes frustratingly so. The best example may be negotiations in the 24-Nations Belt (otherwise known as the Treaty of Fort Niagara), the Indigenous solemnization of the Royal Proclamation of 1763. Following the Seven Years' War (1757–1763) and British defeat of the French for colonial control of North America, a peace offering was made to First Nations west of the eastern English colonies. If the English sought new lands, they required the permission of the local Indigenous nations and a formal agreements would be created (i.e. a treaty).

Many Anishinaabe communities accepted this offer, but others refused, notably Pontiac, who continued to wage war for a subsequent two years (Parmenter, 1997). The Anishinaabeg were split. But this was not an uncommon phenomenon. During US expansion into Minnesota in the 1850s, some communities viewed collaboration with the Americans as an opportunity to increase their share of trade goods. This was at odds, of course, with many other communities who kept their distance and advocated isolation (Treuer, 2010).

How political communities acted in international politics has not been firm, predictable or even consistent. Rather, it is flexible and required to be so by desire for freedom. In the story of the emergence of the Three Fires Confederacy, the political alliance of the Ojibwe, Odawa and Pottawatomi, the 'nations' are referred to as brothers, born and raised together but often going their separate ways (Corbiere, 2013). Imagining the waxing and waning alliances of Anishinaabeg communities as a relationship of siblings brings into focus the desire for unity, when required, but also the inherent independence of siblings from each other. This reading indicates that the overarching concept structuring Anishinaabe politics, the nation, may not exist. Or rather, it exists on deeply contrasting terms than any approximation of a traditional IR conceptualization. This contrast is the result of a political community that is dynamic, defined by fluidity and layers of fluctuating autonomy.

Anishinaabe Akina: the border of everything, in unity

The standard greeting for Indigenous peoples across Canada is often 'Where are you from?' The same is true for Anishinaabeg, for people are bound to each other through relationships and, importantly, bound to the land. People are seeking each other out after many years of separation. The expected response is the community you come from. In Anishinaabem one would say: *aaniin, booozhoo, Biidwewidem n'diiznakaaz, migizi n'dodem, Gchi'mnissing n'donjibaa, Ojibwe ay Pottowatomi n'daaw.* The rough translation is 'Hello, my name is "He Who Comes Speaking", I of the Eagle Clan, the Great Sturgeon Island is where I am from. My nations are Ojibwe and Pottowatomi'. This information situates me within Anishinaabeg territory broadly, identifies my specific community, denotes my neighbors, highlights my relatives and obligations towards them, and finally from which branch of the Anishinaabeg family tree I come. There is a very clear relationship in this individual orientation to geography and even a sense of borders. On the surface, this appears to approximate an orthodox IR conception of sovereignty, especially paired with the principle of non-interference described above.

Yet, much like political communities, borders are very difficult to establish in concrete terms. They, too, shift. Or rather, they blur. There is evidence to indicate that clearly defined territories were important to Anishinaabeg during the post-contact treaty era. For instance, Darlene Johnson's (2006) research on clans and the Dish with One Spoon treaty indicates that there was a rigid border between clans and between the Anishinaabe and Haudenosaunee respectively, though this is an outlier in the literature. Meanwhile Alan Corbiere (2012) interprets squares on wampum belts as denoting territory. The nuance here is that in Anishinaabeg conceptualizations of territory – and jurisdiction over it – there could be a sharing relationship with diverse political communities. In some cases, we could sit, and/or lay, on one another's mats. This conceptualization of sovereignty as *inclusive* is most apparent in the history of post-contact Great Lakes treaty-making.

The first contact era treaties in what is now Canada took the shape of gift exchanges. In Migmagi, the baptism of Membertou was very likely considered a treaty (Miller, 2009). The first institutional treaty was very likely between the Haudenosaunee and the Dutch. The *Treaty of Tawatgonshi*, which would become known as the *Two Row Wampum* is a part of the *Guswenta*, the Iroquian system of treaty making. In the early 1600s the first waves of settlers were arriving in Kanien'kehá:ka (or *Mohawk* land), the eastern portion of Haudenosaunee[1] territory. Reflecting the pragmatism of Indigenous diplomacy, the Mohawk entered into an agreement with these newcomers that they hoped would shape the long-term relationship. Oren Lyons describes the agreement:

> The row of purple wampum on the right represents the Ongwahoway or Indian people, it is their canoe. In the canoe along with the people is our government, our religion or way of life. The row of purple wampum on the left is our White brethren, their ship, their government, and their religions for they have many. The field of white represents peace and the river of life. We will go down this river in peace and friendship as long as the grass is green, the water flows, and the sun rises in the east…You will note the two rows do not come together, they are equal in size, denoting the equality of all life, and one end is not finished, denoting the ongoing relationship into the future.
>
> (Lyons, 1986, 119)

Building on Lyons' interpretation, Mitchell (1989) elaborates on the parallel lines in the wampum. They signify the mutual sovereignty embedded in Indigenous treaty making: distinct nations travel the river of peace together but the vessels are independent, the people from one boat not permitted to steer the other. While the *Two-Row Wampum* is one agreement connected to many others in the vast canon of Haudenosaunee diplomacy, it is a powerful and simple description of our relationship. While *The Two Row Wampum* did not initially involve the Anishinaabek, it has been included in many subsequent treaties Anishinaabek have been party to. Among the most significant are the *Covenant Chain*, an alliance of the English, Haudenosaunee and Anishinaabe through the mid-eighteenth century and the 1764 *Treaty of Niagara* (Parmenter, 2007). While not often admitted by Anishinaabek, the *Two-Row Wampum* is one of many aspects of Haudenosaunee diplomacy adopted. In fact the use of wampum belts to record treaty agreements was very likely adopted from the Haudenosaunee. This is not surprising given the long history as enemies and allies.

Negotiated nearly 100 years after the *Two Row Wampum* was the *Dish With One Spoon*, which elaborates on the nature of Indigenous sovereignty. This is an agreement initially struck between the Anishinaabek and Haudenosaunee but later extended to Indigenous and non-Indigenous nations in the Great Lake area and Ohio Valley following The Seven Years War. Its purpose then was to re-establish peace in the region. Like the *Two Row Wampum* it requires a mnemonic reading: it is a wampum of nearly all white beads with a purple 'lozenge' in the center representing a bowl or dish. The *Dish with One Spoon* effectively recognized that a number of distinct nations live in the dish and have obligations to ensure it never runs empty. That does not mean we surrender authority or jurisdiction, but that we recognize mutual obligations and responsibilities to each other and importantly to the land. It is also important to note there are no sharp objects on the wampum (or the table) with which we might stab each other (Johnson, 2004). In other words, the *Dish With One Spoon* recognizes that distinct peoples with distinct ways of life can share the same territory in peace.

The principles of the *Dish with One Spoon* treaty are reflected in relationships of the western Anishinaabek as well, which were just as tumultuous through the eighteenth and nineteenth centuries as they were on the eastern side of the Great Lakes. Our primary conflict was with the Dakota whom the Anishinaabek had been pushing steadily out of their lands since at least 1740, a conflict rooted in a resource war while under pressure from American settler colonialism. The interesting feature of this conflict was the practice of *biindigodaadiwin*, which translates as: 'to enter one another's lodges'. The practice was to create temporary truces in the midst of conflict in order to hunt, often together, and to eat in each other's lodges (Treuer, 2010). For the Anishinaabek and the Dakota warriors, condoning starvation or limiting access to the land was unthinkable. There were obligations to each other to allow hunting and eating, sustenance – economic activity – even on territory we conceived of as 'ours' (a philosophy that flowed from expansionist pressures). In fact, all efforts throughout the conflict to create rigid borders between the two peoples failed. It took the emergence of the Grandfather Drum, a gift from the Dakota to the Anishinaabeg, which helped re-connecting men to empathy to finally end the conflict (Vennum, 2009). Many more years of American reservation policy afterward to truly separated the Dakota and Anishinaabek geographically.

The themes that emerge from this reading of Anishinaabek treaty making (and among First Nations generally) are manifold. In contrast to notions of exclusive sovereignty, Anishinaabek have practiced a politics that emphasized shared jurisdiction and inclusive or mobile sovereignty. Coming up again and again throughout diplomatic symbols on wampum belts: 'their council fire was made one', and they 'ate out of the same dish', 'sat on the same mat', 'sat beneath the shade of the same forests and swamps' (Warren, 110). Borders are not rigid but rather they are fuzzy, amorphous, if they exist at all. As Margaret Noodin (2014, 2) reminds us, aki, the Anishinaabem for land, comes from the root akina, or 'in unity, everything'. Distinct peoples and 'nations' may come and go within aki, as long as they observe commonly agreed upon truths and thus become united in the land. This is the second theme: a sustainable *sharing* of the land is a permanent condition. It is not a one-time transaction but a durable, never-ending pact. As Yellowhead said during a recitation of the *Dish with One Spoon*, the Council Fires representing peaceful relations between the Anishinaabe and Haudenosaunee shall burn for 'as long as the world stood' (Johnson, 2006, 11), or, as follows on Indigenous interpretations of the Numbered Treaties, 'as long as the sun shines' (Grand Treaty Council #3). This consensus is indeed self-interested, but in contrast to realists who strive to maximize gains in a world of zero sum gains, this is self-interest, but one that acknowledges that our survival depends on the survival of the land.

Gchi'naaknigawin: the law of reciprocity

When any ceremony begins, in many Indigenous traditions, and increasingly at conferences and academic meetings, even at provincial legislatures like Ontario's, there is a land acknowledgment. In the latter case it happens during the Throne Speech. This adapted version usually thanks the nation on whose land x or y university sits. While it seems the practice is just beginning to take hold, critics argue it is hollow and performative. This is partly because it misses the core purpose of the acknowledgement. In community settings, the 'opening' is a thanksgiving directed to the land, not merely the nation. We acknowledge the land for all it provides – our sustenance, our education, our medicines, and so on – and we commit to honoring that gift. Outsiders often assume this is a spiritual invocation, indeed in some cases the creator is mentioned. But it is a deeply pragmatic practice. We are reminding each other and ourselves that we have responsibilities to the land. And if we neglect those obligations, if we do not recognize the power and agency of land, we will suffer grave consequences; it may even lead to our destruction.

Of course, it is the land that foregrounds everything in Anishinaabeg life. This is largely true of the IR concept anarchy; in the orthodox tradition, it foregrounds all that comes after, the state and sovereignty. Anarchy is the natural condition of the international. There are no laws that bind people or communities, with nothing to govern the relationship between distinct political communities. In some cases, among Indigenous thinkers, anarchy is a desirable condition. There is a strain of Indigenous Studies that could be described as anarcha-Indigenism which advocates for a 'cultural and spiritual rootedness in this land and the Onkwehonwe (Indigenous) struggle for justice and freedom, and the political philosophy and movement that is fundamentally anti-institutional, radically democratic, and committed to taking action to force change: anarchism' (Alfred 2005, 45). There is a distinction to be made between a movement that finds advocates within Indigenous activism and the concept of anarchy in IR, to which this chapter strives to find an equivalent. For Anishinaabeg the closest approximation may be Gchi'naaknigawin, or the great law, a decidedly rules-based world.

A critical feature of the Anishinaabek social organization that helps understand conceptualization of an Anishinaabeg version of anarchy (or lack thereof) is the clan system, which has been discussed here but not yet at length. For the Anishinaabek society internally, each community was (and in some cases still is) organized by a series of clans. Each clan – represented by an animal totem and in rare cases a phenomenon like the Northern Lights or a tornado – is usually a collection of families in a given community or region. Democratically, a clan representative speaks on behalf of clan members at the council table. But more important for the purposes here, are the organizational benefits of the clan. Each clan and clan member serves the community in a specialized way. For instance, Bear Clan members are keepers of community peace (as well as the medicine people); Loon and Crane clan members provide internal and external leadership, respectively. Fish Clan members offer education, Eagle Clan members are spiritual advisors, and so on. Each clan receives teachings from their clan animal, observed and distilled over many years to help facilitate these specialized roles in communities. In exchange for these teachings, people are obliged to honor the animal: to feast it regularly, to never hunt or eat it, to advocate on its behalf, and so on. This relationship illustrates a conception of the land not only as economic but also educational and political. In other words, the clan system reveals a worldview that holds up the land as an entity with agency, rights, even sovereignty, and which demands accountability of humans. Leanne Simpson (2011) describes species of animals as nations in their own right.

A more specific example of this relationship comes from among the most well known extra-community political and economic agreements, the story of the breaking and re-negotiation of an agreement between the deer, moose, and humans that would govern our relationships for centuries after its creation. The story goes that one day, very long ago the people lost track of the deer and the moose. The creatures simply vanished. After searching for many weeks and having their queries rejected by other creatures, the humans discovered that the crows and the owls had kidnapped the deer and moose. So the humans embarked on a campaign to free the hooved creatures. After dispersing the birds and reaching the deer and moose, they learned that the latter had not been captured at all but went voluntarily with the crows and the owls because the humans had forgotten their obligations. They spoke of a legal principle which stipulated that in exchange for sacrificing themselves to feed, clothe, provide tools, and educate the people, the people would have responsibilities to maintain the integrity of their homes for generations to come (Borrows, 2002; Simpson, 2008). The people agreed to correct their behavior as well as make reconciliation with the winged creatures and the treaty was renewed. This is not merely a quaint tale, for there are real consequences for humans who abandon notions of *reciprocity*: their treaty partner held them accountable by potentially depriving them of sustenance, of life.

Aaron Mills (2009) recounts yet another story that reflects the notion of reciprocity with more clear indications of what he calls *boundaries* (not to be confused with borders). In the story, two young men catch a glimpse of a pair of thunderbirds, perched atop Animki Wajiw (Mount McKay in Thunder Bay, Ontario). They knew not to approach the sacred beings but could not resist the opportunity and as they got closer, one of the birds shot lightening from its eyes and struck one of the men dead. Mills (2009, 120) explains that he was killed for violating protocol. Linking this to reciprocity, the subtext of the story is that the 'Anishinaabe (aren't) meant to have unfettered access to satisfaction of his desires wherever he pleases'. The consequences for violating the sacred, breaching the rights of the land, the creatures we share it with, the spiritual realm, come with the harshest of penalties. The story is not meant to be interpreted literally, but for the Anishinaabeg to accept there are limits on our actions. This applies, too, to relations to other political communities. When examining written versions of treaties, from the Great Peace of Montreal in 1701 through to Canadian confederation, the Anishinaabe leaders sign with their clan designation. This is an indication that they are there representing their communities, but also the land. Their adherence to the law of reciprocity is always prioritized.

When considering from an Anishinaabe perspective, the IR concept of anarchy is called into question. Instead of a lawless international order where we must compete to survive, the Anishinaabeg have historically considered the power of non-human entities as the *de facto* and overarching authorities. Despite a deep desire for freedom described earlier, we are nonetheless bound by our relationships and responsibilities, the first of which is reciprocity.

Conclusion

Anishinaabe conceptions of the international require reciprocity and responsibility. First, everything taken from the land must be given back, in one form or another. This rests on the recognition of the **sovereignty of the land** and the non-human creatures we share it with. Secondly, autonomy in this articulation is privileged. Among diverse people and the land, there are multiple legal and economic orders that must be respected. Thirdly, the borders and boundaries that separate distinct political and economic practices are not rigid but flexible and dynamic. In this sense, autonomous people can share the same geographic region, making for a terrain mapped by *inclusive* sovereignties. Finally, these are long-term relationships, permanent even, as all the parties are required to renew the norms and obligations that permit a relationship with the land. This philosophy is put into practice to varying degrees today. After four hundred years of sustained contact with settlers, often characterized by conflict, Indigenous peoples are living in a time of renewal: re-establishing relationships to one another and non-Indigenous neighbors. And parallel to these re-connections, Indigenous peoples are refusing to accept the distortions caused by the discourses of conquest. These politics espouse pragmatic and principled inter-national relations among distinct communities, inside the rigid borders of the discipline and out.

Box 8.1: Key points

- There is a direct relationship between the stories we tell ourselves about Indigenous peoples – and correspondingly settlers – in popular culture and the international politics we practice.
- The theoretical frameworks that drive the discipline of International Relations ignore and marginalize Indigenous thought and action. If considered at all, Indigenous peoples are misrepresented.
- International Relations is embedded in a process of settler colonialism. Where colonization has yet to end, the discipline and the practice of IR encourages and reinforces ongoing dispossession of Indigenous peoples.
- Indigenous diplomacy through time challenges foundational International Relations concepts of the state, sovereignty and anarchy to produce divergent conceptions of the international.
- An articulation of Indigenous international relations conceives political communities as fluid in structure, decentralized in the exercise of sovereignty, and bound by obligations to the land.

Short definition of 'Indigenous'

Indigenous is a concept emerging from international human rights activism over the past fifty years. It denotes a people natural to a specific place and is the preferred general term for the diverse Indigenous communities that populate the planet. But Indigenous is also very general and can homogenize those diverse peoples. Students should always strive to be as locally specific as possible when referencing or discussing Indigenous peoples (i.e. Anishinaabe or Haudenosaunee, etc.).

Short definition of settler colonialism

Settler colonialism refers to the variant of colonialism where settlers arrive and do not leave. In settler contexts, foreign institutions and populations strive to permanently replace the original Indigenous societies through violence or assimilation. In this sense, as Patrick Wolfe notes, settler colonialism is a structural phenomenon. Throughout the international community, there are a handful of settler states, from Canada and the United States to Palestine, Australia and New Zealand.

Note

1 The Haudenosaunee, sometimes referred to as the Iroquois, are a confederacy of six nations including the Mohawk, Seneca, Onondaga, Cayuga, Oneida and Tuscarora. They have been the long-time neighbors of the Anishinaabek to the southwest of the Great Lakes.

Further reading

Borrows, J., and Coyle, M. (Eds.). (2017). *The right relationship: reimaging the implementation of historic treaties*. University of Toronto Press. An edited volume highlighting the insconsistent approach to treaty implementation in the past and charting myriad ways forward in the relationship using the treaty as an organizing principle for domestic and international politics between Indigenous peoples and Canadians.

McCarthy. (2016). *In divided unity: Haudenosaunee reclamation at grand river*. University of Arizona Press. Hyper-local in context, McCarthy examines the reclamation of Six Nation lands from a real estate developer and the conflict that ensues. Over the ten years that followed, this text considers the actions of the Haudenosaunee as international politics.

Simpson, A. (2014). *Mohawk interruptus: Political life across the borders of settler states*. Duke University Press. Anthropologist Audra Simpson theorizes settler colonialism as an unfinished project that Indigenous nations can exploit to pursue their own sovereignty, resulting in a messy international politics characterized by tensions and conflict.

Simpson, L.B. (2017). *As we have always done: Indigenous freedom through radical resurgence*. University of Minnesota Press. Breaking from mainstream theorizing about Indigenous politics, this text crafts a unique orientation for thinking about and acting on Indigenous resurgence grounded in Anishinaabe thought and moving towards prescriptions for structural change.

Vowel, C. (2016). *Indigenous writes: A guide to first nations, Métis and Inuit issues in Canada*. Highwater Press. A broad overview of the relationship between Indigenous peoples and settler colonialism, ranging from foundational myths and stereotypes, proper terminology and a range of policy issues that dominate contemporary discussions.

Bibliography

Alexander, W. (1992). Anarchy is what states make of it: The social construction of power politics. *International Organization*, 46, 391–425.

Alfred, T. (2005). Wasáse: *Indigenous pathways of action and freedom*. Toronto: University of Toronto Press.

Beier, M. (2005). *International relations in uncommon places: Indigeneity, cosmology, and the limits of international theory*. New York: Palgrave Macmillan.

Benton-Banai, E. (1988). *The Mishomis book: The voice of the Ojibway*. Harvard, WI: Indian Country Communications.

Borrows, J. (2002). *Recovering Canada: The resurgence of indigenous law*. Toronto: University of Toronto Press.

Burrows, J. (1997). Wampum at Niagara: The royal proclamation, Canadian legal history and self-government. In M. Asch (Ed.) *Aboriginal and treaty rights in Canada: Essays on law, equity, and respect for difference*. Vancouver: University of British Columbia Press.

Copway, G. (1847). *The life, history and travels of Kah-ge-ga-gah-bowh*. Albany, NY: Weed and Parsons.

Corbiere, A.O. (2013). Ojibwe Chief Shingwaukonse: One who was not idle. *Muskrat Magazine*. http://muskratmagazine.com/ojibwe-chief-shingwaukonse-one-who-was-not-idleojibwe-chief-shingwaukonse-one-who-was-not-idle/

Corbiere, A. (2012). Their own forms of which they take the most notice: Diplomatic metaphors and symbolism of wampum belts. In The Ojibwe Cultural Foundation (Ed.) *Anishinaabewin Niiwin: Four rising winds*. M'chigeeng: Ojibwe Cultural Foundation.

Duffy, E.M., and Metcalf, A.C. (2011). *The return of Hans Staden: A go-between in the Atlantic world*. Baltimore: Johns Hopkins University Press.

Edmunds, R.D. (2006). *Tecumseh and the quest for Indian leadership*. London: Pearson.

Francis, D. (1992). *The imaginary Indian: The image of the Indian in Canadian culture*. Vancouver: Arsenal Pulp Press.

Grand Council Treaty #3. The Paypom Treaty. www.gct3.ca/about/history/paypom-treaty/.

Henderson, J. (Sa'ke'j) Y. (2008). *Indigenous diplomacy and the rights of peoples: Achieving UN recognition*. Saskatoon: Purlich Publishing.

Hixon, W.L. (2013). *American settler colonialism: A history*. New York: Palgrave Macmillan.

International Labour Organization. (1957). Convention 107: Indigenous and Tribal Populations Convention. http://ilo.org/ilolex/cgi-lex/convde.pl?C107

Jáuregui, C.A. (2010). Hans Staden's true history: An account of cannibal captivity in Brazil. *Luso-Brazilian Review*, 47, 219–223.

Johnson, B. (1976). *Ojibway ceremonies*. Toronto: McClelland & Stewart.

Johnson, B. (1982). *Ojibway heritage*. Toronto: McClelland & Stewart.

Johnston, D. (2006). Connecting people to place: The power and relevance of origin stories. In J.S. Linden. *The Ipperwash Inquiry*. Volume Two. www.law.utoronto.ca/documents/lectures/religion-johnston-0611.pdf

Lyons, O. (1986). Indian self-government in the Haudenosaunee constitution. *Nordic Journal of International Law*, 55, 117–121.

Lyons, S. (2010). *X-Marks: Native signatures of assent*. Minneapolis: University of Minnesota Press.

Miller, J.R. (2000). *Skyscrapers hide the heavens: A history of Indian-white relations in Canada*. Toronto: University of Toronto Press.

Mills, A. (2009). Aki Anishinaabek, kaye tahsh crown. *Indigenous Law Journal*, 9, 109–162.

Mitchell, M. (1989). An unbroken assertion of sovereignty. In B. Richardson (Ed.). *Drumbeat: Anger and renewal in Indian country*. Toronto: Summerhill Press.

Parmenter, J. (1997). Pontiac's war: Forging new links in the Anglo-Iroquois covenant chain, 1758–1766. *Ethnohistory*, 44, 617–654.

Parmenter, J. (2007). After the mourning wars: The Iroquois as allies in colonial north American campaigns, 1676–1760. *William and Mary Quarterly*, 64, 39–82.

Ruoff, A.L.B. and Smith, D.B. (2006). *Life, letters and speeches*. Lincoln: University of Nebraska Press.

Said, E. (1993). *Culture and imperialism*. New York: Vintage Books.

Shaw, K. (2002). Indigeneity and the international. *Millennium Journal of International Studies*, 33, 55–81.

Simpson, L. (2008). Looking after Gdoo-naaganinaa: Precolonial Nishnaabeg diplomatic and treaty relationships. *Wicazo Sa Review*, 23, 29–42.

Simpson, L. (2011). *Dancing on our turtle's back: Stories of Nishinaabeg re-creation, resurgence and a new emergence*. Winnipeg: ARP Books.

Sokolow, J.A. (2003). *The great encounter: Native peoples and European settlers in the Americas, 1492–1800*. New York: Routledge.

Stam, R., and Shohat, E. (2012). Whence and whither postcolonial theory? *New Literary History*, 43, 371–390.

Stark, H.K. (2012). Marked by fire: Anishinaabe articulations of nationhood in treaty making with the United States and Canada. *The American Indian Quarterly*, 30, 119–149.

Treuer, A. (2010). *The assassination of hole in the day*. Minneapolis: Borealis.

Turner, D. (2006). *This is not a peace pipe: Towards a critical indigenous philosophy*. Toronto: University of Toronto Press.

Venne, S. (1999). *Our elders understand our rights: Evolving international law regarding indigenous peoples*. Penticton: Theytus Books.

Vennum, T. (2009). *The Ojibwe dance drum: History and construction*. Minneapolis: Minnesota Historical Society Press.

Veracini, L. (2010). *Settler colonialism: A theoretical overview*. New York: Palgrave Macmillan.

Vizenor, G. (1984). *The people named the Chippewa: Narrative histories*. Minneapolis: University of Minnesota Press.

Vizenor, G. (1993). *Summer in the spring: Anishinaabe lyric poems and stories*. Omaha: Oklahoma University Press.

Warren, W.W. (1885). *History of the Ojibway people*. St. Paul: Minnesota Historical Society Press.

Weatherford, J. (1993). *Indian givers: How the Indians of the Americas transformed the world*. Toronto: Random House.

Wendt, A. (1992). Anarchy is what states make of it: The social construction of power politics. *International Organization*, 46, 391–425.

Williams, R. (1990). *The American Indian in western legal thoughts: Discourses of conquest*. New York: Oxford University Press.

Witgen, M. (2007). The rituals of possession: Native identity and the invention of empire in seventeenth-century western North America. *Ethnohistory*, 54, 639–668.

Wolfe, P. (2006). Settler colonialism and the elimination of the native. *Journal of Genocide Research*, 8, 387–409.

9 Security studies, postcolonialism and the Third World

Randolph B. Persaud[1]

Introduction	155
The postcolonial approach to security	156
Conquest and intervention	158
Democratic peace, sanctions, humanitarian interventions, terrorism, and war	162
Conclusion	174

Introduction

A postcolonial approach to security is only now emerging in the field of International Relations. To understand why this is so we need to acknowledge that international theory, and especially security studies, far from being purely academic undertakings, are in fact politically oriented knowledges that come from within the Western academy, and both intentionally and inadvertently, are written from a Euro–American perspective. Most importantly, these perspectives have justified, legitimized, or simply explained global security from a Western angle, broadly defined. According to Barkawi and Laffey (2006, 330) the problem is not simply one of bias, but '...thinking derived from conventional studies...[that] is at best a poor basis for understanding and action in contemporary security studies'. Postcolonialism does not offer a flat-out rejection of mainstream security studies. Rather, the key point is security studies in their modern institutional forms were developed in universities mostly in the United States and the United Kingdom, much of it based on their own national interests combined with selective readings of history and philosophy. Along these lines Acharya (2014, 648) observes that '...it is universities, scholars, and publishing outlets in the West that dominate and set the agenda'.

A postcolonial perspective on Third World security, if not world security, cannot be carried out without a critique of Western-centric security studies. This is so because security studies do not only offer *explanations* about world security, but also provide historiographies of world development, almost invariably starting with some variation of Thucydides, Greece and Rome, then moving through the European Enlightenment, and the Industrial Revolution (in Europe), only to proceed to the European balance of power system, then on to the Cold War, and ending with American global leadership (George 1994; Gill & Mittelman 1997; Ayoob 2002; Grovogui 2010; Hobson 2012; Pasha 2013; Anievas, Manchanda, and Shilliam 2014; Henderson 2017). Important to note is that postcolonialism is not the only tradition that critiques mainstream security studies. Challenges have also come from gender studies (Enloe 1990), human security (Tadjbakhsh & Chenoy 2007), neo-Gramscian international theory (Cox 1981 & 1983; Ayers 2008), peace studies (Abu-Nimer 2002), and climate change scholars (Homer-Dixon 2007). Recently, a call for 'global international relations' has been put forward by Acharya. The task of postcolonial theory is to unmask the biases embedded in securitizing histories from a *global* point of view, or through what Bhambra has called connected histories, and more recently 'connected sociologies' (Bhambra 2014). Consistent with Robert Young's work, Gandhi is right to suggest that '...postcolonialism can best be thought of as a critique of history' (Gandhi 1998, 170; see also Seth 2013).

The chapter proceeds through three major sections. The first identifies and describes the main ideas of a postcolonial approach to security, much of it through an engagement with key concepts prevalent in Eurocentric security studies, such as anarchy and survival. This section also has a general overview of the ways in which Third World security is deeply embedded in the histories of colonialism and imperialism, followed by continuing forms of intervention both violent and otherwise. Section two elaborates on conquest and intervention as important concepts and practices that are relevant and more historically accurate (than just anarchy and survival) in describing and analyzing the security and insecurity of the Third World in relation to Euro-America. Section three engages five issue areas from the perspectives of mainstream security studies, and from a postcolonial position. The issue areas are the democratic peace, sanctions, humanitarian intervention, terrorism, and war against the Third World. The conclusion calls for postcolonial scholars to engage, or even *confront* Eurocentric security analysis more directly.

The postcolonial approach to security

While there is no postcolonial *theory* of international, global, or even Third World security, there is an existing body of work that can help in identifying the key aspects and, when combined, provide a broad outline of a postcolonial perspective. For Laffey and Nadarajah (2016, 123) 'Postcolonial analysis exposes the embedded Eurocentrism...which structures both IR and security studies – conceptually, empirically, and normatively'. They pin-point three specific positions of a postcolonial approach relevant to security. First, they note that postcolonialism '...is distinctive because of the central role of violence in world politics' (Laffey and Nadarajah 2016, 124). They emphasize the 'sheer scale of material violence unleashed by European colonialism against populations in the Americas, in Africa, and in Asia...' (2016, 125). Their second element is that postcolonialism is also concerned with 'epistemic violence, understood as the imposition of European knowledge systems unto other people and places' (Laffey and Nadarajah 2016, 125). The third dimension is that 'postcolonialism is not predominantly or exclusively a European form of knowledge...' (Laffey and Nadarajah 2016, 125). In totality, these authors advance an approach to postcolonial security that is at once historical, epistemological, and material.

For postcolonialism, 1648 is a historically contingent rather than necessary point of departure in understanding the modern world system. The analysis of International Relations need not necessarily commence with the emergence of the European states system, or for that matter with Europe, where the latter is seen as a compartmentalized, self-contained geo-political and geo-civilizational space, with an inner core (Barkawi 2013, 99). Europe as the center and the beginning of world history is rejected not only by postcolonial scholars writing about international security. Frank and Gills (1993), for instance, provided a seminal critique of Euro-centeredness, arguing that the European states system is only the latest phase in a more *connected* set of historical systems. Nor would adding in non-Western histories or doing comparative studies do the trick. Instead of Eurocentrism, they call for a *world history*, as distinct from a history of the world, where the latter can be, and has been, composed of various installments that are regional or 'civilizational'. Their '...wider world-historic humanocentric alternative' (Frank and Gills 1993, 11) envisages a history of the 'same time', which means a rejection of historical development as a set of sequential compartmentalized enclaves. It is for this reason Frank and Gills posit that globalization began five thousand, rather five hundred years ago.

Beginning with Europe is also a grand epistemological project which not only sees the world through European values and beliefs, but also distributes these as if they were universal (George 1994). Acemoglu and Robinson have shown that while economic progress is sometimes catapulted forward by 'creative destruction' and introduction of these foreign values, foreign interference as in the case of Kongo reinforced not only extractive industries, but also 'political absolutism' (Acemoglu and Robinson 2012, 90). Cultural interference also accompanies democracy promotion. These include attempts to modify gender roles, consumption practices, and at the broadest level, the advancement of the ideology of individualism. It is out of these concerns that Acharya's six main dimensions of Global IR advance the idea of 'pluralistic universalism' and '*world history, not just Greco-Roman, European, or US history*' (Acharya 2014, 649; emphasis in the original). And further, even scholars working within realism/liberalism have called into question the overreach and the adequacy of mainstream security approaches in dealing with the Third World. For instance, Mohammed Ayoob, a proponent of **'subaltern realism'**, is convinced that those who favor the international over the domestic level of analysis, and the bipolar over the multipolar '...ignore the fact that stability in Europe was achieved at the expense of stability and order in much of the rest of the world' (Ayoob 2002, 36).

No single example is ever sufficient to illustrate major claims and propositions and it is no different here. Yet, the rise and expansion of the Mongol Empire under the indefatigable leadership of Genghis Khan serves as a case worth exploring, not only because of the connectedness which ensued through several centuries, but due to the unique circumstances of emergence and development. Instead of 1648, one could just as well begin in the steppes of Central Asia where a couple of remote tribes rose from absolute historical irrelevance only to build one of the largest and most powerful empires of all time (Keegan 1993, 200–207). What is most remarkable is that although the Mongols did not have an ideology or universal world view, they became the engine for *longue durée* transformations, including but also well beyond the emergence of the European Renaissance, economic modernization, and military innovation (Weatherford 2004, 233). While some historians such as R.R. Palmer (1960) argue that the Mongols were responsible for the delayed modernization of countries like Russia, Weatherford has shown quite the opposite for Europe itself, and also for China. The vast Mongol Empire was tantamount to a free-trade zone in which goods, ideas, and technologies, moved in a system that simply did not exist before the thirteenth century. Weatherford writes:

> In conquering their Empire, not only had the Mongols revolutionized warfare, they also created the nucleus of a universal culture and world system. This new global culture continued to grow long after the demise of the Mongol Empire, and through continued development over the coming centuries, it became the foundation for the modern world system with the original Mongol emphasis on free commerce, open communication, shared knowledge, secular politics, religious coexistence, international law, and diplomatic immunity.
>
> (Weatherford 2004, 234)

Perhaps the most enduring aspect of Genghis Khan and the Mongols is in warfare, and especially devastatingly effective war of maneuver tactics. They developed sophisticated re-supply systems and had mastered it to such a level that Genghis Khan was able to defeat armies at great distances, armies with already dug-in, and solid defensive positions, and with vast resources. Thus, the Mongols also mastered the art of the siege, a strategy that would have profound impact of subsequent warfighting. Genghis Khan's use of lightning speed in his horse-archer wars of maneuver is arguably the basis for major transformation in European militaries. Halford Mackinder (1904), a geographer, and the founder of the geopolitics of grad strategy was significantly influenced by the Mongols. Their devastating military victories in Europe led Mackinder to develop the geographic 'pivot' which theorized that whoever controlled the European heartland, would become the most significant world power. Mackinder hypothesized that Russia would become the new Mongols. It is obvious that Mackinder favored 'boots on the ground' over navies. He could not, of course, speculate about airpower given that his pivot lecture was delivered in 1904.

Conquest and intervention

As noted above, mainstream security studies are partly built on a philosophy of survival. This is not simply a matter of physical survival, or protection of territory, or even of core economic values. The philosophy of survival is a general organizing principle around which numerous aspects of society are organized. These include, but are not restricted to, the construction of people-hood, nationhood, the definition of friends and enemies in the international system, and other material issues such as strategies of defense and offense, force structure, alliances, and how wars are fought. Moreover, the centrality of the discourse of survival in traditional Western-centric security analysis is also the basis for the very constitution of the 'West' as an idea. For instance, during the late nineteenth century and early twentieth century there was great fear that the 'West' was being overtaken by a 'rising tide of color', a development then thought to be the basis of growing international anarchy. We can therefore affirm that the ways scholars and politicians talk about survival of the West amidst global anarchy is also important in the making and remaking of the West, and also how it thinks and approaches supposed threats to the 'civilized world', an expression still routinely used in European and American contemporary political discourses.

As a central concept in Western IR, therefore, survival has had a peculiar kind of cultural and political status. This is so because survival is not a universal concept, meaning that it does not always apply to all. The employment of the concept of survival as a discourse has always implied the exact opposite for the Others – with consequences ranging from formal or informal subjugation to outright destruction. While one can understand that any state would want to defeat enemy states wishing to do harm, the history of Western states with the Third World does not bear this out. The record shows rather, that **conquest**, colonialism, expansionist imperialism, imperialist competition, and other forms of intervention, have been the principal drivers regarding security matters with the Third World. The postcolonial position on security, therefore, is that two of the foundational concepts in explaining Western security practices, namely survival and anarchy, are too ambiguous to be analytically useful. Moreover, the insightful constructivist work of Vucetic (2011) has shown that the dynamics of cooperation between two of the principals of the West – the United Kingdom and United States – formed the Anglosphere not out of balance of power considerations, or fears of existential survival, but on the basis of racial perspectives of world order, that is to say, the racial ideology of Anglo-Saxonism (Vucetic 2011, 136). Let us explore this argument in greater detail.

While colonialism and imperialism usually get consigned to footnotes in Western-centric IR, they really ought to be at the very start of any modern historical analysis of world orders (Said 1993; Grovogui 2001; Inayatullah & Blaney 2004; Jones 2006; Agathangelou & Ling 2009; Krishna 2009; Biswas & Nair 2010; Matin 2011; Sajed & Inayatullah 2016). Conquest, expansionism, and empire-building should replace survival as the *explanatory* leitmotiv of Western state policies and practices as far as the Third World is concerned, especially in terms of security, and especially since 1492. In this regard, the work of Achille Mbembe is of tremendous importance. Mbembe (2001, 25) argues that 'colonial sovereignty rested on three sorts of violence' – these being, 'the founding violence'; violence related to legitimation; and the use of violence to institute, spread, and maintain authority. He makes the telling point that colonial violence had become 'banal', day-by-day practices. In actuality, violence is imposed on the body politic, therefore institutionalizing what Foucault sees as biopolitics through governmentality. In this instance '…sovereignty is exercised within the borders of a territory, discipline in exercised on the bodies of individuals, and security is exercised over a whole population' (Foucault 2007, 11). The daily, mundane use of violence, however, should not mask the numerous instances of outright violence, including dramatic massacres such as happened in British Guiana in 1823, Jamaica in 1865, at Wounded Knee, South Dakota in 1890, Jallianwala Bagh, Amritsar, in (India) 1919, at No Gun Ri (South Korea) in 1950, My Lai (South Vietnam) 1968, Haditha, Iraq 2005; or by the Japanese at Nanjing in 1937 – just to name a few. R.J. Rummel estimates that the Japanese Army murdered some three to six million people between 1937 and 1945 – most of whom were Chinese, Indonesians, Koreans, Filipinos, and Indochinese – and some Western soldiers. Nor should violence be confined to either subduing, harming, or killing the 'natives'. Violence also took the form of hard labor, sexual assault, regular beatings as part of a system of disciplinary governmentality, forced/coerced migration either for military or labor purposes, famines, and so on. In many instances, the violence was also visited on the population of the colonizing state, as in Japan's forced migration of rural Japanese to Manchuria (Young 1998, 392–393).

Some historians and IR scholars have indeed underlined expansionism and empire in US foreign policy (Hunt 1987; Deconde 1992; Bacevich 2002; Manela 2007; McDougall 1997 & 2016). Walter McDougall argues that expansion has been part of the DNA of American notions of freedom. He makes a distinction between 'expansion' as a 'practical' matter and *expansionism* as an ideology. Importantly, in this revisionist perspective, Americans had an expansionist mindset well before *Manifest Destiny* emerged as a policy legitimatizing ideology, and well after its rhetorical twilight. The ideology of expansionism is based on eight assumptions first delineated by Albert K. Weinberg in 1935, and elaborated on by McDougall. All of these demonstrate that the war against First Nation peoples in the United States, and against Mexico had nothing to do with security, but everything to do with *conquest*. Further, the idea of conquering foreign lands was just that – an idea born of pure desire, and with absolutely no connection to national security, and zero connection to US survival in the existential sense of that concept. Much the same can be said for all the European powers that sat in Berlin and divided up Africa.

Here are the eight justifications identified by Weinberg and elaborated on by McDougall (McDougall 1997, pp. 82–84):

1. Natural right – meaning that expansionism is a divine right given to American Christians to simply take and own land. This justification is ensconced in virtually all the other reasons below, though in a variety of forms.
2. Geographical predestination

3. Natural growth
4. Natural overseas expansion
5. Cultivate idle lands
6. Increased liberty
7. Manifest destiny I
8. Manifest destiny II

This list confirms that the ideology of expansionism was a combination of both claims to divine appointment anchored in Christianity and what David Campbell (1998, 118) called the 'evangelism of fear'. The first three justification are based on religious and geographical determinism. The taking of land presumed to be idle, is a generic theme in imperialism, one touted as late as the presidency of Theodore Roosevelt. Manifest Destiny is rendered in two parts, where according to McDougall (1997, 84), the first is the pure form: peaceful, automatic, gradual, and governed by self-determination. The second form is the abstract conceptual form of the will to empire, where expansionist Americans felt it their responsibility to conquer foreign peoples for the benefit of the conquered.

The inadequacy of survival as a pivotal element of Western security discourse viz-à-vis the Third World is also to be found in the scale and duration of colonial and imperial rule, these last running for hundreds of years, and still very much alive today despite formal sovereignty. To add to that, the manner of conquest which involved mass killings were offensive rather than defensive. The overkill factor in wars against the Third World is an ongoing problem, and this despite step-level innovations in military technology (Kaplow 2010). And yet further, the conquered throughout the world had to wage long, difficult, and bloody liberation struggles, with enormous loss of life to actually win the very freedom that the colonizers were supposedly there to establish (Doty 1996). One of the most important claims of postcolonial security scholarship is that wars of liberation and resistance to imperialism have played decisive roles in the democratizing of democracy, and thus, in the making of democracy as lived freedom.

While the record of conquest, occupation, and the refusal to 'give-up' foreign possessions are thoroughly documented, the reasons for the nearly five hundred years of empire and other forms of foreign rule are still in dispute. We have already seen that the concept of survival as an integral element of Western-centric security theory does not hold up. Racism rather than reason and rationality have been key European drivers in the securitized construction and prosecution of war with non-Europeans, first indigenous peoples worldwide, and then the Third World (Mills 1997). In addition to the racialized reason for conquest, the act of conquest and subsequent colonial/imperial rule was marked by violence, a good example of which occurred in Amritsar in 1919.

Brigadier General Dyer's testimony points to a singular fact of the colonizing mind, namely, that the Indians, as all the other colonized, needed to be taught a hard lesson, a lesson in the prevailing colonial order of things that meant

---

Box 9.1: Massacre at Amritsar, India, 1919

On Sunday April 13, 1919, soldiers under the command of British Brigadier General Reginald E.H. Dyer massacred 379 Indians in Amritsar. Events leading up to the massacre were buoyed by the Rowlatt Act which had instituted sweeping wartime emergency measures first put in place in 1915, lifted after the end of World War I, but then reinstated in early 1919. The Act was hastily rammed through the Supreme Legislative Council. Rowlatt, and the manner of its passage, were taken as a betrayal of India which had just fought alongside the British in a long and bloody war that took thousands of Indian lives. By most accounts, the proximate circumstances of the massacre actually began on April 10, 1919 when, in protest against deportation of two stalwart nationalist leaders (Satyapal and Dr. Saif ud-Din Kitchlew) Indians took to the streets where 'several banks and other buildings, either housing government property or otherwise emblematic of British rule, were set fire to, and here and there other acts of incendiarism were committed' (Lal 1993).

Brigadier General Dyer himself not only openly and fully acknowledged that he had masterminded and directed the action from a raised position, firing some 1,650 rounds into a crowd of nearly 15,000–20,000 thousand men, women and children who were essentially trapped in Jallianwalla Bagh with only one exit. Dyer defended it without apology or grief. More than that, Brigadier General Dyer stated that his actions were a matter of duty, a claim that was backed up by the British Lieutenant Governor who stated that 'Your action is correct. Lieutenant Governor approves' (Lal 1993). The British general is on record that the crowd, most not part of the protest, could have been dispersed without any bloodshed.

---

violence. That was then, but 'master/slave violence' both preceded that day, and many soon followed, in India and elsewhere.

Democratic peace, sanctions, humanitarian interventions, terrorism, and war

The democratic peace and democracy promotion

Democratic peace theory illustrates the gulf that exists between Western and postcolonial IR (Henderson 2017). First, it is important to acknowledge that the theory of democratic peace seamlessly morphs into practical, real-life policies. Policies based on the democratic peace allow a broad range of foreign policy practices by Western governments either acting in concert *via* multilateral institutions or on their own individual accord. Intervention for the promotion of democracy has been justified in round-about ways including the need to root-out terrorism and corruption, save failed states, protect resources (e.g. oil), remove dictatorships, establish the rule of law, and attend to other issues that threaten the 'international community'. Often, these instances of democracy promotion involve massive loss of life for the targeted country, structural reorganization of economic systems, selling off of nationally owned state assets to Western economic interests, and in contradiction to the stated objectives, installation of Western-friendly regimes. But what is the claim of the democratic peace?

According to Harvey Starr (1997, 153) the core of what he calls the democratic peace proposition (*DPprop*) is '*there is a virtual absence of war among dyads of democratic polities*'. He argues that according to the statistical data it is '... an empirical fact that democracies never, or almost never, go to war with each other' (1997, 154). He joins many other theorists who suggest that the broader *explanation* of the 'liberal peace' is that the state in democratic societies is restrained by the institutions of transparency and accountability. Another key argument is that the democratic peace is part of a larger whole, namely, integration among democratic states. In this regard, democratic states participate with other democratic states in a larger set of interactions. These interactions, when undergirded by the same democratic values, produce *security communities* that is a public good for the world community. The narrow construction of the *DPprop* can be also understood as the proposition of a 'separate peace', meaning that while democracies do not fight each other, they do go to war with other forms of state (Henderson 2017, 101).

Critics of the democratic peace from *within* liberalism, such as Sebastian Rosato (2003), argue that the causal logic of the democratic peace is flawed. The word *causal* here is important because while Rosato accepts that democracies rarely go to war with one another, he rejects the *explanations* provided for the absence of war among democratic nations. Several arguments are leveled against the democratic peace. There are issues with the data, and specifically, with coding. Here, democratic peace theorists are charged with having a flexible definition of democracy which allows them to include, exclude, or classify cases for theoretical 'convenience'. The data then, while largely reliable, are susceptible to non-scientific manipulation.

With regard to the argument that trust and respect inform democratic decision-making and thus act as a constraint on war, Rosato notes that mature democracies have overthrown democratically elected governments in developing countries, this being a core postcolonial position as well. This is an empirical fact that weakens the arguments that democratic values and norm externalization are constitutive elements of the democratic peace. There are also real problems with arguments about accountability. On this count, it is noted that democracies often go to war despite the lack of popular support. Moreover, the data also show that autocratic leaders are just as likely as democratic leaders to be removed from office due to an unpopular war, and are certainly more likely to be killed. Still on the issue of accountability-restraint, Rosato argues that sometimes nationalist sentiments by the people may actually push leaders to fight wars or engage in other forms of violent conflict (such as armed intervention) upon pain of being voted out.

Democratic peace theorists respond to the charge of what is essentially foreign interference by arguing that while a state may be democratic, the issue is that it might not be a mature democracy, or that it is a question of how they are seen, that is, a question of perceptions by the leaders of the intervening state.

At work here, is a clear case of paternalism where the Western intervening state sees itself as having some kind of higher duty to oversee the democratic progress of those not ready for self-government, an argument that goes well back in the imperial encounter. Rosato himself points to the cases of Guatemala (1954), Indonesia (1957), British Guiana (now Guyana) (1961), Brazil (1961, 1974), Chile (1973), and Nicaragua (1984) – where in all except one instance (Nicaragua), democratically elected leaders were toppled and replaced by authoritarian leaders.

Beyond internal critiques of the democratic peace, postcolonialism has shown that democracy promotion based on the democratic peace have been only pretexts for foreign intervention, or more benignly, platforms for the continuity of civilizational hegemony. Moreover, as Armstrong and Prashad (2006, 34–35) have shown, intervention in the name of democracy has peripheralized the concerted action of Third World women in the democratization process – first against the foreign power, and then in their respective countries. They point to women's democratic activism in India (1905, 1909, 1919, 1920–21 and 1930–1931; Iran 1907–1911 and 1919; and among others – Afghanistan – 1880, 1920, and 1960. The same must be said for women in nearly all decolonization movements.

Sanctions

Sanctions are a form of coercion employed by states, groups of states, or by the international community through the UN Security Council. In theory, the intended purpose of sanctions is to get the targeted state to change its behavior. It is important to understand that states often use sanctions because of the limited options available short of the use of force, or outright war. When used this way, sanctions can clearly signal to the offending state the resolve of the international community or of the state/s that have initiated the action. Critics argue that the historical record shows that sanctions have enjoyed only limited or qualified success. Others argue that sanctions are a prelude to war, and for postcolonialism, it is a form of centrally directed violence that is a continuation of the colonial administration.

In February 2012, the United States placed new sanctions on Iran. The US Treasury noted that the sanctions which target Iran's financial assets in the US will communicate to Iran that 'it will face ever-increasing economic and diplomatic pressure until it addresses the international community's well-founded and well-documented concerns regarding the nature of its nuclear program'.

It is worth noting that economic sanctions are usually coupled with diplomatic maneuvers aimed at isolating the targeted state.

Critics of sanctions make the following arguments: (1) that analyses of the available data on sanctions show that they are not that effective; (2) that sanctions hurt the civilian population more than those who control and directly benefit from state power; and (3) that the targeted state usually finds willing partners to provide critical goods and services denied through the sanctions regime. In addition to the above criticisms, Bahrami and Parsi (2012) also note that sanctions may actually strengthen the hands of authoritarian rule. This may happen because the targeted state may blame the suffering of the people on those who employ the sanctions. Moreover, sanctions can become the basis for mobilizing the domestic population along the lines of aggressive nationalism and in the language of defending the national interest.

These are at least some of the main lines of debate, bearing in mind that the vast majority of sanctions have been leveled against enemies of the West, some legitimate, while many are forms of what Quijano (2000) calls the coloniality of power. A broader view, and one that is closer to a postcolonial position, is that successful sanctions not only incur significant hardships on populations, but also have in the past caused large numbers of deaths both directly and indirectly. Like humanitarian intervention, sanctions are deeply politicized with the targets most likely to be not simply violators of UN resolutions, but also those who pursue policies deemed inimical to Western interests. This is clearly what has happened in Iraq. Sanctions were imposed by the UN Security Council starting August 6, 1990 following Iraq's incursion into Kuwait. These were comprehensive sanctions that were almost total, and which ended blocking the import of the most basic items including medical equipment and other health related necessities. The sanctions were kept in place after Iraq was defeated in February 1991 by a US-led coalition. Despite the contestation of the impact of the sanctions on civilians, numerous studies found that Iraqi civilians died in large numbers due to the UN Security Council action. As early as 1995, researchers found that 'as many as 576,000 Iraqi children may have died' because of the sanctions (Corssette 1995). Although that estimate was later revised downwards, other studies also found intolerable mortality rates due to the sanctions. In November 2001, *The Nation* reported on studies by Richard Garfield ('Morbidity and Mortality Among Iraqi Children', 1999), and by Mohamed Ali (of London School of Hygiene and Tropical Medicine) and Iqbal Shah (of the World Health Organization) published in *The Lancet* in May 2000. Based on the Ali and Shah study, Garfield's initial figure of 227,000 was revised upwards to 350,000 in 2000 – a massive death toll by any measure (Cortright 2001).

Sanctions against Iran have not only been deeply politicized but also subjected to manipulations when it is complying with the requirements needed to lift the sanctions. In July 2015 the P5+1 (US, UK, China, France, Russia, and Germany) arrived at a solid agreement in the form of the Joint Comprehensive Plan of Action (JCPOA) 'to ensure that Iran's nuclear program will be exclusively peaceful'. The US State Department's website notes (until the time of writing, August 2017) that the International Atomic Energy Agency (IAEA) has verified that Iran has implemented its key nuclear-related measures described in the JCPOA, and the Secretary of State has confirmed the IAEA's verification. Implementation of the Plan took effect on January 16, 2016 and the US and EU lifted the sanctions against Iran.

In the meantime, Donald J. Trump as candidate in the 2016 US elections consistently berated the JCPOA, and upon taking office in 2017 immediately set about airing his intention to scrap the agreement although the IAEA has confirmed that Iran has complied. The basis of Trump's accusation is that Iran is not following the 'spirit' of the JCPOA. More than that, the American president in his maiden speech to the UN on September 19, 2017 praised the Security Council Resolution for new sanctions on North Korea, only to go on calling for another Security Council action (JCPOA) to essentially be scrapped. He framed his arguments in terms of Iran being a 'corrupt dictatorship' and 'an economically depleted rogue state whose chief exports are violence, bloodshed, and chaos'. Important to note is that the 'West' in this case as in many others, is not always agreed on policies. Thus, on September 21, 2017 – two days after Trump's speech – the EU foreign policy chief, Federica Mogherini, essentially upbraided the American president's position. She noted that Iran is 'delivering', and further, that the agreement cannot simply be scrapped because it would be a violation of a UN Security Council action.

Humanitarian intervention

Intervention in the Third World took a new twist after the end of the Cold War, framed as it were in the language of humanitarianism, and specifically humanitarian intervention. For postcolonialism the very idea of 'intervention' is problematic because it flies in the face of the international system's sacred value of sovereignty, and also because it is used based on definitions of friends or enemies of the West, or on arguments of national interest which are self-serving. Sovereignty as a norm emerged through the Peace of Westphalia and was consolidated in its subsequent embedding in international institutions, including international law. It is for instance the backbone of the United Nations Charter. Consistent with Chapters VI and VII of the UN Charter, the Security Council can only authorize coercive intervention (including the use of military force) if developments in a state, or between states, pose a threat to international security.

Mahmood Mamdani (2009) underlines the fact that sovereignty is the basis for citizenship, an internal matter that is externally recognized. Subsequently, the norms of multilateral intervention were broadened to include intervention where there is a threat or actual practice of crimes against humanity or genocide, and more broadly, where there is mass violence against civilians. These latter can be broadly subsumed under the norms of a duty to intervene, and the Responsibility to Protect. Recent developments in the Middle East, and specifically in Libya, have led to a further expansion of the necessity of intervention. In the case of Libya, the United States and France provided military and other forms of support to armed insurgents fighting the Libyan army of Muammar Gaddafi (Prashad 2012). Support for insurgent groups aimed at toppling the government of Syria has also been justified on the same basis.

Liberal internationalists have joined some neo-conservatives in making the case for these interventions. Jon Western and Joshua Goldstein, for instance, make a determined case in support of humanitarian intervention, with special emphasis on peace-keeping. They argue that there is a clear record of overall success with UN peace-keeping and humanitarian intervention, and this, despite notable failures in some high-profile missions, such as in Rwanda and Somalia. Western and Goldstein (2011) note that the failures, though catastrophic, led the UN to carefully engage in self-assessment with the aim of becoming more effective. They also point out that many of the missions did not succeed because the international community lacked the political will to intervene *early*, or with *enough strength* on the ground.

Two key elements of successful humanitarian intervention are legitimacy and exit. A typical liberal critique of humanitarian intervention can be found in arguments by Benjamin Valentino (2004) who states that though humanitarian intervention is a 'noble notion', it has too many costs in the way it is currently practiced. The general argument is that humanitarian intervention in the form of armed intervention is neither efficient nor economical. For Valentino, even though no price is too high to save a life, the financial cost of military intervention is too high. Apart from the measurable financial expenditures, there are also opportunity costs. Military interventions also result in accidental deaths of innocent civilians, speed up or increase the violence by the contenting parties, sour relations among great powers, and corrode the legitimacy of international organizations. By contrast, the resources expended on military intervention can be more effectively employed in preventative measures, such as health care, or in disaster-relief efforts (Valentino 2004).

The postcolonial critique is much broader and is perhaps best exemplified by Mamdani's analysis of the genocide in Darfur and also of the activities of the International Criminal Court. The crisis in Darfur according to Mamdani cannot be understood outside of the legacy of British colonialism in Sudan, especially since it was this same colonialism that created the basis for tribal antagonisms and outright conflict, including significant violence. This violence led to the International Criminal Court (ICC) charging Sudan's president, Omar Hasan Ahmad al-Bashir, with crimes of racial polarization, ethnic cleansing of 'Zurga' groups, and 'slow death' 'from malnutrition, rape, and torture in IDP camps' (Mamdani 2004, 270). But Mamdani argues that none of the charges 'can bear historical scrutiny', and that they were politically motivated. There were in fact multiple causes for the violence in Darfur.

Engdahl (1992) has shown that the formation of Iraq as a nation state after World War I was basically the result of British economic and geopolitical calculations, much of it to do with outflanking American financial and oil interests. Germany lost not only the war, but the coveted Berlin–Bagdad Railway which had already begun, underwritten as it were, by a financial powerhouse – Deutsche Bank. The British created a political construct called Iraq out of Mesopotamia, pushing disparate religious sects and tribes under the rule of '… the son of Husain ibn Ali of Mecca, Feisal bin Husain' (Engdhal 1992, 59–60). By contrast, Tilly (1992, 104) has shown that in the case of Europe, '…national standing armies, national states, and direct rule caused each other'. The forces pushing amalgamation of different peoples, tribes, ethnicities, and histories into artificially constructed nation states has played a major role in ongoing so-called ethnic conflicts which occur in the Third World. Some, such as Rwanda, have endured nothing less than genocide. Note that for Mbembe (2001, 40) '… African state entities rested on eminently indigenous social bases', a point that deserves considerable attention when thinking about the endogenous factors in Third World nation building. One hundred years after Iraq came into being through colonial artificial insemination, the British are in a coalition there today, bombing the same Iraq, for much the same reason – oil.

Humanitarian intervention is also seen as a pretext for usurping the sovereignty of Third World countries, but only those that are not friends or allies of the West, and especially the United States. Humanitarian intervention could also be seen as a continuation of the trusteeship system which followed World War I and which was a concoction that allowed the victors in the Great War to snatch territories from the defeated Germans, Italians, and Ottoman Empire. Finally, while humanitarian intervention is conceptually different from preventative and preemptive wars, the three have become muddled at times. This is clearly what happened when the justification for invading Iraq in 2003 switched from preemptive attack against Iraq's WMD, to saving Iraqis from Saddam Hussein (Colhoun 2016, 149). Preventative war which is built on the principle of Just War Blanket Prohibition, and which is supported in some instances by neoliberal institutionalists (Buchanan & Keohane 2004) has also been rejected by postcolonial scholars such as Neta Crawford who argues that fear alone of attack, even if rational, cannot be the basis for preventative attack (Crawford 2003).

Terrorism

Since September 11, 2001, few topics in international politics have animated more intense public discussions than terrorism. The catastrophic attacks of that day also pushed IR scholars into sustained examination about the causes, consequences, and ways of combating terrorism. The United States declared a 'war on terror'. Broadly speaking three distinct lines of arguments have been developed in the scholarly literature, namely, those based on culture/ideology, economics, and politics. The cultural-ideological approach puts emphasis on general belief systems as the basis for action. This approach also incorporates religion with considerable emphasis on fundamentalism, and specifically Islamic fundamentalism. The economic approach has two inter-related dimensions. First, poor economic conditions can form the basis for individuals to be recruited into radical movements. And secondly, poor economic conditions can prevent a weak state from fully discharging the responsibilities of both domestic and international security (Rice, Graff, and Pascual 2010).

The culture and ideology explanation of terrorism, and specifically Islamic terrorism, is motivated by what Bernholz describes as Supreme Values. 'Supreme values are typically ingredients of an ideology comprising a *Weltanschauung*, a comprehensive world view, which purports to be absolutely true' (Bernholz 2006, 224). Bernholz further states that in order to reach the truth, or the goals, '…everything and everybody has to be sacrificed if this is necessary to reach them' (Bernholz 2006, 224). Still in this narrative, while terrorism motivated by values has been around for a long time, in the past decades it has been dominated by Islamic terrorism, much of it influenced by thinkers such as Ibn Tamiyya, Mawdudi, and Syyid Qutab. The views of these Islamic thinkers have been revived by charismatic leaders such as Osama bin Laden. Bernholz strongly believes that the West is vulnerable to radical immigrant Islamists. Most scholars within American and European liberalism are hesitant to cast such a broad net, but the rise of right-wing populism in the United States, has actually tightened the link between terrorism and Islam.

The liberal argument as exemplified by Ehrlich and Liu (2002) is that terrorism has economic roots. First, they state that there is a geopolitical logic to terrorism. This dimension is linked to the historical dependence of developed nations and especially the West on oil from the Middle East. In order to secure guaranteed supplies of oil the West has for decades either turned a blind eye, or actively supported dictatorial regimes in the oil supplying Middle Eastern countries. 'That's why there are American troops in Saudi Arabia, whose presence has enraged some Moslems, especially Osama Bin Laden' (Ehrlich and Liu 2002, 184). Secondly, poverty combined with a demographic 'crisis' – meaning millions of unemployed young men in poor countries – has set the stage for the emergence of radical ideas, and for recruitment to take place.

Those who place ideology or Islam at the center of terrorism dismiss poverty as a source of action. For US grand strategist Thomas P.M. Barnett (2004), however, hostility, including terrorism is a product of 'the gap', meaning those places in the world that have been cut off from globalization. Implied in the argument is that economic (self) marginalization is both indicative of, and a reinforcer of, cultural aversion to modernity. Despite the grandiose theory of globalization and conflict, Barnett falls back into many of the familiar cultural tropes of pinning aversions to Western modernity on 'religion', and how women are treated. More than that, he comes very close to advocating the use of military power to spread Western style ways of life, both economic and cultural. Thus, he argues that '…our military interventions will be judged by the connectivity they leave behind, not the smoking holes' (Barnett 2004, 137). Put differently, war is a justifiable means of spreading globalization broadly defined as free market capitalism and Western values.

Postcolonial scholars take a long-term view of terrorism, and more specifically, prefer to examine it in the context of colonialism, imperialism, and empire, rather than mono-causal explanations based on a spectrum of issues from the geopolitical and economic, to the ideological, or religious. One of the enduring legacies of empire is the construction of resistance to foreign domination as acts of terror, a label used so broadly that it engulfs slave revolts (Morant Bay Rebellion), wars of liberation (Algeria's war of independence against France), attempts at repelling foreign invasion (the Vietnamese defense of their country against the French and then the United States), and even determined efforts to remove foreign installed military dictatorships (the struggles against the Shah of Iran). Doty (1996) has shown how the production of African peoples in the languages of madness, immaturity, and needing modernization, set up the basis for a wide range of violations from simple abuse to torture against the Mau Mau in Kenya (Doty, 106–115). The political argument has been most eloquently stated by Mahmood Mamdani, an anthropologist at Columbia University. Mamdani argues that Islamic terrorism is largely the result of Cold War politics. The grand strategy that would come to characterize the War on Terror was actually already on its way since the 1980s in the Reagan Doctrine which took the form of Low Intensity Conflict. Mamdani (2004) argues that well before the War on Terror, the United States determined that threats from the Third World were more pressing than that of the Soviet Union. One of the key shifts in the new doctrine was to move from deterrence to offense. A telling argument of Mamdani that actually undercuts the construction of terror as Islamic is the way the West divides the world into 'good Muslims' and 'bad Muslims' (Mamdani 2004). The good Muslims are those who support Western interests, examples being Saudi Arabia, Pakistan, the Gulf Emirates – all of which actually have long histories of cooperation with colonial and imperial rulers. Fanon (2005, 86) is clear that colonialism would not have been possible without collaborators.

War fighting against the Third World

In May 2003, the Chairman of the Joint Chiefs of Staff, Richard B. Meyers, delivered an address to the US Air Force Academy in which he essentially made the case for a new American way of war. The crux of the General Meyers' text is that wars of 'annihilation or attrition' are no longer needed because the new strategy can strike the pillars of the enemy with great precision. Wars could be won through a preponderance of air power and because of that there is a gradual 'obsolescencing' of ground wars. What is needed then, is a transformation of military strategy and a reconfiguration of force structure, deployment, and war-fighting tactics. Much has indeed been made about the supposedly humane ways in which modern war is conducted with repeated stress on the ways in which smart weapons are helping to avoid unnecessary deaths. It is along these lines that drone warfare is often praised by politicians and strategists as a more humane way of fighting the War on Terror. Of course, the discourse of drones as being more humanitarian is given succor by the multiple civilian uses to which drones have been put to use.

Many *within* the debates on US grand strategy reject the claims made on behalf of smart-weapons warfare. Pape (2004), for instance, rejects the argument that smart wars can replace the older strategy of a combination of air power and ground forces, or the hammer (air power) and the anvil (ground forces). He acknowledges that smart weapons and developments in information technologies leading to superior intelligence and real-time battle-field 'pictures' have revolutionized contemporary warfare. Yet he argues that a review of the last five American wars does not support the claims of a Revolution in Military Affairs or 'transformationists'. In the case of Kosovo, for instance, he states that it was the use of air power, *plus* the threat of invasion that led Slobodan Milosevic 'to surrender Kosovo to NATO forces…' Nor did 'shock and awe' take out Saddam Hussein or the top Iraqi leadership. In fact, argues Pape (2004), at times, precision strikes can be even counterproductive, such as when the US Air Force strike on Muammar al-Qaddafi not only missed him, but subsequently led to the bombing of Pan Am flight 103 which resulted in 270 civilian deaths.

But even these critiques of smart-weapons war miss the point, which is that Western wars against the Third World have been brutal by any measure, and further the levels of lethality have consistently shown a wanton disregard for Third World lives (Mitamura 2017). The most minimal review of lethality against the Third World, both before and during the age of smart-weapons wars, can quickly substantiate this claim. Consider the data in Box 9.3.

Box 9.2: Snapshot: Violence against the Third World

- 635,000 tons of bombs dropped on Korea
- 6,163,000 tons of bombs were air dropped on Vietnam between August 1965 and August 1973
- 1.5 million tons of bombs dropped on Southeast Asia by the US Navy and Marine Corp – 1965–73
- 89,679 tons of bombs dropped on Iraq in First Persian Gulf War
- 400,000 tons of napalm dropped on Vietnam
- 29,199 tons of bombs dropped on Iraq in Operation Shock and Awe – March 21–April 21, 2003
- Millions of gallons of chlorine gas dropped on Vietnam
- 4,747,587 acres of forest destroyed in Operation Ranch Hand
- 481,897 acres of cropland destroyed

Violence has been the definitive effect of colonial and imperial contact, conquest, occupation, and wars against 'Third World' states and peoples. The original violence began with and lasted throughout the conquest of North America, Meso America, South America, the Caribbean, Australia, New Zealand, and the Pacific islands, where entire peoples of indigenous heritages were completely or almost completely annihilated (Beier 2009). Much the same happened during centuries of colonial rule and in places like the Belgian Congo, where the violence was not only on a scale vastly at odds with any kind of military or security objective, but was systematic in planning and execution (Hochschild 1999). The case of No Gun Ri during the Korean War clearly illustrates the point. On July 26, 1950 the US 7th Cavalry Regiment had several hundred refugees pinned down under a bridge at No Gun Ri, a small village south of Seoul. The refugees were dressed in white and easily identifiable *as* refugees. They were heading south, towards greater safety from a murderous war. Soon some 250–300 unarmed and cowering refugees were systematically killed, many of them blown up beyond recognition as reported by eye witnesses:

> A whine from over the horizon, from the direction of Hwanggan, grew instantly to a roar. Heads turned, looked up. From among the broken clouds American warplanes were dropping down toward them. Ten-year-old Choon-ja was at the brook and culvert when she heard it and looked up, when the ground suddenly shook wildly and everything lifted into the air in an unearthly, deafening thunder, dirt and gravel from the railbed, bags and bushes and white clothing blasted upward, with people and parts of people. Again and again the earth rocked…and suddenly midday was midnight amid dust, dirt and falling leaves, and planes again and again roared in, unleashing bombs or rockets, firing machine guns.

And again:

> Some scratched into the earth trying to hide. Others lay bloody and silent, dismembered, strewn about. Still others lay sprawled crying pitifully for help. Cows screamed. The limbs of people and animals rained down.
>   (Hanley, Choe, and Mendonza 2001, 119–120)

Box 9.2 provides only the most minimal glimpse of the extent to which violence against Third World peoples must trouble the historiography in which Western states spread values that are universal and civilized. Note that more than six million tons of bombs were dropped on Vietnam alone, and when combined with hundreds of thousands of tons of napalm, and millions of pounds of chlorine gas, and saturation with Agent Orange, the picture of absolute devastation should be clear. Turse (2013) provides vivid details of the use of 'pineapple' and 'guava' cluster bombs in Vietnam which can and did cause death by a 'thousand cuts'. 'From 1964 to 1971, the US military ordered at least 37 million pineapples, and between 1966 and 1971 it bought approximately 285 million guava bomblets – nearly seven for each man, woman, and child in Vietnam, Laos, and Cambodia combined' (Turse 2013, 85). There are also credible reports of the use of white phosphorous in the battle of Fallujah in late 2004, and against ISIL in June, 2017. The weapons are widely known to cause grievous burns and it is against international law to drop them on civilian populations as happened in both cases noted here. As Kumarakulasingam (2017) has shown, the greatest legacy of violence is horror.

In a critique of neoliberal institutionalism's theory of hegemony as a form of leadership, and neo-Gramscian theory of hegemony as essentially consensual, this author has framed Western power over the Third World as 'primitive hegemony', meaning the employment of massive violence is the preferred way of 'dealing' with Third World peoples who are not allies or friends (Persaud 2004). For over five hundred years the Third World when not under direct occupation of the West, and Japan, has been subjected to multiple forms of warfare, and the lethality continues notwithstanding claims about the new American way of war (Persaud 2016). Soviet occupation of Afghanistan resulted in nearly one million Afghan deaths. Japan's Empire in South East Asia was every bit as murderous as the widespread killings associated with Western colonialism and imperialism. Yukiko Koshiro (1999) has shown how, in fact, Japanese notions of civilizational superiority propelled its imperialism of Co-Prosperity. Thus, '... racial superiority became an ideological force to legitimate Japan's rule over non-Japanese peoples in Asia' (Koshiro 1999, 7).

The claims of a precise warfare based on smart weapons have been belied by the continuing carnage and indiscriminate killing, the latter evidenced by

---

Box 9.3: Key points

- Theories and approaches to security are overwhelmingly derived out of Western sources, and promote Western interests.
- A world-historical and global approach to security needs to replace the existing Eurocentric literature.
- Colonialism and imperialism were definitive in shaping the internal structures affecting Third World security, as well as the relationship between Empire and its Others.
- Since 1492 violence against the Third World and resistance against this violence have been consistent themes in North/South relations.
- Race and gender, not only reason and rationality, have informed all manner of Eurocentric thinking and strategies about the Third World.
- Although Euro-Americans have benefitted from colonialism, imperialism, and empire, significant criticism and resistance to these practices have come from within Euro-America.
- Some Global South scholars (Mahbub ul Haq and Amartya Sen) have contributed to the concept of human security, which is a more comprehensive idea compared to 'national security', and which was officially adopted by the UNDP in 1994.
- The Western peace since 1945 has come at the price of Western wars in the Third World.

numerous bombs dropped by drones on individuals and groups who have no connection to terrorism (Ahmed 2013). From 'signature strikes' to 'crowd killing' the US Predator drone killing program has resulted in 'thousands killed by Hellfire missiles' (Calhoun 2016, 139). These killings have been followed by denial, standardized apologies, and token compensations. Between August 2014 and August 2015, some 22,478 weapons were dropped on Iraq and Syria, a staggering figure given that between January 2010 and August 2015, the comparable figure was 20,237. In 2016, the last full year of the Obama administration, the US dropped seventy-two bombs a day, for the entire year (Benjamin 2017). Kaplow (2013) notes that the US is now actively pursuing usable nuclear weapons and has also revived cluster bombs.

Conclusion

Postcolonialism, states Siba Grovogui (2010, 239) offers '…new ways of thinking about techniques of power that constrain self-determination' in former colonies. In the case of security, we may add that postcolonialism is a recognition of the long and agonizing efforts of colonized peoples to secure their sovereignties at costs often times unbearable to repeat, but still there, dignified and resilient. Mindful of the ways in which Euro-centric security studies nonchalantly uses its own history to make universal claims, postcolonialism is insistent on 'provincializing' these claims, and embarking on a reconstructive historiography founded in global pluralism.

It is now exactly thirty years since Azar and Moon (1988) warned that traditional security analyses are '…distortive of objective reality' when it comes to understanding the security of the Third World. Their volume in 1988 – *National Security in the Third World* – in part, anticipated a broadening of security, one that is 'organic' to the challenges of the Third World.

The specificity of Third World security must become a priority for postcolonial scholars. There is vast potential to build on the work of Mohammed Ayoob (1995 & 2002) even if his work does not typically fit the postcolonial tradition. Ayoob's central claim that the key issues for Third World security are internal, and directly related to the disrupted process of state formation that occurred in the Third World due to colonial intervention and foreign rule, often indirect rule, still remains true. Acharya's (1997) spatial reordering of security studies where the 'periphery is the core' advances the connected histories thesis adumbrated by Frank and Gills, and by Bhambra and others. Writing with Ayoob's contribution in mind, Acharya emphasizes the importance of understanding the problem of weak states inherited from colonial rule, as well as the need to go below the level of the state in order to flesh out the very real problems of human development that continue to affect so many countries in Asia, Africa, the Middle East, and Latin America and the Caribbean.

Important strides have been made. Thus, the emergence of human security in the early 1990s was a productive shift to questions and concerns afflicting the vast majority of humanity. Human security shifts the focus of attention away from foreign threats, military solutions, and a fixation on the state. Instead, human security is people centered, grounded in multiple levels of action – local, national, and global, and includes an array of actors and issues hitherto marginalized, or all together shut out.

Note

1 My sincere thanks to Amitav Acharya, John Hobson, Craig Murphy, and Mustapha Kamal Pasha for their feedback on some parts of this chapter. My thanks also to Srdjan Vucetic from whom I benefitted a great deal during this writing.

Suggested readings

Barkawi, T. and Stanski, K. (Eds.). (2012). *Orientalism and war.* New York: Cambridge University Press. An excellent collection of essays on the ways in which Orientalism as a scholarly endeavor and a mindset has affected ways of thinking about war.
Koshiro, Y. (1999). *Trans-pacific racisms and the US occupation of Japan.* New York: Columbia University Press. This book shows how the domestic racisms in the United States and Japan facilitated post-World War II relations, including the occupation of Japan.
Mamdani, M. (2009). *Saviors and survivors: Darfur, politics and the war on terror.* New York: Pantheon Books. A detailed historical and contemporary analysis of the forces that led to the crisis in Darfur, as well as the ways in which the crisis has been maneuvered for narrow political interests.
Porter, P. (2013). *Military orientalism: Eastern war through western eyes.* New York: Oxford University Press. This book will deepen your knowledge about postcolonialism and war, not least because it takes a critical perspective on Orientalism.
Weatherford, J. (2004). *Genghis Khan and the making of the modern world.* New York: Three Rivers Press. This book makes a compelling case that we should not necessarily begin IR with 1648, or for that matter, 1492. Exhaustive in detail, and very clearly written.

Bibliography

Abu-Nimer, M. (2002). *Nonviolence and peace building in Islam: Theory and practice.* Gainesville, FL: University Press of Florida.
Acemoglu, D. and Robinson, J. (2012). *Why nations fail.* New York: Crown Business.
Acharya, A. (1997). The periphery as the core: The third world and security studies. In K. Krause, and M.C. Williams (Eds.). *Critical security studies: Concepts and cases* (pp. 299–327). Minneapolis: University of Minnesota Press.
Acharya, A. (2014). Global international relations (IR) and regional worlds: A new agenda for international studies. *International Studies Quarterly,* 58, 647–659.
Agathangelou, A.M. and Ling, L.H.M. (2009). *Transforming world politics: From empire to multiple worlds.* London: Routledge.
Ahmed, A. (2013). *The thistle and the drone: How America's war of terror became a global war on tribal Islam.* Washington, D.C.: Brookings Institution Press.
Anievas, A., Manchanda, N., & Shilliam, R. (Eds.). (2014). *Race and racism in international relations: Confronting the global color line.* New York, NY: Routledge.
Armstrong, E. and Prashad, V. (2006). Bandung women: Vietnam, Afghanistan, Iraq, and the necessary risks of solidarity. In Riley, R. and Inayatullah, N. (Eds.). *Interrogating imperialism.* New York: Palgrave Macmillan.

Ayers, A. (2008). *Gramsci, political economy, and international relations theory: Modern princes and naked emperors.* Basingstoke: Palgrave Macmillan.

Ayoob, M. (2002). Inequality and theorizing in international relations: The case for subaltern realism. *International Studies Review,* 27–48.

Azar, E.E. and Moon, C. (Eds.) (1988). *National security in the third world: The management of international and external threats.* Cheltenham: Edward Elgar Publishing Ltd.

Bacevich, A.J. (2002). *American empire: The realities and consequences of U.S. diplomacy.* London: Harvard University Press.

Bahrami, N. and Parsi, T. (2012). Blunt instrument: Sanctions don't promote democratic Change. *Boston Review,* February 6, 2012.

Barkawi, T. (2006). *Globalization and war.* Lanham, MD: Roman & Littlefield.

Barkawi, T. (2013). War, armed forces and society in a postcolonial perspective. In S. Seth (Ed.). *Postcolonial theory and international relations.* New York: Routledge.

Barkawi, T. and Laffey, M. (2006) The postcolonial moment in security studies. *Review of International Studies,* 32, 329–352.

Barnett, T.P.M. (2004). *The Pentagon's new map.* New York: Berkley Books.

Beier, J.M. (2009). *International relations in uncommon places: Indigeneity, cosmology, and the limits of international theory.* London: Palgrave Macmillan.

Benjamin, M. (2017). America dropped 26,171 bombs in 2016. What a bloody end to Obama's reign *The Guardian,* January 9.

Bernholz, P. (2006). International political system, supreme values and terrorism, *Public Choice,* 128, 221–231.

Bhambra, G.K. (2014). *Connected sociologies.* London: Bloomsbury Academic.

Biswas, S. and Nair, S. (Eds.) (2010). *International relations and states of exception: Margins, peripheries, and excluded bodies.* New York: Routledge.

Buchanan, A. and Keohane, R.O. (2004). The preventive use of force: A cosmopolitan institutional proposal. *Ethics & International Affairs,* 18, 1–22.

Campbell, D. (1998). *Writing security: United States foreign policy and the politics of identity.* Minneapolis: University of Minnesota Press.

Colhoun, L. (2016). *We kill because we can: From soldering to assassination in the drone age.* London: Verso.

Cortright, D. (2016). A hard look at Iraqi sanctions. *The Nation* (November 15). Online www.thenation.com/article/hard-look-iraq-sanctions/

Crawford, N.C. (2003). The slippery slope to preventive war. *Ethics & International Affairs,* 17, 30–36.

Crossette, B. (1995). Iraq sanctions kill children, UN Reports www.nytimes.com/1995/12/01/world/iraq-sanctions-kill-children-un-reports.html?mcubz=0

Cox, R.W. (1981). Social forces, states, and world orders: Beyond international relations theory. *Millennium,* 10, 126–155.

Cox, R.W. (1983). Gramsci, hegemony, and international relations. *Millennium,* 12, 162–175.

Deconde, A. (1992). *Ethnicity, race and American foreign policy: A history.* Boston: Northeastern University Press.

Doty, R.L. (1996). *Imperial encounters: The politics of representation in North-South relations.* Minneapolis, MN: University of Minnesota Press.

Ehrlich, P.R. and Liu, J. (2002). Some roots of terrorism. *Population and Environment,* 24, 183–192.

Engdahl, F.W. (2004). *A century of war: Anglo-American oil politics and the new world order.* London: Pluto Press.

Enloe, C. (1990). *Bananas, beaches and bases: Making feminist sense of international politics.* Los Angeles: University of California Press.

Fanon, F. (2005). *The wretched of the earth.* New York: Grove Press.

Frank, A.G. and Gills, B.K. (Eds.) (1993). *The world system: Five hundred years or five thousand?* London: Routledge.

Foucault, M. (2007). *Security, territory, population.* (Trans. by G. Burchell). New York: Palgrave Macmillan.

Gandhi, L. (1998). *Postcolonial theory: A critical introduction.* New York: Columbia University Press.

George, J. (1994). *Discourses of global politics: A critical (re)introduction to international relations.* Boulder: Lynne Rienner.

Gill, S.R. and Mittelman, J.H. (Eds.). (1997). *Innovation and transformation in international studies.* Cambridge: Cambridge University Press.

Grovogui, S.N. (2001). Come to Africa: A hermeneutics in international theory. *Alternatives*, 26, 425–448.

Grovogui, S.N. (2010). Postcolonialism. In T. Dunne, M. Kurki, and S. Smith (Eds.). *International relations theories* (2nd edition) (pp. 238–256). New York: Oxford University Press.

Hanley, C.J., Choe, S., and Mendoza, M. (2001). *The bridge at No Gun Ri.* New York: Henry Holt.

Henderson, E. (2017). *African realism? International relations theory and Africa's wars in the postcolonial era.* Lanham, MD: Roman & Littlefield Publishers.

Hobson, J.M. (2012). *The eurocentric conception of world politics: Western international theory,* 1760–2010. Cambridge: Cambridge University Press.

Hochschild, A. (1999). *King Leopold's ghost.* New York: Mariner Books.

Homer-Dixon, T.F. (2007). *The upside of down: Catastrophe, creativity and the renewal of civilization.* London: Souvenir Press.

Hunt, M. (1987). *Ideology and US foreign policy.* New Haven: Yale University Press.

Inayatullah, N. and Blaney, D.L. (2004). *International relations and the problem of difference.* London: Routledge.

Jones, B.G. (Ed.). (2006). *Decolonizing international relations.* Lanham, MD: Roman & Littlefield, Publishers.

Kaplow, D.A. (2010). *Death by moderation: The U.S. military's quest for useable weapons.* New York: Cambridge University Press.

Keegan, J. (1994). *A history of warfare.* New York: Vintage.

Koshiro, Y. (1999). *Trans-Pacific racisms: and the US occupation of Japan.* New York: Columbia University Press.

Krishna, S. (2009). *Globalization and postcolonialism.* Lanham, MD: Rowman and Littlefield.

Kumarakulasingam, N. (2017). Metropolitan killings: Laundering a scandal. Paper presented at the 58th *International Studies Association Convention*, Baltimore, Maryland, February 22–25.

Laffey, M. and Nadarajah, S. (2016). Postcolonialism. In A. Collins (Ed.). *Contemporary Security Studies* (4th edition), pp. 122–138.

Lal, V. (1993). The Incident of the crawling lane: Women in the Punjab disturbances of 1919. *Genders*, No. 6 35–60. Online version (downloaded 9/23/2017) www.sscnet. ucla.edu/southasia/History/British/Crawling.html.

McDougall, W. (2016). *The tragedy of US foreign policy.* New Haven: Yale University Press.

McDougall, W.A. (1997). *Promised land, crusader state.* Boston: Houghton Mifflin Co.

Mackinder, H. (2004/1904). The geographical pivot of history. *The Geographical Journal*, 170, 298–321 (original Vol. XXXIII, No. 4).

Mamdani, M. (2009). *Saviors and survivors: Darfur, politics, and the war on terror*. New York: Pantheon Books.

Mamdani, M. (2004). *Good Muslim, bad Muslim: America, the cold war, and the roots of terror*. New York: Pantheon Books.

Manela, E. (2007). *The Wilsonian moment: Self-determination and the international origins of anticolonial nationalism*. New York: Oxford University Press.

Matin, K. (2011). Redeeming the universal: Postcolonialism and the inner life of Eurocentrism. *European Journal of International Relations*, 19, 353–377.

Mbembe, A. (2001). *On the postcolony*. Los Angeles: University of California Press.

Meyers, R.B. (2003). The new American way of war. *Military Technology*, June 2003, 64–74.

Mills, C. (1997). *The racial contract*. Ithaca: Cornell University Press.

Mitamura, E. (2017). Provoking humanity: Afterlives of mass violence in Cambodia and the United States. Paper presented to the 58th *International Studies Association*, Baltimore, Maryland, February 22–25.

Palmer, R.R. (1960). *A history of the modern world*. New York: Alfred A. Knopf.

Pape, R.A. (2004). The true worth of air power. *Foreign Affairs*, pp. 116–130.

Pasha, M.K. (2013). The 'Bandung impulse' and international relations, in S. Seth (Ed.). *Postcolonial theory and international relations* (pp. 144–165). London: Routledge.

Persaud, R.B. (2003–2004). Shades of American hegemony: The primitive, the enlightened, and the benevolent. *Conn. J. Int'l L*, 19, 263.

Persaud, R.B. (2016). Neo-Gramscian theory and third world violence: A time for broadening. *Globalizations*, 13, 547–562.

Prashad, V. (2012). *Arab spring, Libyan winter*. Baltimore: A.K. Press.

Quijano, A. (2000). Coloniality of power and Eurocentrism in Latin America. *International Sociology*, 15, 215–232.

Rice, S., Graff, C., and Pascual, C. (Eds.). (2010). *Confronting poverty: Weak states and US national security*. Washington, DC: Brookings Institution Press.

Riley, R. and Inayatullah, N. (Eds.). (2006). *Interrogating imperialism*. New York: Palgrave Macmillan.

Rosato, S. (2003). The flawed logic of democratic peace theory. *American Political Science Review*, 97, 585–602.

Rummel, R.J. (1998). Statistics of Democide: genocide and Mass Murder since 1900 (Chapter 3). Online www.hawaii.edu/powerkills/SOD.CHAP3.HTM

Said, E. (1993). *Culture and imperialism*. New York: Alfred A. Knopf.

Sajed, A. and Inayatullah, N. (2016). On the perils of lifting the weight of structures: An engagement with Hobson's critique of the discipline of IR. *Postcolonial Studies*, 19, 201–209.

Seth, S. (2013). *Postcolonial theory and international relations*. London: Routledge.

Starr, H. (1997). Democracy and integration: Why democracies don't fight each other. *Journal of Peace Research*, 34, 153–162.

Tadjbakhsh, S. and Chenoy, A.M. (2009). *Human security: Concepts and implications*. London: Routledge.

Tilly, C. (1992). *Capital, coercion, and European states: AD 900–1992*. Oxford: Blackwell Publishers.

Turse, N. (2013). *Kill anything that moves: The real American war in Vietnam*. New York: Picador.

Valentino, B.A. (2011). The true cost of humanitarian intervention. *Foreign Affairs*, 90, 60–73.

Vucetic, S. (2011). *The Anglosphere: A genealogy of racialized identity in international relations.* Stanford, CA: Stanford University Press.

Weatherford, J. (2004). *Genghis Khan and the making of the modern world.* New York: Three Rivers Press.

Western, J. and Goldstein, J.S. (2011). Humanitarian intervention comes of age. *Foreign Affairs*, 90, 48–59.

Young, L. (1998). *Japan's total empire: Manchuria and the culture of wartime imperialism.* Los Angeles: University of California Press.

10 'It is not about me...but it kind of is'

Celebrity humanitarianism in late modernity

Aida A. Hozic, Samantha Majic, and Ibrahim Yahaya Ibrahim

Introduction	180
Current developments in celebrity humanitarianism	181
Celebrities in action: a brief history	183
Pros and cons of celebrity humanitarianism	188
Illustrations and narratives of celebrity engagement: human trafficking and famine	189
Conclusion	194

Introduction

How we know *what* we know in the domain of the *international* defines and structures our interests, responses, and engagements in world politics. Unlike the realm of *domestic* politics where we are led to believe the effects of political decisions are immediate and localized, events in the international domain appear distant and remote, hardly relevant to our day-to-day activities. In addition, they are generally known to us only through media – we learn about the international by watching or reading the news and/or through documentaries, movies, or other works of popular culture and/or arts. Occasionally, we travel abroad – but even in such instances our exposure to things international may be limited to food, tourist landmarks, shopping or entertainment. Of course, the very distinction between *domestic* and *international, inside* and *outside* of the state is predicated upon the existence of borders (Walker 1993). These distinctions are then reiterated through exercises of state power and various forms of knowledge production (including the study of *international* relations), which prioritize and order our experiences. Therefore, what appears close or distant from us, familiar or foreign, worthy of empathy or hardly interesting, very much depends on *how* we learned about it and *how* we had been taught to think about it.

These days, young people around the world are often educated about global events by celebrities (Mostafanehzad 2013). The practice of relying upon famous people from the world of popular culture and the arts (actors, popular singers, sports figures, famous artists) as participants in and conveyors of international events dates far back in history. Their activities and performances have long co-mingled with war efforts and imperial projects, religious and civilizing missions, affirming the role of (white) saviors against the background of barbaric or victimized others. Colonialism, in particular, was normalized through travelogues, such as the well-documented and popularized journeys of Dr. Livingston in Victorian times, when many explorers became celebrities in their own right. But it was also celebrated as in the staging of Giuseppe Verdi's opera 'Aida' at the opening of the Suez Canal (the opera written expressly for that purpose). And it is the echoes of these often sentimental but always racialized and gendered colonial practices and images which necessitate that we explore *and* problematize contemporary celebrity humanitarianism in that context.

Current developments in celebrity humanitarianism

Contemporary celebrity humanitarianism is a relatively recent phenomenon. It is generally acknowledged that it commenced in the 1980s, when images of Ethiopian famine (which we will discuss later in more detail) prompted a number of Western music stars to raise funds for the hungry by organizing a series of Live Aid concerts. Ever since, numerous celebrities, especially in the Global North, have turned to humanitarian causes – famine, disease, violence against civilians, including rape and genocide, child soldiers, refugee crises, human trafficking. International organizations, especially the United Nations, and non-governmental organizations (NGOs), which are increasingly tasked to deal with humanitarian crises (in lieu of states), welcome celebrities' involvement. In their view, celebrities can effectively spread the message about humanitarian crises to the wider public, they can be enormously helpful in fundraising efforts, and they can provide that often-missing affective link between audiences and events in faraway places. Because celebrities have already made it into our living rooms and/or onto our computer screens, because we already care about their personal lives – relationships, children, illnesses, even weight loss or gain – it is assumed that they can make us care about the plight of distant others as well. The intimacy that exists between celebrities and their fans (itself a product of careful public relations campaigns) is expected to translate into an emotional investment in causes that celebrities support. In short, celebrities trade in distant suffering (Boltanski 1999), making the unfamiliar and boring worthy of our attention and time. And therein lies the problem.

Barbie, the world's most famous white blonde, can help us visualize and understand the tropes that make celebrities' humanitarianism so questionable. In 2016, two young women (who preferred to remain anonymous) created an Instagram account where they posted pictures depicting Barbie on her imaginary volunteer travels and works in Africa. The tongue-in-cheek photos of 'Barbie Savior' – many of them 'selfies' – resembled photos of celebrities well known from the Western media: Barbie surrounded with happy (and/or hungry) *African* children, Barbie on a safari, Barbie giving talks in *African* villages, Barbie modeling the latest fashions against the background of *African* landscapes. An instant Internet hit, the visuals echoed the wonderfully humorous and poignant essay by Kenyan author Binyavanga Wainaina 'How to Write About Africa.'

'In your text', wrote Wainaina,

> treat Africa as if it were one country. It is hot and dusty with rolling grasslands and huge herds of animals and tall, thin people who are starving. Or it is hot and steamy with very short people who eat primates. Don't get bogged down with precise descriptions. Africa is big: fifty-four countries, 900 million people who are too busy starving and dying and warring and emigrating to read your book. The continent is full of deserts, jungles, highlands, savannahs and many other things, but your reader doesn't care about all that, so keep your descriptions romantic and evocative and unparticular.

And, indeed, in one of the photos, Barbie described her experiences as follows:

> What a year! It was my first year taking up residency in the country of Africa. Some may say I have done good, but there is still so much to do and so many to save! I am excited to share my New Year's resolution with you all. By the end of 2017 I will love on 153 million orphans. It's a lofty goal, but I believe I am up for the challenge.

Barbie's ID on Instagram summed up her ambitions nicely:

> Barbie Savior: Jesus. Adventures. Africa. Two worlds. One love. Babies. Beauty. Not qualified. Called. 20 years young. It's not about me…but it kind of is.

'It is not about me…but it kind of is!' In this chapter, we grapple with serious questions that Barbie Savior so cheerfully presses upon us: Who is celebrity humanitarianism about and for? When Hollywood stars and volunteer humanitarians travel to faraway places to raise awareness about a crisis – are they trying to help others or building their own resumes? When photos and videos of their journeys appear on magazine covers and Internet feeds – who is it that we are really seeing? Who is in the foreground and who is turned into landscape? What is emphasized and what obscured by mediating crises through celebrities' engagement? And last but not least – what kind of audiences and publics are being produced through circulation and consumption of such visuals and narratives?

The first section of the chapter offers a brief history of celebrity humanitarianism. In the second section, we discuss some of the common pros and cons for celebrity engagement in things international. In the third section, we look at two issues – human trafficking and famine – and examine how celebrity focus and Western media engagement shape their representation and perception. At the end, we suggest some additional texts and activities that can help you articulate your own answers to the questions posed by this chapter.

Box 10.1: Key points

- Famous people have long been engaged in international politics, but celebrity humanitarianism is a recent − *late modern* − phenomenon, which aligns well with neoliberal/neoconservative tenor of the time.
- Celebrities can effectively spread the message about humanitarian crises to a wider public but the narratives that they produce tend to reinforce existing global hierarchies.
- Celebrities tend to favor individualized, often market-based solutions to international problems rather than solutions that would transform the politics that caused the crises in the first place.
- Celebrity humanitarianism stems from but also produces certain kinds of audiences: politically disengaged but emotionally super-charged and convinced of their own ability to resolve crises through enthusiasm.

Celebrities in action: a brief history

Famous people − by the standards of their time − have been involved in international politics for a very long time. Ever since antiquity, poets, musicians, actors, playwrights and athletes have been called upon or volunteered to celebrate wars and mobilize people in their support. Just as often, they have argued for peace, led protests, participated in liberation and anti-colonial movements, and lent their voices to those who otherwise might not have been politically heard.

Celebrities, however, at least in the way the term is now commonly used, are a modern phenomenon. They are products of expanding global communication technologies and mass media, especially radio, film and television. In the 1920s and 1930s, building upon the strategies already known from vaudeville and theatre but adapted for mass media markets, Hollywood studios developed the so-called 'star system' which enabled the US film industry to flourish even during the harsh times of the Great Depression. Movie actors were placed on long-term, exclusive contracts with Hollywood studios and treated as their property. They had carefully cultivated on-screen and off-screen personas. Studio executives and gossip columnists, often working in cahoots with each other, fed movie audiences with a constant stream of stories about stars' roles, love lives, friendships, hobbies, and interests. However, fearful of censorship and dodging calls for moral regulation of the entertainment industry, studio executives kept their stars away from overt engagement in politics. Other countries were not that shy − Germany, Italy, Japan, even the Soviet Union − built their own film industries in the 1920s and 1930s, with their own film stars and their own fandoms, openly relying upon them to prop up their regimes. As World War II approached, all the Great Powers realized the immense propaganda potential of celebrities and of the intense emotional relationship they had developed with their fans. German, Italian, Soviet, Japanese and US film studios put themselves in service of their states' interests, thus transforming entertainment into an apparent – and mass mediated – political project.

With the end of World War II and the beginning of the Cold War, that political capacity of the entertainment industry turned into a liability, at least in the United States. Of course, movie stars and other celebrities were still expected to promote US power. The CIA funded exhibitions of American art abroad (Saunders 2013). The US government stimulated exports of American movies. Bob Hope, a famous vaudeville and film comedian, entertained the US troops during the Korean War so often that he became the synonym of Hollywood's servitude to the military. But in the age of the paranoid politics of Cold War era, which prevailed in the United States in the 1950s, this affinity between politics and arts/entertainment also invited suspicions. Hollywood screenwriters, directors and actors came under a vicious attack by the House Committee on Un-American Activities, whose charge was to investigate disloyal or subversive actions of American citizens. Senator Joseph McCarthy, the leading anti-communist crusader of the time, singled out Hollywood as the hotbed of communism in America. As a result of these pressures, Hollywood studios blacklisted a number of their most talented creative workers. The movies themselves turned bland, losing viewers to television and foreign films. By the beginning of the 1960s, the Hollywood studio system lost its grip on the stars and on its audiences. The blacklist had cast a longer shadow on the entertainment industry than anyone expected (Hozic 2002).

Paradoxically, the end of the studio system also allowed many actors who were formerly constrained by studio contracts to become 'free agents', while the mounting social turmoil in the nation – the Civil Rights movement, anti-Vietnam protests – set the stage for them to become politically active. Many embraced this opportunity enthusiastically, such as Jane Fonda, who visited Vietnam to express her opposition to the war, and Charlton Heston and Paul Newman, who debated nuclear disarmament on national television (Demaine 2009; Gamson 1994).

Since then, celebrities have entered the political realm *en masse* and made direct appeals to the broader public's political consciousness (Marks and Fischer 2002; Demaine 2009), beginning with Bob Geldof's 1984 recording of 'Do They Know It's Christmas' and the related Live Aid concerts in 1985, which we mentioned in the introduction. From here, as scholars have documented, celebrities have become increasingly politically active, advocating for environmental conservation and LGBT rights (Meyer and Gamson 1995); promoting engagement in political campaigns and get-out-the-vote efforts (Payne, Hanlon, and Twomey 2007; Nolan and Brookes 2013); giving testimony before Congressional committees (Demaine 2009); and participating in international diplomacy (Choi and Berger 2010), development (Biccum 2011; Brockington 2014), and humanitarian aid (Repo & Yrjölä 2011). Arguably, as Marks and Fischer (2002) wrote, we live in the era of the celebrity activist.

Alongside the decline of the Hollywood studio system, various conditions of 'late modernity' have facilitated celebrities' political ascendance. Following sociologist Anthony Giddens (1991), we understand 'late modernity' as an extension and intensification of modernity, exemplified by compression of time and space and loss of tradition. The *first* manifestation of these 'late modern' conditions is the changing 'media-scape', as indicated by the introduction of the Internet, cell phone technologies, the proliferation of cable channels, and increasingly plentiful tablet/laptop computers (van Elteren 2013). This media-scape ensures 24–7 access to current events/news and other people, thereby facilitating what Douglas Kellner calls the rise of the media spectacle, where 'competition for the audience's attention is ever more intense' and the corporate media is increasingly compelled to attract maximal audiences for as much time as possible until the next spectacle emerges (Kellner 2009, 716). Celebrities, with their penchant for dramatization and their large fan-bases, provide the perfect draw for audiences in this context. As a result, corporate media has increased its 'infotainment' output, providing evermore celebrity news and gossip.

Within this media-scape, social media use has also grown through the development of Facebook, Twitter, and Instagram, among other popular platforms, thus providing an alternative to and competition for more traditional corporate media. In fact, 'the number of social networking site users has grown from 33 percent of the online population in 2008 to 69 percent of the online population in 2012' (Smith 2013, 7). Not surprisingly, celebrities are prolific social media users who mobilize their considerable resources and communications talents to draw audiences to their various Twitter feeds, etc., which has drawn closer links between them and topical issues (Biccum 2011) and collapsed the distance between celebrities and ordinary life, as the popularity of reality TV and YouTube attest (Bystrom 2011). Consequently, as van Elteren (2013) writes, 'intimacy at a distance' now characterizes the relationship between celebrities and their fan-like audiences.

A *second* and related 'late modern' condition, which facilitates celebrities' ascendance in the polity, is public disengagement from the political process. Many scholars, following the lead of Robert Putnam, argue that civic participation peaked in the 1960s and has decreased ever since (Putnam 1995). Recent empirical research suggests that ordinary Americans' knowledge about politics, trust in political institutions, and voting participation have declined significantly (Majic 2011, 821). Of course, many scholars argue that participation has not declined but in fact shifted forms from 'duty-based' activities, such as voting and military service to more 'engaged' forms of citizenship, such as boycotts (Dalton 2008). As well, the locations of political engagement have shifted, with a growth in organized advocacy groups (Skocpol 2003; Strolovitch 2007) and nonprofits (Majic 2014b; Berry and Arons 2003).

But as political engagement has shifted, the public has become closer to and more knowledgeable about celebrities (Brockington 2014), who are often visible through new media technologies expressing support for advocacy groups, nonprofits, and boycotts, and other 'engaged' forms of activity. As they are often charismatic performers and highly skilled communicators with access to vast networks of adoring fans (Demaine 2009), celebrities can capture (social) media attention for various issues and present themselves as concerned spokespeople. And political leaders have taken note – they are often as star-struck as the general population, and they know that bringing a celebrity to speak at an event or testify before a legislative body will engage their constituents. Therefore, even as celebrities are not democratically elected, their high profiles and fan-base place them in a position to promote political engagement by directing public attention to various issues, shaping how the public understands them and, at times, influencing policy developments. In effect, in a changing media environment with shifting and more varied forms of political engagement, celebrities have become the ultimate supporters of causes and movements to 'reinvigorate the masses' (Marks and Fischer 2002, 380).

Underlying and operating alongside the changing media environment and patterns of political engagement are neoliberal and neoconservative political rationalities (or, logics/ways of being), a *third* condition that has facilitated celebrities' political engagement. Let us briefly examine these two important concepts. As well documented, neoliberalism is generally associated with preferences for a marketized organization of economic and other societal activity and a minimal state that is oriented towards deregulation and privatization of services (Larner 2000). It is 'neo' because it is not presumed to be natural but something that is achieved, whether by law or other measures; as such, it is a specific and consequential organization of the social, the subject and the state (Brown 2006). Yet neoliberalism is not found in a coherent, distinctive set of policies, but in practices that facilitate governing from a distance, and in political discourses about how to best rule a society (Larner 2000). As such, neoliberalism is less of an ideology and more of a rationality – a form of political reasoning that governs all aspects of life (Brown 2006) – which casts citizens as individualized, active subjects who are responsible for enhancing their own well-being and exercising autonomous choices (Larner 2000). And in the political and social spheres, market principles emphasizing profitability and productivity are appropriate ways to discuss and conceptualize governance (Brown 2006). If one looks at the US and globally, she can see neoliberalism everywhere, from the privatization of Bolivian water supplies, to broader discussions of government programs as 'products' for consumption.

In the United States, as Wendy Brown (2006) writes, neoliberalism has developed alongside a flourishing neoconservative rationality. Like neoliberalism, this particular conservatism is not ideologically or socially unified but a product of seemingly disparate interests, ranging from those of conservative feminists to religious Christians and right-wing politicians, among others. Neo-conservatism supports a strong, state-led moral and political vision, but it is 'neo' – meaning a new or revived form – because it affirms (moralized) state power yet abandons classical conservative commitments to modest libertarianism, frugality, refinement, education and discipline, among others (Brown 2006). The result, then, of neoliberalism and neo-conservatism, Brown (2006) compellingly argues, is a combination of market and moral political rationalities, with a business model of the state on the one hand, and a theological (i.e. related to a notion of God or 'the divine') model of the state on the other. She writes that the clash of these rationalities is apparent in, for example, the level of debt generated by military expenditures: while neoconservatives support this, it is less acceptable to cost-conscious neo-liberals who would ultimately like to see the state reduced, not expanded. Similarly, as the proceeding discussion explains, celebrities' engagement in humanitarian issues reflects and reinforces these competing (and contradictory) neoliberal and neoconservative rationalities.

Altogether, in this late modern context, celebrities are the ideal political actors.

Neoliberalism's emphasis on market-based solutions to social problems has led states to broaden the range of voices and actors, namely elites, into the policy-making process, including corporate actors, the charitable sector, and (the focus of this chapter) celebrities, who use their media expertise to convince the public that they have the answers to the problems they face (Hart and Tindall 2009; Brockington 2014). And in keeping with neoliberal self-sufficiency and individual responsibility, celebrities independently mobilize their own considerable resources and engage with new media technologies to shape public and political perceptions of and responses to various issues. Moreover, they often promote market-based solutions to social problems. Here a very prominent example is Project RED, which was founded in 2006 by Bono and Bobby Shriver and used chic consumerism to 'to get businesses and people involved in the fight against AIDS'. Although critics argue that this initiative masked the social, racial and environmental trade and production relations that underpin poverty, inequality and disease, particularly in Africa (Richey and Ponte 2008), it was popular because it used consumerism to 'solve' a social problem.

Celebrities also, if counter-intuitively, satisfy the logics of neo-conservatism. While neo-cons may deplore many celebrities' liberal political leanings, public and private behaviors (e.g. drug use and frequent divorces), and participation in films and other media that promote 'bad values', celebrities can also bolster and support a state's moral and political vision. In effect, in the market language of neoliberalism, they are able to do this as 'norm entrepreneurs': individuals interested in challenging and changing norms, which are broadly defined as beliefs about appropriate behavior for persons with a given identity (Finnemore and Sikkink 1998). In one example, as Alexandra Budabin (2015) shows in her study of Mia Farrow's activism regarding the Beijing Olympics, celebrities engage in norm entrepreneurship to draw attention to an issue (human rights abuses), secure an organizational platform, build state support, and shape policy.

Consequently, celebrities are a large and growing part of the political land-scape, to the extent that, as Steele and Shores (2014) so trenchantly observe, state authority is now shared with celebrities, who are able to capture public and political attention (often through social media technologies) in ways that politicians cannot.

Pros and cons of celebrity humanitarianism

As celebrities' role in international politics becomes more and more prominent, the scholarship about them continues to grow. However, scholars are divided about the impact that celebrities have on things international. On the one hand, in an era of arguably declining and fragmented political engagement, celebrities' high profiles bring issues to the public's attention (Demaine 2009), and they also provide 'information shortcuts' for average citizens (Frizzell 2011). On the other hand, scholars have documented that celebrities often lack the training and knowledge about the issues they address, and they tend to over-simplify issues (Dieter and Kumar 2008; Demaine 2009). Moreover, they detract atten-tion from the local activists who are more familiar with and committed to the issues on the ground (Meyer and Gamson 1995; Cooper 2007). As well, celebri-ties are rarely accountable for the solutions to social problems that they propose (Haynes 2014).

In her book on celebrity humanitarianism and North–South relations, Lisa Ann Richey (2016) suggests that we should organize the scholarship about it along three different dimensions: (1) literature on celebrities and international aid; (2) literature on celebrities and representations of 'Others;' and (3) literature on new actors and alliances in North–South relations. Richey's volume and the essays within it showcase the complexity of the phenomenon and of its impli-cations. But one chapter – Mary Mostafanehzad's essay on Angelina Jolie's work in Burmese refugee camps – seems particularly worthy of emphasis. Through careful ethnographic analysis, Mostafanezhad demonstrates how gossip – both in the camps and in the media – consistently centered on Jolie instead of human rights abuses that were ostensibly the reason for her visit. And, as Richey notes in her introduction, Jolie's humanitarian travels as an international celebrity 'perpetuated a geopolitics of hope that foregrounded sentimental rather than political concern' (Richey 2015, 14). Mostafanehzad's chapter built upon her previous research, which explored the effects of Angelina Jolie's humanitarian work on volunteer tourism, a booming female-dominated from of travel to distressed areas of the world.

Angelina Jolie's humanitarian work – as the Goodwill Ambassador for the United Nations High Commissioner for Refugees (UNHCR), as an advocate for the homeless and the dispossessed, as a producer and director of films about violence against women, and as a mother of adopted refugee children – attracts enormous media attention as well as scrutiny. Her 2016 appointment as a vis-iting 'Professor in Practice' at the London School of Economics' program on Women, Peace and Security caused an outcry among some academics. In their view, numerous other feminist – and especially non-white – scholars would have been worthier of such a prestigious visiting position. Writing in Jolie's defense, Australian professor Laura Shepherd emphasized instead fifteen years of Jolie's service to UNHCR and her 'credentials as a UN official with a long-standing commitment to advancing human rights, particularly the rights of refugees, and even more particularly, the rights of women'. And, in a recent article, feminist researchers Sarah Davies and Jacqui True also convincingly argue that the work of Angelina Jolie and the British Foreign Secretary William Hague on prevention of sexual violence in conflict might have been praiseworthy. Because sexual violence so frequently stigmatizes victims rather than perpetrators, Jolie's media-savvy campaign was crucial in brining light to violence in conflict zones and demanding international action against it.

Illustrations and narratives of celebrity engagement: human trafficking and famine

What do we see and what is missed when celebrities engage in humanitarian crises?

We have learned from the previous two sections that celebrities capitalize on the expanded media-scape to draw attention to humanitarian issues and engage the public. We now look at two such issues which often attract celebrity engagement – human trafficking and famine. By examining them more closely, we will see that while celebrities may indeed draw attention to an issue, they do so in a way that can largely be characterized as a melodrama – a compelling narrative of 'sexual danger, drama, sensation, furious action, wild applause, and…clearly identifiable victims, villains and heroes' (Vance 2011, 904). In the context of human trafficking, celebrities often offer melodramatic representations of this issue, where, for example, a young girl is kidnapped and forced into sexual slavery, only to be rescued later by law enforcement officers. Further, and in line with our earlier analysis, this melodrama is distinctly late-modern in character – it is media-friendly and informed by neoliberal and neoconservative rationalities which appeal to morality and offer individualized, marketized solutions to this problem. Specifically, celebrity anti-trafficking activity tends to over-emphasize sex trafficking of young women and girls, and finds its causes in immoral individuals and cultures. And although there are exceptions, celebrities commonly promote solutions that are oriented towards individual behavior change, and private, market-based activities such as fundraising, foundation creation, and NGO action. Similarly, narratives about famine tend to create a sense of urgency: famine is framed as an emergency, suddenly provoked by natural catastrophes, beyond human control, and preventable only by massive humanitarian intervention, thus legitimizing (indeed, demanding) engagement of outside actors. In respect to both issues, media narratives and celebrity engagement tend to obscure deeper, structural causes of the crises, to privilege external actors over locals, and to offer temporary patches instead of long-term substantive policy transformations.

(a) Human trafficking

Human trafficking is defined as 'the recruitment, transportation, transfer, harboring or receipt of persons, by means of the threat or use of force or other forms of coercion... for the purpose of exploitation' (United Nations 2014).

Human trafficking is a popular issue for celebrities. Samantha Majic (2016) has found in her preliminary research that numerous celebrities (182 to date, by her count) have engaged in at least one incidence of anti-human trafficking activity between 2000 and 2015; however, there is a racialized and gendered dimension to this, in that the majority of celebrities who participate in this are women (104) and white (80 of 104). White men are the next most likely group of celebrities to engage in this activity (51 of 78 total men). Among all the celebrities, actors were the most prominently engaged with the issue, having 229 of 330 unique instances of engagement; musicians came next with 71 instances. However, not all celebrities participated at the same level, which was apparent in the data about the celebrities who have engaged in two or more incidents of activity. Approximately two dozen celebrities had at least two instances of activity, and of these, the following celebrities – again, the majority of whom are white women – stand out for the duration and volume of their actions regarding human trafficking: Darryl Hannah, Ashely Judd, Ashton Kutcher, Ricky Martin, Demi Moore, Julia Ormond, Jada Pinkett Smith, Mira Sorvino, and Emma Thompson.

Celebrities also favor some activities over others. In principle, they privilege those that receive significant media attention and/or are more easily broadcast and covered by social media such as fundraisers, awareness campaigns, documentaries, public service announcements followed by panels or forums and legislative work. A number of those most active celebrities have also done highly visible work or on behalf of the United Nations. However, the bulk of the most popular celebrity anti-trafficking activity emphasizes that women, and young non-Western girls of color, are the primary victims of sex trafficking in particular. The focus on girls and sex is apparent in the titles and focus of many of these campaigns that are popular with celebrities, such as *Real Men Don't Buy Girls* (Majic 2017) and *Girls* are not for Sale (our emphasis). In addition, celebrity anti-trafficking activity reflects and reinforces both neoliberal and neoconservative rationalities by emphasizing how bad individuals and corrupt cultures cause human trafficking. This individual emphasis aligns with the melodramatic human trafficking narrative which, as Carol Vance writes, must be about *people*, and not states, institutions or structural conditions, all of which are too complicated or confusing to portray *and* may actually implicate the state (or other structures of power) as complicit if discussed in too much depth (Vance 2011). In short, a neoliberal melodrama needs a 'bad guy', and for celebrities, particularly actors, sharing stories of 'bad people' (and bad men in particular) aligns with their skill set.

Not surprisingly, in terms of solutions, most anti-trafficking activities supported by celebrities, emphasize modifications in individual behavior with a moral imperative – telling individual men to act differently by not purchasing sex from girls or appealing to the public to make more informed consumption choices in order to prevent human trafficking. They also tend to promote market-based initiatives such as sale of goods to raise money for the cause and/or to create their own foundations. For example, Ashton Kutcher and Demi Moore created the DNA Foundation (now THORN Digital Defenders) in 2012, the same year that Jada Pinkett Smith and Selma Hayek created the organization and accompanying website Don't Sell Bodies. Most notable is the example of Ricky Martin: he was the first to get involved publicly with the issue, after he visited Cambodia and 'witnessed this heinous crime' and also India, when he 'witnessed the horrors of human trafficking as we rescued three trembling girls living on the impoverished streets of India' (CNN). Since then, he has become one of the most active celebrities regarding human trafficking, particularly that regarding children. In 2003, he was named a UN Goodwill Ambassador, and in 2004 he created the Ricky Martin Foundation, whose principal project, People for Children, is an 'ongoing effort to combat the exploitation of children' (RMF.org). The RMF has, since its founding, variously conducted a variety of anti-trafficking activities, commonly in Central America, including research projects (namely about human trafficking in Puerto Rico), working to make online environments safer for children, and public service announcements (PSA). Ricky Martin has also testified before Congress about human trafficking, and in 2005 the State Department named him one of its 'Heroes in Ending Modern Slavery'.

To sum, the narrative about human trafficking offered by celebrities suggests that innocent girls are victims, dangerous males are predators, and moral rectitude, law enforcement and private organizations are the solution. Such narratives, presented – for the most part – by white women and men, have gendered and racialized implications, such as activism focused on young girls and women of color as victims of sex trafficking at the hands of non-Western men, which reinforces gender norms of female passivity and male agency (Majic 2014a). And it revives the 'white slavery' panics that emerged in the Progressive Era (Doezema 2010) to promote a white, Western moral superiority, whereas Gayatri Spivak so famously noted 'white [wo]men sav[e] brown women from brown men' (Spivak 1998, 93).

What these melodramatic narratives fail to acknowledge is that young women and girls are not often the primary victims of human trafficking. In fact, men, women, boys, and trans people also have experiences in sex work and other forms of labor that fit the definition of human trafficking (Marcus and Curtis 2016; Marcus et al. 2014; Ditmore, Maternick, & Zapert 2012; Gozdziak & Collett 2005). Moreover, by many estimates, sex trafficking is not the most common form of human trafficking; instead, trafficking into domestic labor, agricultural work, and garment production are far more common (ILO 2012). As well, the causes of human trafficking are not simply a predatory man or criminal ring of traffickers. In fact, many individuals who may be categorized as trafficking victims are actually migrating for labor in the face of war, anti-immigrant sentiments, and unemployment, among other factors, and oftentimes they were not tricked or duped into their movement (Agustín 2007; Andrijasevic 2007; Chapkis 2003; Kempadoo, Sanghera, & Pattanaik 2012; Milivojevic & Pickering 2013; Saunders 2000; Sharma 2003).

(b) Famine

Famine – and particularly famine in Africa – is probably the best-known and the most obvious cause of (and for) celebrity humanitarianism. In fact, it was the Ethiopian famine of 1983–1985 that prompted Bob Geldof, lead singer of a punk-rock group The Boomtown Rats, to compose 'Do They Know It's Christmas' in 1984. The song is now regarded as the milestone in the development of celebrity humanitarianism. It was recorded in a single day by Band Aid, a group of mostly British and Irish musicians. It became an instant hit and the proceeds of its sales, which were intended to raise funds for Ethiopia, far exceeded Geldof's original expectations. The song has since had multiple iterations. Its 2014 version was used to raise funds to alleviate the consequences of the Ebola crisis in West Africa. However, as Tanja Müller (2013) argues, the Band Aid representation of famine was also 'instrumental in establishing a hegemonic culture of humanitarianism in which moral responsibility towards impoverished parts of an imagined "Africa" is based on pity rather than demand for justice.'

Wainaina's article 'How to Write About Africa', mentioned in the introduction to this chapter, highlights some of the frequent tropes in such representations of famine, designed to prompt humanitarian responses:

> Among your characters you must always include The Starving African, who wanders the refugee camp nearly naked, and waits for the benevolence of the West. Her children have flies on their eyelids and pot bellies, and her breasts are flat and empty. She must look utterly helpless. She can have no past, no history; such diversions ruin the dramatic moment.

In reality, however, famines – including the 1983–1985 Ethiopian famine – are not natural catastrophes but man-made events, with a past and with history. The famine in Ethiopia, Müller notes, was caused by 'a combination of drought, exhausted soils, forced agricultural collectivization, forced resettlement schemes, and a counter-insurgency campaign by the Ethiopian army in Wollo, Tigray and Eritrea'. Armed conflict raged around the hamlet of Korem, whose images compelled Geldof to act, but it was never mentioned in Band Aid's media campaign. Instead, Geldof and his activist friends played up the emotionally-wrenching images of 'The Starving African'; they adopted the view of the famine 'as a result not of particular couplings of power that would demand a political response, but of natural (Biblical) outside human control leading to final breakdown' (Müller 2013).

These representations have now become standard, repeated in the last few decades of Western media coverage of famines in Somalia, South Sudan, Nigeria, Yemen and Niger. The contrast between Western and local interpretations of the 2005 famine in Niger seems particularly useful here, allowing us to see what is missed if the very notion of famine is simply taken for granted.

In 2005, the population of Niger was once again hit by the phenomenon of massive starvation. Ongoing food insecurity is chronic in Niger and affects some of the population annually at differing scales and magnitudes, but this was the third widespread event with high levels of food insecurity since the mid-1990s. The causes of starvation in Niger were both structural and circum-stantial. The structural factors included chronic poverty, an endemic agricul-tural crisis, and the continuous inflation of food prices. The inflation altered traditional strategies of survival of the local population and established a lin-gering situation of precariousness, which can easily transform into large-scale starvation when food deficit occurs (Gado 1993). The food deficit is mainly caused by circumstantial factors such as the drought and locust invasions. But, it is important to note, food deficit does not result in the absence of food in the market, but in the increase of food prices, which then makes it unafford-able to low-income households. It is this inability to access high-priced food in the market that push low-income families to resort to migration, changing or reducing their normal dietary habit, and raise the level of malnutrition, particularly among children (Olivier de Sardan 2007). In 2004 a combination of drought and a locust invasion created an estimated food deficit of 223,500 tons, representing 7.5 percent of the total need of the population, but the starving populations were estimated at 3.2 million – 32 percent of the total population (SAP Report 2005).[1] This deficit was aggravated by the fall in the price of livestock which constitutes an important source of income for most Nigerien households. The confluence of the rise of food prices and the fall of incomes created massive starvation that resulted in the migration of thousands from rural to urban area, and an increase in the rate of malnutrition among children (Olivier de Sardan 2007).

The crisis sparked an unprecedented rush of media and humanitarian organizations in Niger which propelled the country into the headlines of the largest media outlets in the world. Suddenly, a country that is rarely men-tioned in the West (with the possible exception of its rich uranium mines), that is easily confounded with Nigeria and whose widespread stigmatized image is that of being 'the poorest country in the world', became the interest of the most prestigious media, which engaged in publishing alarming images and papers, trying to rise indignation and emotion in the West (Tidjani Alou 2008, 39).

Importantly, however, the media coverage of this event differed between Western and local media. In the Western media's narrative, what happened in 2005 in Niger was a situation of *famine* that caused a massive death toll among the starving population. The famine was described as a phenomenon suddenly provoked by drought and the locust invasion which destroyed the crops of 2004 leaving thousands of people to starve to death. The phenomenon is, therefore, portrayed as an emergency that could only be prevented by a massive humanitarian intervention. The portrayal of the event as an emergency gave legitimacy to the humanitarian agencies to intervene despite the disagreement of the government, prioritizing the principle of humanitarian imperative over the principle of sovereignty.

The local media, however, had a different interpretation of the phenomenon. They portrayed it as a '*food crisis*' that increased migration of starving populations toward the cities, obliged people to change their dietary habits, and brought some local, national and international networks of solidarity into action. Unlike the Western media, the local media considered the 'food crisis' as a structural problem that lays bare the failure of the current democratically elected government to conceive and implement policies capable of resolving the problem. Therefore, rather than a call for a humanitarian emergency, this narrative suggests that the solution to the phenomenon of starvation was only conceivable through long-term policies conceived and implemented by Niger's government.

Conclusion

In the beginning of this chapter, we mentioned Barbie Savior, Instagram celebrity humanitarian and the intrepid traveler through *Africa*. In her Instagram life, Barbie Savior painted *African* villages, celebrated Christmas with *African* children and advertised T-shirts whose sales would then support her *African* friends. We may laugh or cringe at these photos but the truth is that many of us have journeyed to – or even become passionate about – some part of the world or some humanitarian crises because celebrities took us there. Thus, the last question we need to raise in this chapter is: Who have we become as audiences in this humanitarian spectacle? The answer is not easy. As we have seen through analysis on previous pages, celebrity humanitarianism thrives on a disengaged public and it fundamentally de-politicizes the events and the crises that celebrities choose to cover. But it also produces emotionally super-charged audiences, other Barbie Saviors, who are convinced that their individual actions – donations, consumption of the right products, 'likes' and retweets on social media – might change the world for the better. In some instances, we have seen, such actions may make a difference. More frequently, they will reproduce political passivity and disengagement as well as the existing – racialized and gendered – hierarchies of international politics. Those who hope that Barbie can effectively portray *and* transform conditions in Africa (a country) are deceiving themselves and the public at large.

Box 10.2: Story box: Teju Cole – 'The White-Savior Industrial Complex'

In 2012, Invisible Children, a non-profit organization based in San Diego, released a sleek, exceptionally well produced video entitled *Kony2012*. The video sought to raise awareness about Joseph Kony, a central African warlord whose Lord's Resistance Army enlisted – and brutally exploited – children within its ranks. At the time when the video was released, Joseph Kony had already been indicted for war crimes and crimes against humanity by the International Criminal Court in The Hague. Yet the broader public in the US and the Global North was largely unaware of his actions. Within days, the video went viral thanks in part to its clever targeting of celebrities and billionaires ('CultureMakers') such as George Clooney, Angelina Jolie, Rush Limbaugh, Tim Tebow, Oprah Winfrey, Bill Gates and others. Many celebrities shared the video, endorsed it, and made financial contributions to Invisible Children. Within a year, the video raised more than 30 million dollars for Invisible Children's activities.

Almost immediately, however, *Kony2012* was also met with sharp criticism. Some expressed concerns that by focusing on Joseph Kony as an individual, the video distracted from structural problems that had made Kony and his Lord Resistance Army possible in the first place. Others demanded transparency in Invisible Children's finances. The most powerful critique was articulated by Nigerian-American writer Teju Cole, who argued that Invisible Children's Kony campaign should be viewed as a part of a 'White Savior Industrial Complex'. In Teju Cole's words, the White Savior Industrial Complex was 'not about justice'. It was 'about having a big emotional experience that validates privilege'. 'If Americans want to care about Africa', wrote Cole, 'maybe they should consider evaluating American foreign policy, which they already play a direct role in through elections, before they impose themselves on Africa itself'.

Teju Cole – 'The White-Savior Industrial Complex' – www.theatlantic.com/international/archive/2012/03/the–white–savior–industrial–complex/254843/

Note

1 SAP: Systeme d'Alerte Precoce is the government agency in charge of following food security issues in Niger.

Suggested readings

Explore Barbie Savior Instagram photos and the website and analyze them in conjunction with Binyavanga Wainaina's essay 'How to Write About Africa' and Teju Cole's essay 'The White-Savior Industrial Complex'.

Hozic, A.A. (2002). *Hollyworld: Space, power and fantasy in the American economy.* Ithaca: Cornell University Press. Provides an overview of interlocking relations between the film and media industries and American hegemony.

Richey, A. (Ed.). (2015). *Celebrity humanitarianism and North-South relations: Politics, place and power.* New York: Routledge. This volume includes a variety of excellent essays about celebrities' engagement in international politics.

Bibliography

Agustín, L. M. (2007). *Sex at the margins: Migration, labour markets and the rescue industry.* London and New York: Zed Books.

Andrijasevic, R. (2007). Beautiful dead bodies: Gender, migration and representation in anti-trafficking campaigns. *Feminist Review*, 86, 24–44.

Barbie Savior website and blog – www.barbiesavior.com.

Barnett, M. (2011). *Empire of humanity: A history of humanitarianism.* Ithaca: Cornell University Press.

Berry, J., and Arons, D. (2003). *A voice for nonprofits.* Washington, DC: Brookings Institution Press.

Biccum, A. (2011). Marketing development: Celebrity politics and the 'new' development advocacy. *Third World Quarterly*, 32, 1331–1346.

Boltanski, L. (1999). *Distant suffering: Politics, morality and the media.* Cambridge: Cambridge University Press.

Brockington, D. (2014). The production and construction of celebrity advocacy in international development. *Third World Quarterly*, 35, 88–108.

Brown, W. (2006). American nightmare: Neoliberalism, neoconservatism, and de-democratization. *Political Theory*, 34, 690–714.

Budabin, A.C. (2015). Celebrities as norm entrepreneurs in international politics: Mia Farrow and the 'Genocide Olympics' campaign. *Celebrity Studies*, 1–15.

Bystrom, K. (2011). On 'humanitarian' adoption (Madonna in Malawi). *Humanity: An International Journal of Human Rights, Humanitarianism, and Development*, 2, 213–231.

Chapkis, W. (2003). Trafficking, migration, and the law: Protecting innocents, punishing immigrants. *Gender & Society*, 17, 923–937.

Choi, C.J., and Berger, R. (2010). Ethics of celebrities and their increasing influence on 21st century society. *Journal of Business Ethics*, 91, 313–318.

Cole, T. (2012). The white-savior industrial complex. *The Atlantic*, March 21. Available at www.theatlantic.com/international/archive/2012/03/the-white-savior-industrial-complex/254843/ and accessed on August 19, 2017.

Cooper, A. (2007). Beyond Hollywood and the boardroom: Celebrity diplomacy. *Politics and Diplomacy*, Summer/Fall, 125–132.

Dalton, R. (2008). Citizenship norms and the expansion of political participation. *Political Studies*, 56, 76–98.

Davies, S.E., and True, J. (2017). Norm entrepreneurship in foreign policy: William Hague and the prevention of sexual violence in conflict. *Foreign Policy Analysis*, 13, 701–721.

Davies, S.E., and True, J. (2017). Ending sexual violence in conflict: What can UK efforts tell us? IPI Global Observatory. Available at https://theglobalobservatory.org/2017/03/sexual-violence-conflict-sri-lanka/ and accessed on August 19, 2017.

Demaine, L. (2009). Navigating policy by the stars: The influence of celebrity entertainers on federal lawmaking. *The Journal of Law and Politics*, 25.

Dieter, H., and Kumar, R. (2008). The downside of celebrity diplomacy: The neglected complexity of development. *Global Governance*, 14.

Ditmore, M., Maternick, A., and Zapert, K. (2012). *The road north: The role of gender, poverty and violence in trafficking from Mexico to the US*. New York: Sex Workers Project.

Doezema, J. (2010). *Sex slaves and discourse master: The construction of trafficking*. London and New York: Zed Books.

Drake, P., and Higgins, M. (2006). 'I'm a celebrity, get me into politics': The political celebrity and the celebrity politician. In S. Holmes and S. Redmond (Eds.). *Framing celebrity: New directions in celebrity* culture (pp. 87–100). Abingdon: Routledge.

Finnemore, M., and Sikkink, K. (1998). International norm dynamics and political change. *International Organization* 52, 887–917.

Frizzell, C. (2011). Public opinion and foreign policy: The effects of celebrity endorsements. *The Social Science Journal*, 48, 314–323.

Gado, B.A. (1993). *Une histoire des famines au Sahel: Étude des grandes crises alimentaires (XIXème–XXème siècles)*. Paris: L'Harmattan.

Gamson, J. (1994). *Claims to fame: Celebrity in contemporary America*. Berkeley: University of California Press.

Giddens, A. (1991). *Modernity and self-identity: Self and society in the late modern age*. Stanford, CA: Stanford University Press.

Gozdziak, E., and Collett, E. (2005). Research on human trafficking in North America: A review of the literature. *International Migration*, 43, 99–128.

Hart, P. and Tindall, K. (2009). Leadership by the famous: Celebrity as political capital. In: J. Kane, H. Patapan, and P. 't Hart (Eds.) *Dispersed leadership in democracies*. New York: Oxford University Press.

Haynes, D.F. (2014). The celebritization of human trafficking. *The ANNALS of the American Academy of Political and Social Science*, 653, 25–45.

Hozic, A.A. (2002). *Hollyworld: space, power and fantasy in the American economy*. Ithaca: Cornell University Press.

ILO (2012). ILO global estimate of forced labour: Results and methodology. Geneva: International Labour Office.

Kapoor, I. (2012). *Celebrity humanitarianism: The ideology of global charity*. New York: Routledge.

Kellner, D. (2009). Barack Obama and celebrity spectacle. *International Journal of Communication,* 3, 715–741.

Kempadoo, K., Sanghera J., and Pattanaik, B. (2012). *Trafficking and prostitution reconsidered: new perspectives on migration, sex work, and human rights* (2nd edition). Boulder, CO: Paradigm Publishers.

Larner, W. (2000). Neo-liberalism: Policy, ideology, governmentality. *Studies in Political Economy*, 63, 5–25.

Littler, J. (2008). 'I feel your pain': cosmopolitan charity and the public fashioning of the celebrity soul. *Social Semiotics*, 18, 237–251.

McGough, M. (2013). Ending modern-day slavery: Using research to inform US anti-human trafficking efforts. *NIJ Journal*, 271, 26–32.

Majic, S. (2011). Serving sex workers and promoting democratic engagement: Rethinking nonprofits' role in American civic and political life. *Perspectives on Politics*, 9, 821–840.

Majic, S. (2014a). Beyond 'victim-criminals': Sex workers, nonprofit organizations, and gender norm resistance. *Gender and Society*, 28, 463–485.

Majic, S. (2014b). Sex work politics: From protest to service provision. In *American governance: Politics, policy, and public law*. Philadelphia: University of Pennsylvania Press.

Majic, S. (2016). Lights! Camera! Misinformation? Celebrities and the movement to end human trafficking. Paper presented at the 2016 Annual Meeting of the American Political Science Association Philadelphia, PA.

Majic, S. (2017). Real men set norms? Anti-trafficking campaigns and the limits of celebrity norm entrepreneurship. *Crime, Media and Culture: An International Journal*. First published July 12. doi: 10.1177/1741659017714518

Marcus, A., Horning, A., Curtis, R., Sanson, J., and Thompson, E. (2014). Conflict and agency among sex workers and pimps: A closer look at domestic minor sex trafficking. *The ANNALS of the American Academy of Political and Social Science*, 653, 225–246.

Marcus, A., and Curtis, R. (2016). No love for children: Reciprocity, science and engagement in the study of child sex trafficking. In D. Siegel and R. de Wildt (Eds.). *Ethical Concerns in Human Trafficking Research*. New York: Springer.

Marks, M., and Fischer, Z. (2002). The king's new bodies: Simulating consent in the age of celebrity. *New Political Science*, 24, 371–394.

Meyer, D., and Gamson, J. (1995). The challenge of cultural elites: Celebrities and social movements. *Sociological Inquiry*, 65, 181–206.

Milivojevic, S., and Pickering, S. (2013). Trafficking in people, 20 years on: Sex, migration and crime in the global anti-trafficking discourse and the rise of the 'global trafficking complex'. *Current Issues in Criminal Justice*, 25, 585–604.

Mostafanehzad, M. (2013). Getting in touch with your inner Angelina: Celebrity humanitarianism and the cultural politics of gendered generosity in volunteer tourism. *Third World Quarterly*, 34, 485–499.

Müller, T.R. (2013). The long shadow of band aid humanitarianism: Revisiting the dynamics between famine and celebrity. *Third World Quarterly*, 34, 470–484.

Nolan, D., and Brookes, S. (2013). Populism in theory and practice: Analysing celebrity politics. *Media Asia Research*, 373–383.

Olivier de Sardan, J-P. (2007). Analyse rétrospective de la crise alimentaire au Niger en 2005. Niamey: LASDEL.

Payne, J.G., Hanlon, J.P., and Twomey, D.P. (2007). Celebrity spectacle influence on young voters in the 2004 presidential campaign: What to expect in 2008. *American Behavioral Scientist*, 50, 1239–1246.

Putnam, R. (1995). Tuning in, tuning out: The strange disappearance of social capital in America. *Political Science and Politics*, 28, 664–683.

Repo, J., and Yrjölä, R. (2011). The Gender politics of celebrity humanitarianism in Africa. *International Feminist Journal of Politics*, 13, 44–62.

Richey, L.A. (2015). *Celebrity humanitarianism and north-south relations: Politics, place and power*. New York: Routledge.

Richey, L.A., and Ponte, S. (2008). Better (red)™ than dead? Celebrities, consumption and international aid. *Third World Quarterly*, 29, 711–729.

Saunders, F.S. (2013). *The cultural cold war: The CIA and the world of arts and letters*. New York: The New Press.

Saunders, P. (2000). Working on the inside: Migration, sex work and trafficking in persons. *Legal Link*, 11.

Sharma, N. (2003). Travel agency: A critique of anti-trafficking campaigns. *Refuge*, 21, 53–65.

Skocpol, T. (2003). *Diminished democracy: From membership to management in American civic life*. Norman: University of Oklahoma Press.

Smith, A. (2013). Civic engagement in the digital age. Washington, DC: Pew Research Center.

Spivak, G.C. (1988). Can the subaltern speak? In C. Nelson and N. Grossberg (Eds.). *Marxism and the interpretation of culture* (pp. 271–313). Chicago: University of Illinois Press.

Steele, S., and Shores, T. (2014). More than just a famous face: Exploring the rise of the celebrity expert-advocate through anti-trafficking action by the Demi and Ashton Foundation. *Crime Media Culture*, 10, 259–272.

Strolovitch, D.Z. (2007). *Affirmative advocacy: Race, class, and gender in interest group politics*. Chicago: University of Chicago Press.

Tester, K. (2010) *Humanitarianism and modern culture*. University Park: Pennsylvanian State University Press.

Tidjani Alou, M. (2008). La crise alimentaire de 2005 vue par les médias. *Afrique contemporaine*, 1, 39–74. DOI: 10.3917/afco.225.0039 www.cairn.info/revue-afrique-contemporaine-2008-1-page-39.htm

Tsaliki, L., Frangonikolopoulos, C.A., and Huliaras, A. (Eds.) (2011). *Transnational celebrity activism in global politics: Changing the world?* Bristol, UK: Intellect.

United Nations (2014). United Nations convention against transnational organized crime and the protocols thereto. Edited by United Nations.

US Department of State (2013). USG TIP Projects with funds obligated in FY2012. Edited by State Department. Washington, DC.

van Elteren, M. (2013). Celebrity culture, performative politics, and the spectacle of 'democracy' in America. *Journal of American Culture*, 36, 263–283.

Vance, C. (2011). Twelve ways to do nothing about trafficking while pretending to. *Social Research*, 78, 933–948.

Wainaina, B. (2005). How to write about Africa. *Granta*, 92. Winter. Available at https://granta.com/how-to-write-about-africa/ and accessed on August 19, 2017.

Walker, R.B.J. (1993). *Inside/outside: International relations as political theory*. Cambridge: Cambridge University Press.

Wheeler, M. (2012). The democratic worth of celebrity politics in an era of late modernity. *British Journal of Politics and International Relations*, 14, 407–422.

White House (2013). Federal strategic action plan on services for victims of human trafficking in the United States, 2013–2017. President's interagency task force to Monitor and Combat trafficking in Persons.

Yrjölä, R. (2012). From street into the world: Towards a politicised reading of celebrity humanitarianism. *British Journal of Politics and International Relations*, 14, 357–374.

Index

Note: Page references in **bold** refer to boxes; page references in *italic* refer to tables.

Abu-Lughod, L. 89
Acemoglu, D. 157
Acharya, A. 155, 156, 157, 174
Ackerly, B. 87
Africa 21, 45, 47, 71, 138, 160, 182, 192, 194, **195–196**; Ethiopian famine 181, 192–193; Indigenous peoples 25, 37, 40, 41, 71, 117, 121; Niger famine 193–194
African-American women 65–66, 68, 74, **75**
Akbari-Dibavar, A. 10
Algeria 72
Amerindians 117, 119, 121
Amritsar massacre (1919) 161–162
anarchy 19, 20, 47, 139–140, 141, 148, 150, 160
Anderson, B. 86
Andro-Eurocentrism 61, 71
Anievas, A. 11, 126, 127
Anishinaabek Nation 142–144, 145, 146–148, 149, 150
Anthias, F. 93
anti-immigrant politics 45
Armstrong and Prashad 164
Armstrong and Smith 83
Australia 30, 43, 93, 151
autonomy 5, 83, 144, 145, 150
Ayoob, M. 157, 174

Barbie Savior 181–182, 194
Barkawi, T. 48, 49, 50, 155
Barnett, T.P.M. 169
Beier, M. 137, 139
Bengal famine (1943-1945) 23, 49

Bernholz, P. 169
Bhabha, H.K. 10, 86
Bhambra, G.K. 111, 156, 174
biological racism 40, 41
black feminism 8–9, 10, 59, 68, 71, **76**
Blaney, D. 11, 37–38
Bosia, M.J. 100
Britain 22–23, 25, 160, 167–168; India 8, 23, 42, 49, 161–162; Palestine 27; United States 48, 49
Brown, E.B. **75**
Brown, W. 186, 187
Brus, H. 95
Budabin, A. 187
Butler, J. 10, 88, 89, 95

Canada 28, 30, 45, 151; Indigenous peoples 67, 138, 141–150
capitalism 3, 4, 6, 11, 21–22, **31**, 27, 31, 52, 122–125, 127; global 11, 15, 21, 44, 45; inequality 7, 117, **131**; wealth production 117, 122–123, 124, 125, 128–129, 130; women 9, 63, **70**
care workers 69, 70
Catholicism 37, 47
celebrities 13, 180–181, 183–186, 187–189, 194, **195**; famines 182, 189, 192–193; human trafficking 189, 190–191
celebrity humanitarianism 12–13, 181, 182, **183**, 184, 187, 188–189, 194, **195**
Césaire, A. 3
China 21, 29, 47
Chowdhry, G. 74
civilization 41–42, 43, 71, 99

clan system 145, 149
class 5, 7, 8, 9, 40, 122, 123–124
climate change 28, 30, 156
Cohn, C 63–64
Cold War 7, 21, **29**, 44, 45, 170, 184
Cole, T. **195–196**
colonialism 2–5, 9, 14–15, 21–22, 24,
     27, 52, 67, 85, 111–112, 170, 181;
     European 2, 3–4, 42, 71–73, 119–120,
     121, 124–125, 126; gender 6, 104;
     North America 138; security 159,
     161, **173**; settler 104, 137, 138, 139,
     140–141, 143, 144, 151
colonialization 42, 50, 71–73, 137,
     138, **151**
colonial violence 4, 50, 125, 127, 128,
     129, 137, 160, 167, 172–174
Commonwealth 100
competition 116, 118, 119, 126, 128,
     129, 130
competitiveness 19, 20, 21, 22
conflict 1, 11, 47, 49, 60, 121, 150,
     167, 169
conquest 3, 4, 12, 50, 52, 156, 159,
     160, 161
conquest discourses 137, 139, 150
consensus 7, 51, 81
constructivism 13–14, 141
cooperation 1, 83, 159, 170
Copway, G. 142
'countries' exports, Third World 130–132
Cox, R.W. 7
Crawford, N.C. 168
Crenshaw, K. 9, 10, 64–65, 95
critical security theory 50
critical theory 5–7, 11–12
cultural racism 40, 41
culture 1–2, 5–6, 13, 36, 84, 93

Dakota Nation 147
Dalla Costa, M. 63
Darfur 167
Das Gupta, M. 14, 15
Davies, S. 189
Davis, A.Y. 9
decolonization 5–6, 44–45, 50, 52, 128,
     137–138
de Haan, L. 10
dehumanization 4, 40, 41
democracy 11, 24, 161, 162–164
democracy promotion 157, 162–163, 164

democratic peace 12, 48, 156, 162–164
democratic states 83, 163
dependency theory 44
development 9, 15, 23, 37–38, 71, 117,
     125, 126–127, 129
discourses of conquest *see* conquest
     discourses
Dish With One Spoon treaty 147, 148
domestic workers 70
domination 2, 4, 5, 7, 9, 11, 14, 15, 84,
     121, 129
Doty, R.L. 170
drone warfare 170, 174
Du Bois, W.E.B. 5, 38, 40
Dyer, E.H. 161–162

economic development 15, 23, **31**, 45–47,
     52, 128
Ehrlich, P.R. 169
el-Malik, S.S. 14
empire 3, 9, 15, 48, 52, 159, 160, 169–170
Engdahl 167–168
England *see* Britain
Enloe, C. 91
equality **51**, 62, **62**, 107, 116, 120
ethics 117
Ethiopian famine (1983-1985) 181,
     192–193
ethnicity 6, 39–40, 101, 110, 113
ethno-symbolism 10, 82, 83, 85, 86
EU (European Union) 100, 111
eugenics 41, **51**
Euro-America 9, 12, 52, 53, 156, **173**
Eurocentrism 9, 14–15, 24, 25–26, 41, 45,
     53, 61, 85, **94**, 157, **173**, 174
Europe 3–4, 19–20, 24, 41–42, 47, 121,
     126, 128, 157; nation 84, 86
European colonization 2, 3–4, 42, 71–73,
     119–120, 121, 124–125, 126
European expansionism 40, 41–42, 50
exclusion 84–85, 86; Indigenous peoples
     135–136, 140
expansionism 40, 41–42, 50, 146, 159,
     160–161

face mask 67
fairness 116, 118, 119, 129
famines 13, 182, 189, 192–194; Bengal
     23, 49; Ethiopia 181, 192–193;
     India 23; Niger 193–194
Fanon, F. 4, 5, 6, 10, 72, 85, 170

femininity 11, 59, 60, 64, 69, 71, **76**, 87–88, **94**
feminism 9, 59, 61, 73–74, 80, 88–91, **94**, 109; black 8–9, 10, 59, 68, 71, **76**; liberal 61–62, 68; Marxist 61, 63; postcolonial 59, 71, **76**, 87, 90; poststructuralist 61, 63–64; standpoint 61, 62–63; transformative 74, 75, **76**
feminist theories 61–64, 74, **76**, 84, 88–91
Fenton, S. 110
first nations *see* Indigenous peoples
foreign policies 2, 5, 60
Frank, A.G. 6, 44, 157, 174
French empire 143; Algeria 72; Haiti 42–43, 50
Friedman, M. 122

Geldof, B. 181, 184, 192–193
gender 1–2, 6, 7–9, 10, 13, 14, 60–61, **76**, 80, 87–88, **94**, 109; global politics 58–59, 61, 64; inequalities 60, 61, **62**, 69–70; nationalism 91–92, **93**, 95; sex 59–60
gender inequalities 60, 61, **62**, 69–70
gender mainstreaming **65**
gender theories 59, 61–64
gendered discourse 63–64, 69
gendered performance 89
genocide 21, 28, 48, 166, 167
genomics 39–40
Germany 49
Gills, B.K. 6, 157, 174
global capitalism 11, 15, 21, 44, 45
global economic development 10, 36, 43
global economy 2, 3, 128–129, 130
global inequality 117, 127, 128, 129, **131**
global peace 139
global politics 135–136; gender 58–59, 61, 64
global society 36, 128–129
global warming 28, 30
globalization 7, 9, 45, 157, 169
Goldstein, J.S. 167

Haiti 42–43, 50
Harrison, S. 37, 47
Haudenosaunee Nation 145, 146–147, 148
Hayek, F. 11, 122

Hegel, G.W.F. 11, 37, 116–117, 120–121, 122, 125, 128, 129, **131**
hegemonic masculinity 60
hegemony 7, 21, 51, 173
Henderson, J.Y. (Sa'ke'j) 140
heteronormativity 11, **69**, 90, 99, 102–104, 112
heterosexuality **69**, 109
Hill Collins, P. 9, 10, 68, 75
Hobbes, T. 84
Hobson, J. 44
Hollywood studios 183, 184
homocolonialism 11, 99–100, 105, 106, 107, 110, 112, 113
homonationalism 105
homophobia 71, 102, 104, 112–113; Muslim culture 107, 109, 110, 111, 113
homosexuality 101, 103, 105–106
hooks, b. 9, 74, 75
Hozic, A. 12–13
humanitarian crises 181, 182, **183**, 189, 194, **195**
humanitarian intervention 2, 12, 52, 156, 165, 166, 167, 168, 189, 194
humanitarianism 12–13, 166
human rights 25, 30, 43, 100, 101, 102, 105, 106, 109
Human Rights Council, UN 100
human security 50, 156, **173**, 174–175
human trafficking 13, 182, 189, 190–192

ICC (International Criminal Court) 167, **195**
identities 10, 25, **76**
immigration 45, **46**, 53
imperialism 2, 6, 9, 14, 15, 42, **45**, 52, 104, 159, 161, **173**; dehumanization 40, 41
Inayatullah, N. 11, 37–38
incentives 116, 118
India 8, 22–23, 42, 86, 124–125; Amritsar massacre 161–162; Bengal famine 23, 49
indigeneity 11–12, 139
Indigenous 151
Indigenous peoples 25, 30, 40–41, 73, 119–120, 135–137, 139, 140–142, 144, 145–146, 148, 150, 151; Africa 25, 37, 40, 41, 71, 117, 121; Amerindians 117, 119, 121; Canada 67, 138, 141–150; clan system 145, 149; exclusion

135–136, 140; North America
136, 137, 138, 141–142, 145–146;
race wars 48; reciprocity 149–150;
sovereignty 146, 147–148, 150; treaty
making 146–147
individual freedom 116, 117
industrialization 22–23, **31**, 31
inequalities 86, 116, 117–118, 119, 122,
125, 126, 127, 128, 129, 130, **131**;
gender 60, 61, **62**, 69–70
International Criminal Court *see* ICC
(International Criminal Court)
international law 139, 140, 166, 172–173
international political economy 7, 69, **70**
international politics 141, 146;
Indigenous peoples 137, 139, 140,
141–142; LGBT rights 100, 112
International Relations *see* IR
(International Relations)
international security 43, 45, 157,
166–167
international society 41, 42, 43
international system 2, 21, **31**, 52, 159
international trade 128
intersectionality 9, 10, 64–65, 70, **76**,
90–91, 95, 107–108
intervention 156, 159, 162–163, 164,
166–167; humanitarian 2, 12, 52, 156,
165, 166, 167, 168, 189, 194; military
167, 169; Third World 52, 159, 166, 168
Invisible Children **195**
IR (International Relations) 2, 6–7,
13–15, 19–21, 24–26, 31, **131**,
139–140; gender 59, 60–61;
Indigenous peoples 135–136, 138,
139, 141, **151**; race 35–36, 38,
43–44, **51**, 53
Iran 164, 165–166
Iraq 14, 52, 165, 167–168, **171**, 174
Irma (Puerto Rico hurricane) 13
Islam 15, 25, 105, 107, 111, 112
Islamic terrorism 169, 170
Islamophobia 99, 107, 111, 112–113
Israel 27

James, S. 63
Japan 43, 160, 173
JCPOA (Joint Comprehensive Plan of
Action) 165–166
Johnson, B. 144
Johnson, D. 145

Jolie, A. 188–189
Judaism 93

Kant, I. 11, 116, 120, 122, 129, **131**
Kapoor, I. 71, 90
Khan, G. 157–158
Khosla, S. 130
Kilomba, G. 66–67, 75
King, H. 11–12
Klein, N. 28
Kollontai, A. 63
Kony, J. **195**
Kony2012 (video) **195**
Korean War 172
Krishna, S. 9, 61

Laffey, M. 155, 156–157
Landes, D. 47
Lange, S. 95
'late modernity' 185, **195**
Lazreg, M. 50–51
Lentin, A. 39
LGBT identities 102, 104, 105,
106–107, 109
LGBT Muslims 99–100, 107–108, 109,
110, 111, 112
LGBT politics 99, 100, 101, 104, 105,
107, 110, 113
LGBT rights 11, 99, 100–101, 102, 104,
105–106, 109, 111, 112–113
liberal feminism 61–62, 68
liberalism 156, 163
Libya 166–167
Liu, J. 169
Live Aid concerts 181, 184, 192
logic of elimination 138, 139
Loomba, A. 3
Lorde, A. 67–68
Lyons, S. 143

McClintock, A. 6, 72
McDougall, W. 160–161
Mackinder, H. 158
McLaughlin Mitchell, S. 95
Majic, S. 12–13, 190
Mamdani, M. 48, 166, 167, 170
Manchanda, N. 10
mandate system 43
Manifest Destiny 160, 161
markets 116, 117, 118–119, 122, 126,
128, 130

Martin, R. 191
Marx, K. 11, 44, 117, 122, 123–125,
    128, **131**
Marxism 5, 6, 44, 52, 84
Marxist feminism 61, 63
masculinity 10, 11, 59, 60, 64, 69, 71, 72,
    76, 87, 88, **94**
Mbembe, A. 159–160, 168
media *see* social media
Meer, N. 110, 111
merit 116, 118, 122, 125, 127
methodological nationalism 19, 22, 24,
    25, 27, 28
Meyers, R.B. 170
Middle East 15, 25, 26, 166–167, 169
migrant workers 45, **46**, 70
militarization 92
military interventions 167, 169
Mills, A. 149–150
modernism 10, 82, 83, 85, 87
modernity 11, 99, 102–105,
    111–112, 113
modernization 99, 101, 102–104, 105
modernization theory 24, 37–38
Modood, T. 110, 111
Mohanty, C.T. 8, 10, 89, 90, 95
Mongol Empire 12, 157–158
Mostafanehzad, M. 188
Müller, T. 192
Muslim countries 11, 105–107, 109
Muslim culture 72, 106–107, 113;
    homophobia 107, 109, 110, 111, 113;
    homosexuality 105–106; sexual
    diversity 105, 109–111
Muslims 11, 15, 105–106, 107, 110,
    111, 112

Nadarajah, S. 156–157
Namibia genocide 48
nation 10, 80, 81–83, 84–85, 85–87, 122;
    gender 84, 91, 92–94
national identities 85, 85
national interest 19, 20
nationalism 10, 13, 80, 81, 82, 85,
    85, 86, **94**; gender 91–92, **93**, 95;
    methodological 19, 22, 24, 25, 27, 28
national security 19, 160, **173**
neoconservatism 186–187
neo-Gramscian theory 7, 156, 173
neoliberal globalization 69–70
neoliberalism 73, 186, 187

neorealism 7
Niger famine (2005) 193–194
Niş ancioğlu, K. 11, 126, 127
No Gun Ri (Korean War) 172
North America 136, 137, 138, 141–142,
    145–146

oil 15, 168, 169
Ontario, Canada 28
oppression, coloniality of 10, 12, 14
Organization of Islamic Co-operation
    100–101, 109, 111
Orient 4, 26
Orientalism 4–5, 36, 37, 111, 112, 113
Orientalist 36–37
Otherness 1, 9, 12, *37*, 49, 86, 92,
    113, 159
Özkirimli, U. 82

Palestine 27, 151
Pape, R.A. 171
Parry, B. 8
patriarchy 59, 63, 68–69, 70, 73, **76**, 87
Peloponnesian wars 21, 47
Persaud, R.B. 9–10, 12
Pew Research Center 101
political communities 12, 127, 135, 138,
    140, 141, 142–144, 146, 148, **151**
political economy 7, 44, 45–47, 69, **70**
political engagement 62, 185–186
political theories 80, 81–83, 90
popular culture 12, 180–181
Porter, P. 51
postcolonial feminism 59, 71, **76**, 87, 90
postcolonial scholars 14, 15, 46, 48, 51,
    157, 169–170, 174
postcolonial studies 4, 7–8, 38, 40
postcolonial theory 7, 9, 24, 50, 71,
    84, 156
postcolonialism 2–5, 14–15, 19, 21, 24,
    25, 27, 28, 31, 156–157, 174; security
    155, 156, 159, 161
poststructuralist feminism 61, 63–64
poverty 23, 39, 119, 125–126, 128, 169
power, coloniality of 45
power hierarchies 68, 87–88
Prashad, V. 164
preventative war 168
primordialism 10, 82, 83, 85
progress model, modernization 101,
    102–104, 105

Project RED 187
Protestantism 37, 47
Puar, J. 105
Puerto Rico 13

queer theory 90
Quijano, A. 45, 165

race 1–2, 5, 6, 8–10, 13–14, 35–36, 38–40, 43–44, **46**, **51**, 52–53, 73, 110, 119
race alliances 48, 49
race wars 48, 49
races 41, 49, 104, 120, 121, 122
racial minorities 30, 31
racial supremacy *see* white supremacy
racialization 12, 38–39, 43, 45–46, 47, 119, 121, 129
racism 2, 4, 9, 10, 12, 35, 36–38, 39, 40–41, 43, 44–47, **51**, 52–53, 110, 161
Rahman, M. 11
rape 92
rationality 20
Reagan Doctrine 170
realism 20–21, 157
reciprocity 149–150
refugees 53, 113, 172, 188
Richey, L.A. 188
Robinson, J.A. 157
Rodney, W. 44, **45**, 52
Rosato, S. 163–164
Rostow, W.W. 46–47
Rwandan genocide (1994) 48

Sachs, J. 125, 126
Said, E. 4, 26, 27, 36, 72, 111, 112, 113, 138
sanctions 12, 156, 164–166
sati (India) 8
Saudi Arabia 15, 25
scholarship 24, 26–28
scientific racism 40, 41, 48
security 2, 10, 36, 47, 48, 50, 52, 60, 155, **173**, 174–175; human 50, 156, **173**, 174–175; international 43, 45, 157, 166–167; national 19, 160, **173**; Third World 155, 156, 157, 161, **173**, 174
Security Council, UN 166
security studies 155–156, 158–159, 174
self-interest 20, 21, 28, **31**, 148
settler colonialism 104, 137, 138, 139, 140–141, 143, 144, 151
sex 59–60, 87–88, 90–91, **94**

sex trafficking 65, 189, 190, 191
sexual diversity 99, 103–104, 105, 109–111
sexuality 11, **69**, 90–91, 101, 102–104, 109–110, 113
Sham and Shohot 140–141
Shepherd, L. 59, 189
Shills, E. 82
Shores, T. 188
Simpson, A. 144
Simpson, L. 142, 149
Skalli, L.H. 15
slavery 10, 21, 52, 67, 121
slave trade 21, 40, 41, 50, 121
smart-weapons warfare 170–171, 173–174
Smith, A. 11, 117, 120, 122–123, 125, 128, **131**
'Social Darwinism' 20
social media 185, 186, 190, 194
social problems 187, 188
social relations 9, 65, **70**, 84
social reproduction 69, **70**
socialist feminism *see* Marxist feminism
SOGI rights 100–101, 105–106, 109
Solow, R. 26
sovereignty 51, 83, 127, 130, 140, 145, 166, 168, 174; Indigenous peoples 146, 147–148, 150
Spivak, G.C. 8, 74–75, 89, 191
Staden, H. 136
standpoint feminism 61, 62–63
Stark, H.K. 143, 144
Starr, H. 163
states 2, 9, 81, 83–85, 91, 92, 127–129, 130, 139, 140
Stavrianos, L.S. 11, 126, 127
Steele, S. 188
subaltern 7, 8, 36, **73**, 74–75
Subaltern Studies School, India 7
subaltern turn 36
subordination 86, 90
suffrage movements 65–66
Summers, L. **29**
superiority 4, 15, 41, 90, 113, 121, 128, 136
survival 158–159, 161
Syria 167, 174

terrorism 12, 72, 156, 168–170, 173–174
Thapar-Björkert, S. 91

Third World 2, 11, 12, 14, **29–30**, 36–37, 45, 46–47, 53, 71, 128, 172; 'countries' exports 130–132; intervention 52, 159, 166, 168; security 155, 156, 157, 161, **173**, 174; violence 12, 50, 52, 168, 170–172, **173**; women 8, 89, 164
Three Fires Confederacy 142, 144, 146
Thucydides 21, 47
Tilly, C. 168
torture 51
transformative feminism 74, 75, **76**
Treaties of Westphalia (1648) 19–20, 157, 166
treaty making, Indigenous peoples 146–147
Treaty of Tawatgonshi see Two-Row Wampum
Trouillot, M.-R. 35
True, J. 10, 87, 189
Trueur, A. 143–144
Trump, D.J. 13, 43, 53, 166
Truth, S. 58, 65, **66**
Turse, N. 172
Two-Row Wampum (Treaty of Tawatgonshi) 146

underdevelopment 23, 52, 117, 125, 128
unequal rewards 117–118, 119, 128
United States 5, 14, 15, 30, 42, 53, 65, 151, 168, 169, 169–170, 186; black feminism 9; Britain 48, 49; drone warfare 172–174; expansionism 50, 146, 160–161; immigration **46**; Indigenous peoples 135, 137, 141, 160; Iran 164, 165–166; Korean War 172; LGBT rights 100, 109; Middle East 25; Vietnam War **171**, 172

Valentino, B.A. 167
Venezuelan crisis (1895) 48
Venezuelan crisis (1902-1903) 49
Vietnam War **171**, 172
violence 1, 12, 30, 47–48, 50–51, 52, 72–73, 130, **131**, 159–160, 166; Amritsar massacre 161–162; colonial 4, 50, 125, 127, 128, 129, 137, 160, 167, 171; Third World 12, 50, 52, 168, 170–173, **173**
Vitalis, R. 38

Vizenor, G. 143
Vucetic, S. 9–10, 159

Wainaina, B. 182, 192
Wallerstein, I. 44
war on terror 72, 92, 168, 170
wars 2, 12, 60, 121, 170; Third World 156, 161, **173**
wealth production 117, 122–123, 124, 125, 128–129, 130
Weatherford, J. 158
Weber, M. 46–47, 83
Weinberg, A.K. 160–161
Weiss, M.L. 100
West 5, 9, 12, 15, 36, 37tbl, 41–42, 45, 47, 71, 111–112, 129
Western, J. 167
Western Europe 21, **45**, 84, 126, 161
Western societies 101, 104, 105, 106, 159
Westphalia Treaty (1648) *see* Treaties of Westphalia (1648)
White Savior Industrial Complex **195–196**
white supremacy 38, 42–43, **45**, 46, 48, 50–51, 53, 73
Whitworth, S. 60, **65**, 69
Williams, R. 137
Witgen, M. 143, 144
Wolf, E. 11, 126, 127
Wolfe, P. 138, 151
women 64, 65–66, 67–68, 72, 88–89, 91–92; capitalism 9, 63, **70**; Third World 8, 89, 164
women of color 9, 58, 61, 65–66, 67, 68, 70, 72, 73, 74, 75
women's rights 58, **62**
Women's studies 14, 15
world politics 5, 10, 11, 12, 47, 59, 60–61, 64, 180
world system, modern 2, 6, 9, 11–12, 14, 44, 157
world systems theory 6, 44, 52
World War II 49

Yahaya Ibrahim, I. 12–13
Young, R. 73, 156
Yuval-Davis, N. 93

Zalewski, M. 60